CHRISTIAN HERITAGE COLLEGE
BY HIM ALL THINGS CONSIST
SAN DIEGO, CALIFORNIA 1970

MARK TWAIN'S NOTEBOOK

MARK TWAIN DICTATING, 1906; 21 FIFTH AVE., NEW YORK

MARK TWAIN'S NOTEBOOK

PREPARED FOR PUBLICATION
WITH COMMENTS

BY

ALBERT BIGELOW PAINE

COOPER SQUARE PUBLISHERS, INC.
NEW YORK CITY
1972

Originally Published, 1935 by
Harper and Brothers

Published 1972 by Cooper Square Publishers, Inc.
59 Fourth Avenue, New York, N. Y. 10003
International Standard Book No. 0-8154-0418-2
Library of Congress Catalog Card No. 72-77127

Printed in U.S.A. by
NOBLE OFFSET PRINTERS, INC.
New York, N.Y. 10003

CONTENTS

CONTENTS

ILLUSTRATIONS

FOREWORD

A SUPERSTITION, nursed and nourished by a number of persons—most of them too young to have known Mark Twain, too perverse to accept the simple and the obvious, is that because of restrictions laid upon him by his wife, by W. D. Howells, and later by those to whose care he trusted his manuscripts, he has not been permitted to have his say.

Now this is a good way from the truth. Mark Twain had his say; as much as any author could have it, thirty, forty, fifty years ago. When restricted at all it was chiefly through his own expressed wish to observe the conventions and convictions of that more orthodox, more timid and delicate (possibly more immaculate), day.

It is true, as I have elsewhere freely set down, that Howells, and especially Mrs. Clemens, usually "edited" his manuscripts, and it is also true that the manuscripts profited, and never, I believe, suffered through their suggestions. His own taste was unreliable—as unreliable as that of any genius: he was likely to mistake cheap banalities for choice bits of humor. His advisers prevailed upon him to eliminate, on occasion, and knowing this, a suspicious minority, hankering for revelations, call for Mark Twain, unsuppressed, unexpurgated, unedited. The result of such a procedure would be rather dismal: the eliminations would disturb nobody's refined sensibilities: they would do worse: they would sadden, disenchant, and bore the reader. Some of those that got by his editors might better have been spared.

Mark Twain never wrote for publication anything salacious or suggestive or bordering on the indecent. He never wrote anything suggestive at all. What he said was straight from the shoulder. He had been a printer, a pilot, a California miner. He had fed on strong meat, he had a robust imagination and a better command of Anglo-Saxon English than any other man of his time, but when he "let himself go," as he did two or three times, it was for strictly private consumption. The now famous "1601" was written for the amusement of no other person than the Reverend Joseph Twichell, of Hartford. Twichell sent it to John Hay, who had it put in type and a few copies struck off. Other editions followed. Mark Twain's statement that he once submitted it to an editor was one of his jokes. He had not the least desire to present publicly anything of the sort. He had a kind of chivalry which prevented his offering to the readers of another family that which he would not wish offered to his own. A speech which he delivered to the Stomach Club in Paris, another of his excursions into the forbidden land, was never put into type and is not likely to be. A few squibs and verses complete the tale of his transgressions, if that is the word.

The manuscripts printed by Mark Twain after his wife's death—*What Is Man* and *Captain Stormfield's Visit to Heaven*—were neither very important nor very offending to the orthodox mind, though they could have been, say, twenty-five years earlier. *The Mysterious Stranger*, published by Mark Twain's literary executors—his daughter and the writer of these lines—was not completed in Mrs. Clemens' lifetime. That she would have recognized its great literary value is certain, but it contained the sort of thing which in an earlier day she had found objectionable.

A good while ago I wrote a biography of Mark Twain. In that book I drew briefly here and there upon the set of journals, diaries, or commonplace books which through a period of nearly fifty years he had kept and, what is still more remarkable, preserved. These little books are now offered in full. A man in his diary, if anywhere, can have his say. He is talking to himself—his thought and his language are strictly his own. Some of the things that Mark Twain set down in that privacy were hardly suited to the unadorned cheek of polite society in that purer pre-war day. Now all is changed. How tolerant the world has grown in a few years. A spade is no longer just a garden implement: the utterance that twenty years ago was regarded as too highly seasoned for the "general" has become its daily nourriture.

In his journal, Mark Twain recorded in random phrase and fashion whatever seemed to him worth noting. Those expecting the salacious are likely to be disappointed. Those hoping for furtive indecencies are certain to be. As already suggested, Mark Twain was nothing if not frank, and he was a master of Anglo-Saxon word and phrase. He had little taste for the refinements of suggestion. In the pages that follow he pauses here and there to free his mind: politics, religion, the divine right of kings, personalities, he has something to say of these. He is not always consistent—only the dull-minded are that—inconsistency being one of the chief attributes of gods. He doesn't always agree with the world as he finds it—its conventions and its faiths—he doesn't always agree with himself. Tragedy, comedy, heresy—his notebooks make up the record. The entries, whatever their interest, or lack of it —are as he left them, and they bring us about as near as we shall ever get to this remarkable man, easily the most remarkable of his time.

Albert Bigelow Paine

CHAPTER I

The River and the Mines

IN ONE of the final chapters of *The Innocents Abroad,* Mark Twain tells of a diary he once began with the new year: "When I was a boy and a confiding and a willing prey to those impossible schemes of reform which well-meaning old maids and grandmothers set for the feet of unwary youths at that season of the year. . . . Please accept an extract:"

> *Monday*—Got up, washed, went to bed.
> *Tuesday*—Got up, washed, went to bed.

The diary continued this line through the week or at least until Friday, then skipped to the next Friday, and finally to the Friday of the following month. It seems to have been abandoned then. He was discouraged, he says. "Startling events appeared to be too rare, in my career, to render a diary necessary. I still reflect with pride, however, that even at that early age I washed when I got up. That journal finished me. I never had the nerve to keep one since."

That final statement is true so far as any formal and regular diary is concerned. Mark Twain never kept a consistent, orderly journal. He was not as prosaic as that. But he was always making notes, capturing the moment —the occurrence, the theme, the purpose, the fancy that flitted through his mind: whatever came and went, if he could get hold of a notebook and pencil quickly enough, he fixed it to his page; when he couldn't he forgot, and was profane. It is a long record, for it covers, intermittently, about forty years. The only thing uniform about it is the form—the books he kept it in. There are between thirty and forty of them, filled with his neat, beautiful writing, smooth and graceful in the beginning, becoming angular and uncertain with age. Except for the two little black-bound river logs all are nearly of the same size and style—books to fit the pocket—buff-leather-covered during the early years—limp morocco later, evidently made to order, with a projecting ear or flange on each leaf, to be torn off when used, so that he might always, and quickly, find his place. This was his own idea, and my recollection is that it was patented—he was always patenting things. Sometimes he lost a notebook, but for the most part he preserved them. One wonders how he managed it—he had a gift for mislaying his belongings.[1]

In writing *Mark Twain—A Biography* I made some use of the little river notebooks, and quoted from his own record the circumstance that led to their purchase. These things are too important, however, to be ignored here.

[1] He never really lost more than two or three of them. Two were left by mistake at the Hotel Metropole, in Vienna, and turned up nineteen years later, in a New York auction-room. Charles T. Lark, attorney for the S. L. Clemens estate, saw the announcement, and obtained a catalogue of the sale. In it the statement was made that the books had been left behind when Mark Twain gave up his apartment at the Metropole, in 1898. Visiting the auction-room, Mr. Lark was shown the notebooks, with the information that a private bid of fifteen thousand dollars had been received for one of them. He also learned that the books were now claimed by a butler on a Long Island estate, nephew of the former Metropole proprietor.

Mr. Lark promptly filed a claim for the two books, as property of the S. L. Clemens estate and got out a writ of replevin for them. They were seized by the sheriff just before the sale started. There followed a good deal of parleying back and forth, the nephew's lawyer finally agreeing to compromise on payment to his client of one thousand dollars, to which Mr. Lark assented, thus obtaining the precious notebooks for their rightful owners.

Those little books led the long procession that would follow.

He had engaged himself to learn piloting—to familiarize himself with twelve hundred miles of the Mississippi River, "cub" of the great Horace Bixby. In *Life on the Mississippi* he writes: "I entered upon the small enterprise of learning 12 or 13 hundred miles of the great Mississippi River with the easy confidence of my time of life. If I had really known what I was about to require of my faculties I should not have had the courage to begin. I supposed that all a pilot had to do was to keep his boat in the river and I did not consider that that could be much of a trick, since it was so wide."

A day or two later the easy confidence was all gone. Bixby, asking him to repeat some of the instruction we had furnished him, found that he could remember none of it. His head was a mere jumble of "points" and "bends" and "bars" and "crossings."

"My boy," said Mr. Bixby, "you must get a little memorandum-book and every time I tell you a thing, put it down, right away. There's only one way to be a pilot and that is to get this entire river by heart. You have to know it just like A B C."

He probably bought the little memorandum-book at the next landing-place where such things were to be had —at Cairo, most likely, for there his first entry appears to have been made. He began with great diligence and enthusiasm. The first three or four pages are crowded with confused entries, microscopic lead-pencil abbreviations, today all but illegible. Later his enthusiasm waned, or he recognized the futility of such a confusion. He systematized his entries under blue pencil headings, and wrote more legibly:

Delta to head 62 [small pencil sketch of steamboat with the word "Bar," and picture of same]. Coming up, when all the Bar is covered there is ¼ less 2 in chute of

Montezuma. Shape Bar till head of towhead & main point open—then hold open to right of high trees on towhead till get close enough to go up shore of towhead. Channel out past head of towhead.

Outside of Montezuma—use 6 or 8 feet more water. Shape Bar till high timber on tow head gets nearly even with low willows do. do. then hold a little open on right of low willow—run 'em close if you want to, but come out 100 yards when you get nearly to head of T. H.

It means nothing definite to us—it meant little enough to him, a day after he had written it. Yet he had to store that lesson and thousands more like it safely away in his head and keep them there. That a man of Mark Twain's temperament and easy-going nature should have persisted through all the months required to conquer that great, mysterious, eternally changing river is one of the wonders of human achievement.

The next book bears date of 1860—four years later, when he had been for more than two years a full-fledged pilot, with all the intricate knowledge which that fact connotes assembled in orderly arrangement in his unaccountable mind. It is not a lesson that he gives us now, but a record of fact—the story of a day or a night. Of a night he writes:

4 to 6 feet bank on point below foot of Buck. Could have run Buck Island to tow head. Night—didn't.

4 & 5 ft. bank up shore opp. Dark Corner.

Had 1/4 less 3 in foot of Cat I, tow-head. . . .

Hove lead at head of 55—no bottom—ran no channel in

it. 8 ft. bank on point opp. Densford's—or rather up shore at head of timber. . . .

Fall's City came up behind us. Ran Bayou Goule—no lead. Had 3 fathoms in Glasscock's—ran no channel—ran Diamond chute. When any water at all in lower chute, below Diamond good.

All of which has but little interest today, but when one remembers the scene amid which these cryptographic memoranda were made, the rushing black river, the blind channels behind islands, often half choked with logs and uncertain of passage (yet one must chance them) the lonely pilot-house with its single watcher on whom the fate of the steamboat with its cargo of human lives and merchandise depended, there is a kind of tense fascination in the brief, terse, entries.

Mark Twain left the river a year after that last entry was made, and after a brief, unbrilliant war experience found himself in Virginia City, Nevada, a reporter on the *Territorial Enterprise*, the paper owned by Joseph T. Goodman. Probably it was here that he formed the habit of keeping regular notebooks, though the first to be preserved does not begin until the end of 1864, when he had followed his Virginia City experience with some months of newspaper work in San Francisco, and following some complications there, had retired to the remoteness of James Gillis's cabin on Jackass Hill near Tuttletown, California. This was at the end of the year, and on New-Year's night he makes this entry.

New Year's night 1865, at Vallecito, magnificent lunar

rainbow—first appearing at 8 P. M.—moon at first quarter—very light drizzling rain.

> It was about this time that he went to Angel's Camp, to follow pocket mining. It was not cold in January, but it rained a great deal which made mining difficult. The hotel at Angel's Camp was not much more inviting. The food was unsatisfactory.

Beans and coffee *only* for breakfast and dinner every day at the French Restaurant at Angels—bad, weak coffee. J. [Jim Gillis] told waiter he must have made a mistake—he asked for "café"—*this* was day-before-yesterday's dish-water.

Narrow escape, Jan. 25, 1865. Dark rainy night—walked to extreme edge of a cut in solid rock 30 ft. deep and while standing upon the verge for half a dozen seconds, meditating whether to proceed or not, heard a stream of water falling into the cut, and then my eyes becoming more accustomed to the darkness saw that if the last step taken had been a handbreadth longer I must have plunged into it.

January 23, 1865, Angels. Rainy, stormy, beans and dish-water, for breakfast at the Frenchman's; dish-water and beans for dinner, and both articles warmed over for supper.

24th. Rained all day—meals as before.

25th. Same as above.

26th. Rain, beans and dish-water—beefsteak for a change—no use, couldn't bite it.

27th. Same old diet—same old weather—went out to the "pocket" claim, had to rush back.

28th. Rain and wind all day and all night. Chili-beans and dish-water three times today as usual and some kind of "slum" which the Frenchman called "hash." Hash be damned!

29th. The old, old thing. We shall *have* to stand the weather, but as J. says we *won't* stand the dish-water and beans any longer, by God.

30th. Jan.—moved to the new hotel, just opened—good fare and coffee that a Christian may drink without jeopardizing his eternal soul. Dick Stoker came over today from Tuttletown, Tuolumne Co.

> It was just at this time at Angel's Camp that Mark Twain heard the story of the jumping frog and missed a big pocket of gold. The pocket mentioned the 27th. This incident has been related elsewhere[1] but the memorandum which became the basis of the frog story belongs here.

Coleman with his jumping frog—bet a stranger $50.—Stranger had no frog and C. got him one:—In the meantime stranger filled C's frog full of shot and he couldn't jump. The stranger's frog won.

> Across this pencil note he added later, in ink:

Wrote this story for Artemus [Ward]—his idiot publisher Carleton, gave it to Clapp's Saturday Press.

> There is also in this book a memorandum of a story written many years later, "The Californian's Tale." The note reads:

Baden, crazy, asking after his wife who had been dead 13 years—first knowledge of his being deranged.

Feb. 3. Dined at the Frenchman's in order to let Dick see how he does things. Had "Hell-fire" soup and the old regular beans and dish-water. The Frenchman has 4 kinds of soup which he furnishes to customers only on great occasions. They are popularly known among the boarders as "Hell-fire," "General Debility," "Insanity"

[1] *Mark Twain—A Biography*, pp. 272-273.

and "Sudden Death," but it is not possible to describe them.

Feb. 6. Man in San Francisco jumped lot and built house on it; propped on low pins. Hogs used to congregate under it and grunt all night. Man bored holes in the floor and his wife poured hot water through—hogs struggling to get out hauled the house down the hill on their backs and the lot was rejumped by its proper owner early in the morning.

Feb. 25, 1865. Left Angels with Jim and Dick and walked over the mountain to Jack-ass in a snowstorm, the first I ever saw in California. The view from the mountain tops was beautiful.

CHAPTER II

The Sandwich Islands

IT WAS about this time that a new passenger steamer, the *Ajax*, built for the San Francisco-Sandwich Island trade, made its initial trip. Mark Twain was invited to go, as guest of the line, but, because of the daily letter which he contributed to his old paper, the *Enterprise*, of Virginia City, declined. By the time the *Ajax* was ready to sail again he had arranged to go on it, as special correspondent for the *Union*, of Sacramento, "to ransack the islands, the cataracts and volcanoes completely, and write twenty or thirty letters," as he joyously announced in a letter to his mother, then in St. Louis. He began a new notebook and wrote in it:

From San Francisco to the Hawaiian Islands
per Steamer Ajax, Nov. 7th 1866.

At sea, Mar. 9,

Just read letters from home which should have been read before leaving San Francisco. Accounts of oil on the Tenn. land, and that brother of mine [Orion Clemens] with his eternal cant about law and religion getting ready, in his slow stupid way, to go to Excelsior instead of the States; he sent me some prayers as usual.

Mar. 10. We are making about 200 miles a day. Got some sail on, yesterday morning, for first time, and in afternoon crowded everything on. Sea gulls chase, but no catch.

Three or four of the seasick passengers came to lunch at noon and several of the ladies are able to dress and sit up. Capt. reports 325 miles made in past 24 hours.

Found an old acquaintance today; never been anywhere yet that I didn't find an acquaintance.

Nearly everybody out to breakfast this morning; there's not more than half dozen sick now.

> He began to pick up some information concerning the Islands.

S. Islanders never intended to work. Worse off now with all the religions than ever before. Dying off fast. First white landed there was a curse to them.

Whalers like Kanakas better than any other sailors—temperate, strong, faithful, peaceable and orderly.

King always refused to sign constitution—he altered one clause of it from universal suffrage to property qualification, and when they tried to force him and threatened the straits would run blood he bade them good morning, and conference was ended.

House of Nobles appointed by King, and Lower House elective. Under universal suffrage missionaries used to vote their flocks for certain man and then sit at home and control him. One member (missionary's son) said out loud in open House he controlled 11 votes (a majority) in the House.

King not married, well educated and a gentleman. Has a father and sister living, and will appoint successor.

Country will eventually pass into hands of foreigners, probably French.

11th. Fine day, good N.E. breeze. Fore spencer—fore topsail—fore to'-gallant sail—lower stu'nsail and fore-top stun'sail—jib and flying jib—main spencer—gaff top-sail—all canvas set.

> But it was just at this point that he lost his

notebook. We know that this is so, for he began another, setting down whatever he could remember of the vanished record. It requires no gift to imagine him clawing over his stateroom, looking for the missing memoranda, swearing fervently meanwhile—settling down at last to a grim acceptance of his loss, scowling and fuming as with more or less success he recalled his original entries. A memory of the weather and seasickness was about all that remained. Very likely he suspected that his notes had been appropriated, for in the new book he writes on the inner cover, in a bold defiant hand MARK TWAIN.

12th. Monday. Very rough and rainy all forenoon—foresail shredded last night.

Rough weather on this route 7 to 8 months of year—Spring, Fall and Winter—Other 4 months beautiful weather.

Grown white men and women, handsome and well educated born in Hawaii.

Lauai has Mormon establishment—claim 5000 converts—King won't let them practice polygamy, though.

Missionary denominations are four—American, Episcopalian, Catholic and Mormon.

He was a long way from the islands, yet, but was in daily association with a passenger named Brown, who made his home there. There is no mention in the diary of "the Old Admiral" a retired whaleman—a "roaring terrific combination of wind and lightning and thunder," described in the Sandwich Island chapters of *Roughing It*, so we may assume that he was a figment of Mark Twain's rough and ready—his roughest and readiest—imagination, but in the quiet passenger "Williams," who routed the Admiral in argument, destroyed him with his own guns, it is easy to recognize Brown.

We can imagine him sitting with Brown through long afternoons, smoking and drowsily talking, looking out over stretches of sea that become more inviting and mysterious as the storms of the northern latitudes are left behind. The captain and others would join them, no doubt. Mark Twain was a name already well known along the Pacific slope, and known or not, his personality was a magnet that never failed to attract company. As the notes continue it is easy to see that he was falling in love with Hawaii a good while before he reached it.

Hawaiians indolent and no tenacity of life—no vitality. On the least possible excuse will lie down and die.

Tremendous solitudes of the Pacific—a lonely sea—no land in sight for 10 days, and never a solitary ship in sight.

He seems to have begun to make maxims about this time, a habit that would grow on him in later years.

Never refuse to do a kindness unless the act would work great injury to yourself, and never refuse to take a drink—under any circumstances.

Rise early. It is the early bird that catches the worm. Don't be fooled by this absurd saw; I once knew a man who tried it. He got up at sunrise and a horse bit him.

But the rough weather was not all gone.

March 12, Monday. Roughest night of the voyage, last night—ship rolled heavily. Still rougher this morning till 11 o'clock when course was altered to west, which eased her up considerably. Settee fetched away at breakfast and precipitated four heavy men on their backs.

> Next day old travelers were telling yarns of the force of the water, one or two of which he sets down. Then adds, on his own account.

Water taken in moderation cannot hurt anybody.

Mar. 13, Tuesday. Very rough again all night—had head winds and had to take in all sails—made poor run —weather fine this morning, but still head winds and there being not a rag of canvas on to steady the ship she rolls disagreeably, though the sea is not rough.

14th, Wednesday. Good weather. I have suffered from something like mumps for past 2 days.

15th, Thursday. Dress by the latitude and longitude —Capt. and chief eng. came out in full summer rig today because by the sextant we are in lat. 26 though the weather doesn't justify.

15th, Thursday. Mumps—mumps—mumps—it was so decided today—a damned disease that children have. I suppose I am to take a new disease to the Islands and depopulate them, as all white men have done, heretofore.

In Honolulu you can treat a Kanaka as much as you please, but he cannot treat you. No one is allowed to sell liquor to the natives and an infraction of this law is visited with a heavy penalty. It is evaded by using back doors, as is the custom in civilized countries.

It is not lawful to hire out a horse or vehicle on Sunday—all such preparations must be made the day before. This and the liquor law show where Hawaii's system of laws originated (with missionaries) and how firm they hold and how powerful a supremacy these people have gained by their 46 years of breeding and training voters, and clannish law-makers, among their own ever increasing descendants.

16th March, Friday. They say we shall be in sight of

land tomorrow, at noon. Good weather and a smooth sea for the past two days. Dennis the hog was killed yesterday and served up for breakfast this morning.

The water begins to taste of the casks.

Brown's boots are all one-sided with bracing to the lurching of the ship, and his nose is skinned. Thinks he will have cause of action against the company yet. Passengers all *venir pour me voir.*

160 miles from Honolulu at noon.

> He steadily picks up statistics about the Island which would be useful in his articles later; also some political and social phases of the life there.

King strongly favors English, on account of attention shown him in England and the reverse shown him in the U. S. (Virginia planter said wouldn't sit at table with a nigger) and favors all foreigners much more than Americans—so, Americans are at a discount in Honolulu, and possess small influence—on which account, and to curry favor, no foreigner will buy anything of an American which he can get of an Englishman. All money in hands of foreigners circulates *among* foreigners, pretty exclusively, and on the other hand Americans who have any spirit retaliate by dealing with Americans, pretty exclusively. The *American Hotel* is kept by a Dutchman. Ten Americans there to one foreigner, but the influence plays the devil, nevertheless. All English men-of-war foster this partiality of the King by flattering him and showing him royal honors and attention.

CHAPTER III

Honolulu

Arrived at noon Sunday—fired gun—19 days and 6 hrs. out—Could have got in last night, just after dark.

Channel very narrow but straight—well buoyed—not wide enough for 2 ships at once—hardly. Custom House boat came off with flag.

McIntyre, pilot, old burly, gray-headed scout.

King sat in 2-horse buggy alone on wharf—big whiskers—old leather complexion—broad gold band on plug hat—band of gold around lapels of coat. *No*—King's driver—speculation wrong.

Crowd 4 or 500.

Sunday's stillness—natives sitting in shade of houses on the ground.

People here smoke Manila cigars and drink everything.

Long street, darkest in the world, down to the Esplanade —width 3 buggies abreast—couldn't get out of it, and so found my way.

Found Rev. Mr. Rising there. [An old San Francisco friend.]

Hotels gouge Californians—charge sailing passengers $8 a week for board, but steamer passengers ten.

Charley Richards keeps a tremendous spider and two lizards for pets. I would like to sleep with him if he would get a couple of snakes or so.

Honolulu hospitality. Richards said: "Come in—sit down—take off your coat and boots—take a drink. Here is a pass-key to the liquor and cigar cupboard—put it in your pocket—" 2 doors to his house—stand wide open night and day from Jan. till Jan.—no locks on them—march in whenever you feel like it—take as many drinks and cigars as you want and make yourself at home.

13 letters in Hawaiian alphabet—each a distinct sound—3 vowels together sometimes, but each an independent sound—no trouble to learn to pronounce. Have a large lexicon and a small phrase book.

King sitting on barrel on wharf fishing.

King showed Asa Nudd greater attention than he ever showed foreign civilian before—in return for his hospitality in California.

Couldn't understand the bear-skin mats on floors—whalers bring them.

French got possession of the Society [Islands] and more recently the Marquesas, by means of Romish clergy. They sent priests here—King said his people had been rescued from idolatry—wouldn't have any more of it—sent them away. Man-of-war brought another priest, disguised as merchant—found out—ordered away—ships threatened to burn the town—allowed to remain under protest—ship brought back the banished priests from Mexico—one is now bishop here and lives in palace. We all know how France would regard treaty if she could once get possession.

Mark Twain immediately fell in love with Hawaii and remained in love with it his life long. It becomes evident in his notes.

"No careworn or eager, anxious faces in the land of happy contentment—God, what a contrast with California and Washoe. Everybody walks at a moderate gait but, to speak strictly, they mostly ride.

"O, islands there are on the face of the deep,
Where the leaves never fade and the skies never weep."

In *Roughing It* he says:

In place of the grand mud-colored brown fronts of San Francisco, I saw dwellings built of straw, adobes, and cream-colored pebble-and-shell-conglomerated coral, cut into oblong blocks and laid in cement; also a great number of neat white cottages, with green window-shutters; in place of front yards like billiard-tables with iron fences around them, I saw these homes surrounded by ample yards, thickly clad with green grass, and shaded by tall trees, through whose dense foliage the sun could scarcely penetrate; in place of the customary geranium, calla lily, &c., languishing in dust and general debility, I saw luxurious banks and thickets of flowers, as fresh as a meadow after a rain, glowing with the richest dyes; . . . in place of the Golden City's skirting sandhills and placid bay, I saw on the one side a framework of tall precipitous mountains close at hand, clad in refreshing green, and cleft by deep, cool chasm-like valleys; and in front the grand sweep of the ocean: a brilliant, transparent green near the shore, bound and bordered by a long white line of foamy spray dashing along the reef, and farther out the dead blue water of the deep sea, flecked with white-caps, and in the far horizon a single lonely sail—a mere accent mark to emphasize a slumberous calm and a solitude that were without sound or limit. When the sunk sank down—the one intruder from other realms and persistent in suggestions of them—it was tranced luxury to sit in the perfumed air and forget that there was any world but these enchanted islands.

Went home with Mr. Damon, to his cool, vine-shaded *home*—you bet.

This house and chapel where he preaches were built by Seamen's Friends Society of New York 1833—Rev. John Diell here till '40—died of consumption on way home, off Cape Horn, '41. Damon arrived Fall of '42, been here ever since, except visit home, of a year, and to California in '49. He and Gwynn made their début in California at the same time and both officiated at 4th of July in Sacramento that year—he made prayer and G. spoke while they were cutting down trees to build the town—only half a dozen houses then. He preached first sermon ever preached in Stockton—"Whatsoever a man soweth that shall he also reap." A man cleared out his bar for him—only 2 houses there. One of them Weber's—balance tents.

A Mrs. McFarlane tells him some marvelous things of her residence in the Islands:

Mrs. McFarlane: "Volcanoes on Toahi—30 miles from the house—eruption began slowly at dusk—at 4 A.M. was shooting rocks and lava 400 ft. high which would then descend in a grand shower of fire to the earth—crater overflowed and molten waves and billows went boiling and surging down mountain side, just for the world like the sea—stream from ½- to mile-and-a-half wide and hundreds of feet deep, perhaps. Over cattle-houses and across streams to the sea 63 miles distant (7 years ago) ran into sea 3 miles and boiled the fish for 20 miles around—vessels found scores of boiled fish 20 miles out—natives cooked their food there. Every evening for 7 weeks sat on the veranda half the night, gazing upon the splendid spectacle—the wonderful pyrotechnic display. The house windows were always of a bloody hue. Read newspapers every night by no other light than was afforded by this mighty torch, 30 miles away. Crowds of visitors came from the other islands."

Present King is penetrating—sound judgment—dignity—accomplished—has good sense and courage and decision—became acquainted with business by long acquaintanceship as Minister of Interior. Prince Bill is very able man and accomplished gentleman—they have always been a wonderful family and the ablest in the land.

Sea Island cotton picked every day in the year—stalks cut off every Jan.—no frost—sure crop, worth $1 a pound in Liverpool or Havre—worth *any* price—adulterate silk goods with it. 1000 acres this land in bend of head of this island worth $2 to $20 an acre. Raised 30000 lbs. last year—will raise 50000 this. All that is needed is labor—industry—natives won't pick it every day—lazy and shiftless.

Girls here have good home faces.

Found the purser looking at naked women fishing, through spyglass.

> He became too busy, apparently, to make elaborate notes; 1 or 2 lines was the best he could do. Just a word, or a line, trusting to God and his memory when the time came to write about it.

Boys and girls in swimming.
Eating raw fish and poi.
Hoola hoola dance.
Heated term.
$65 income entitles to vote.
Old battleground.
The Salt Lake.
Fish ponds.
Coral reefs.
Another old battleground.

> It is a modernistic poem.

Evidences of remote antiquity.
Fondness for tobacco but not whiskey—laws against it.
Church law against smoking.

> And Sharon waves in silent praise
> Her sacred groves of palms.

Wailing for the sick.
Hawaii a half-way house on the Pacific highway.
Natives pay to get their poetry printed.

Heated term but there are few flies in my room or hotel.

Mosquitoes. 2 kinds—day and night.

Have to take out a license ($10) to have the Hula Hula dance performed, and then if the girls dress for it in the usual manner—that is, with no clothing worth mentioning—it must be conducted in strict privacy.

A larkspur planted alongside any shrub here will protect the same from the prevailing blight.

The King ought to be grateful to the missionaries because during all the years that the English and French were making trouble and creating complications and trying to get an excuse to seize the islands the wise councils of these men saved Kamehamehas II, III, and perhaps V from making any false step.

Mrs. McFarlane thought I was drunk because I talked so long.

No word to express gratitude—can but lamely express virtue of any kind—prolific in epithets to express every degree of and shade of vice and crime. No word to express farewell or good-bye.

Wail for joy and for sorrow with the same noise.

Wash clothes well, but beat them all to pieces.

Takes one a good while to cramp and crowd and screw and diminish himself down to a conception of the smallness of this island—this kingdom. One rides 6 or 8 miles in any direction and here is the ocean bursting upon his view—seems as if he never will get the damned island trimmed down as small as it really is.

Soft voice of native girls—liquid, free, joyous laughter.

Kanakas will have horses and saddles and the women will fornicate—two strong characteristics of this people.

He seems to have been attacked by the general indolence of the islands, a condition which they call there the "boo-hoo" fever. He defines it:

Boo-hoo—feebleness, lassitude, indifference, no appetite, slight nausea, head and neck-ache, achy all over. [It sounds like malaria.]

Kammy's bones hidden at his own request to keep them from making fish hooks of them—a superstition that hooks made of bones of a great chief would concentrate the fish.

Singing of natives very rich and soft—has no sound of S in it.

Well enough for old folks to rise early, because they have done so many mean things all their lives they can't sleep anyhow.

No native beggars.

More missionaries and more row made about saving these 60000 people than would take to convert hell itself.

Americans have given religious freedom, education, written language and Bible—England and France have given insults.

Here he finds the lost notebook and starts in anew.

July 3, 1866. Saw star tonight on which counted 12 distinct and flaming points—very large star—shone with such a pure, rich, diamond lustre—lustrous on a field of dead solid black—no stars very close—where I sat saw no other. Moonlight here is fine but nowhere so fine as Washoe.

All stars shine pure and bright here.

July 4, 1866, Honolulu. Went to ball 8:30 P.M.—danced till 12:30—went home with M.C.—stopped at Gen. Van Valkenbergh's room and talked with him and Mr. Burlingame, Col. Rumsey and Ed. Burlingame, until 3 A.M.

That is to say, Anson Burlingame, Minister to China, General Van Valkenburg, Minister to

Japan, Colonel Rumsey, attaché and Edward L. Burlingame, later for many years editor of *Scribner's Magazine*, then a charming boy of eighteen. Anson Burlingame definitely influenced Mark Twain's future. His example, and his advice to associate with persons of superior intellect were timed to the exact moment when they would do the most good. But the story of all this has been told elsewhere.[1]

Brown calls his horse Haleakala—extinct volcano, because if ever been any fire in him all gone out before he came across him.

If a man ask thee to go with him a mile, go with him, Twain—(Honolulu joke by Ed. Burlingame).

Which entry refers to a morning when young Burlingame called and proposed a walk. When Mark Twain objected the young man declared there was a Scriptural command covering the case. Clemens answered that if he could quote one he'd obey it, which the other promptly did, as above. This joke, often attributed to other sources, had its origin here.

D'n Kanakas ride along with you—walk when you walk, gallop when you gallop—trot when you trot—never say a word—perfect shadows.

If you cut a shark in two you die—a man who was to fish on shares had to cut a shark in 2—said that 20 years ago he would have been afraid—would have died—now believes in "hoola" doctrine. Still he got a little sick, and all the natives came and said: It's because you cut the shark? At last he said it *was,* and died.

"Honolulu, July 18, '66. I got my passport from the Royal damned Hawaiian collector of customs and paid a

[1] *Mark Twain—a Biography,* chapter LIII, pp. 285-288.

dollar for it, and tomorrow we sail for America in good ship *Smyrniote*; we love it, Master,—and I have got a devilish saddle boil to sit on for the first 2 weeks at sea."

> The *Smyrniote* was a sailing-vessel altogether at the mercy of the winds. M. T. had been in the Islands exactly four months, an experience that all his life he loved to remember and hoped to repeat.

All small villages are gossipy, but Honolulu heads them a little. They let me off comparatively easy, though I don't thank them for it because it argues that I wasn't worth the trouble of blackguarding. They only accused me of murder, arson, highway robbery and some other little eccentricities, but I knew nothing of it till the day I started. The missionary (I should say preacher) feature of insincerity and hypocrisy makes the atmosphere of the place.

A woman who keeps a dog won't do, as a general thing.

CHAPTER IV

Honolulu to San Francisco

HONOLULU, July 19, 1866; the Comet, with Howard and Mrs. Spencer and Nellie and Katie on board, left at 2 P.M. with a great firing of cannon and went to windward (unusual)—we left peaceably in the Smyrniote at 4:30 P.M. (Comet out of sight) and went in same direction. Now we shall see who beats to San Francisco.

Made 110 miles up to noon of Friday 20th, but were then only 10 miles from Oahu, having gone clear around the island.

On 21st made 179 miles.

Tuesday, July 24, had calm several times. Are we never to make any longitude, the Trades are weakening—it is time we struck the China winds about midnight—say in lat. 36.

Wednesday, 25th, 3 P.M. We are abreast of San Francisco, but 1700 miles at sea. When will the wind change.

25th July, lat. 29 N. I was genuinely glad this evening to welcome the first twilight I have seen in 6 years. No twilight in the Islands, California or Washoe.

Minister to ship captain who is complaining of deserting sailors: "Don't swear captain, that won't mend the matter." Captain: "Brother Damon, it's all very well for you to say, don't swear, and it's all right too—I don't say anything against it—but don't you know that if you should ship a crew of sailors for Heaven and were to stop at Hell 2½ hrs. for provisions, some damned son-of-a-gun would run away."

Friday, 27. "Caught 2 goneys.—They are all the same size—they measure 7 ft. 1 in. from tip to tip of wings—They made a wooden clog fast to one and let him go—a pitiful advantage for 'Godlike' man to take of a helpless bird. The bird looked reproachfully upon them with his great human eyes while they did him this wrong."

Across the years one's heart aches for that tortured bird.

King of S. I. is a heathen—an old sorceress has him under her thumb—picks out the fish he may eat—tells him in what house he may sleep, etc., accompanies him in all his excursions. He was educated in a Christian school but has never submitted himself to Christianity—discovered his predilection for heathenism in youth.

The next entry refers to the great marine disaster, the burning of the ship *Hornet* "on the line" early in May of that year. Fifteen survivors in an open boat had managed to reach Hawaii, and Mark Twain, ill at the moment, with the assistance of Anson Burlingame and party, had interviewed them, written his report carrying the first news of the disaster to the outside world—there being in that day no cable. It was a great news-beat. Later he turned it into an article "Forty-three Days in an Open Boat" for *Harper's Magazine*. Rewritten, it appears today in his collected works under the title of "My Début as a Literary Person."

In a single voyage they grew old—in a mariner's stormy experience. In this little voyage of 7 months of these 2 fresh young college students, were crowded the sorrows, the bitter hardships and the thrilling adventures of a whole long lifetime before the mast.

Samuel Ferguson is about 28, a graduate of Trinity College, Hartford. B. Henry is 18—a student of same college—Capt. says the boys were good grit—Henry's underlip never quivered but once and that was when he was told that there was hardly the shadow of a chance for their rescue, and then the feeling he showed was chiefly at the thought that he was never to see his college mates any more.

Think of this prayer uttered in an open boat, before uncovered famishing men, in the midst of the Pacific Ocean and in the midst of the sea lashed to fury by the anger of a storm:

"O, most powerful and glorious Lord God, at whose command the winds blow and lift up the waves of the sea and who stillest the rage thereof; we thy creatures, but miserable sinners, do in this hour of our great distress cry unto Thee for help. Save, Lord, or we perish."

5 o'clock, evening before they made land, most magnificent rainbow they ever saw, and spanned the widest space. Capt. sang out "Saved! there is the bow of promise, boys!" When such a thing is seen at sea it is nearly always accompanied by the signs of coming squalls and tempests, but in this instance the sky was marvelously clear and entirely free from such signs.

Conversation between the carpenters of Noah's Ark, laughing at him for an old visionary.

While most men have a manner of speaking peculiar to themselves no arbitrary system of punctuation can apply. Every man should know best how to punctuate his own manuscript.

Monday, July 30. This is the fifth day of dead, almost motionless, calm—a man can walk a crack on the deck the ship lies so still. I enjoy it and believe all hands do, except the baby. I write 2 hrs. a day and loaf the balance. At this rate it will take me a good while to finish Ferguson's log.

I don't think much of Hawaiian royalty. Years ago when the late King and the present King were only Princes—youths—they traveled in U. S. with the premier of the kingdom, Dr. Judd, an American. On one occasion, on board a southern steamer they did not go in to dinner as soon as the bell rang, and then there was no room for them. They were offended. The captain, however, as soon as he knew their national character, had a table set in a private room for himself and the three and entertained them in a manner befitting their high rank. That is Dr. Judd's story, and no doubt the true one. Other accounts say they went in to dinner, but observing their black faces, and uninformed of their rank, the steward enforced the rule of the boat excluding colored persons from the cabin table. They were naturally incensed and all that could afterwards be done failed to wipe from their minds the memory of the affront. Yet, at its worst, it was one which was offered to them as unknown and merely private individuals, and being entirely unofficial could not affect them as Princes or their country through them, and should have been so received and so valued. The men only were insulted, not the Princes, and thus their country was no more insulted than if the affront had been offered to the commonest Kanaka in the realm. The King has never forgotten or forgiven that trifling stab at his little vanity.

But Great Britain officially seized the Islands in 1843, abused, humiliated and insulted their King, K. III in a bullying and overbearing manner. Threatened the destruction of the little helpless capital town when it was utterly at the mercy of his heavy guns; and finally forced the acceptance of terms of so degrading a nature that in the hearts of the spirited people the memory of them would rankle till the end of time. K. V has been caressed and flattered by British men-of-warsmen and so he has forgiven that deadly insult and fawns upon the nation that gave it.

So also with his dear friends the French, who treated his ancestor K. III like a dog—who, through their admiral, marched gallantly upon his thoroughly harmless and entirely ornamental fort, and, unresisted, demolished it and spiked its guns—and then made the poor King sign an agreement the nature of which may best be expressed by saying that through it, metaphorically, the French nation spit in the face of Hawaii. But dusky Queen Emma had been flattered and fêted at the French court and lo, K. V is mollified and the atrocious acts of the admiral are forgotten. This is Hawaiian royalty.

Missionaries have made honest men out of the nation of thieves; instituted marriage; created homes; lifted woman to same rights and privileges enjoyed elsewhere; abolished infanticide; abolished intemperance; diminished licentiousness; given equal laws, whereby chief's power of life and death over his subjects is taken away; in a great measure abolished idolatry; have well educated the people.

Capt. says sailors (of the Hornet) like great stupid children hadn't been an hour ashore till they were growling about the grub and smuggling great slabs of pork through natives to add to their rations of tea and biscuit. One man nearly killed himself first day, eating fruit—came near dying that night. Cox sat beside Capt. on shore and was eating a cocoanut—Capt. confiscated it and threw it away—Cox thought it hard treatment of a poor devil who had been starving 43 days.

Sparkling and Bright

Floating away like a fountain spray
O'er the snow-white bloom of a maiden,
The smoke-wreaths rise to the scarlet skies
With blissful fragrance laden.
Then smoke away till golden ray
Lights o'er the dawn of the morrow
For a cheerful cigar like a shield will bar
The heart from care and sorrow.

Aug. 3. The calm continues—magnificent weather. Men all turned boys. Play boyish games on the poop and quarter-deck. Lay small object on fife-rail of mainmast—shut one eye, walk 3 steps and strike at it with forefinger. Lay small object on deck, walk 7 steps blindfold and try to find it. Kneel, elbows against knees, hands extended along deck—place object against ends of fingers then clasp hands behind back and try to pick it up with teeth, and rise up from knees.

Sunday, Aug. 5, 1866. Everybody cheerful—at daylight saw the Comet on our lee—it is pleasant in this tremendous solitude to have company.

Aug. 13. San Francisco. Home again. No *not* home again—in prison again and all the wide sense of freedom gone. The city seems so cramped and so dreary with toil and care and business anxiety. God help me, I wish I were at sea again.

D'n it—when you go to sea, take some cans of condensed milk with you.

I never was cheerfully and cordially received but at 3 or 4 places on the Islands. I think they must have heard of me before—and yet in nearly every case I was treated with such kind and considerate politeness that I seldom had cause to feel uncomfortable. Most Americans who have lived any considerable time there all seem to have lost whatever of impulsiveness, frank openness and warmth of feeling they may have possessed before, and become calculating, suspicious, reserved, cold and distant. They have cased themselves in a shell—don't believe they would welcome anybody and if by chance they are betrayed into coming out of it and displaying their old-time vivacity and naturalness for an hour they will draw into it again as soon as they cool down. There is little sociability and genuine friendship existing among the families of foreigners living in the Islands, though there is some show of it by way of keeping up appearances. One would expect the opposite from a class shut out as they are from the rest of the world. They live within themselves—within their shell and are not, if I may be allowed to suggest it—not happy. I thought differently, at first. I thought they were the happiest people I had ever seen. They do look serene and contented, but they are not. Their hearts are not dead, but far away—at home. They think often of home, and this absence of man's life—essence—his feelings, his affections, his interests has much to do with their seeming so indifferent and reserved, no doubt.

A man never reaches that dizzy height of wisdom when he can no longer be led by the nose.

Hornet's Sailors

These boys have been mourned as dead for nearly 4 months. Think of the thrill of the first telegram to that home circle—"Crew and passengers of Hornet arrived safe."

Capt. knew for days that murderous discontent was brewing, by the distraught air of some of the men, and he stayed on guard. Slept no more—kept his hatchet hid and close at hand.

Notes on Henry Ferguson's Log

From day after the ship burnt till the 12th he put simply the (to him) eloquent word "doldrums."

The storms during the first fortnight he called the awfulest wind squalls, the most terrific thunder and blinding lightning he ever saw, and black as ink in absence of lightning—caused to steer in all directions—Rained 5 times as hard as in the States.

Saw waterspout on 17th. Thinks it might be a pleasant sight from a ship—Mentions the star mistaken for ship's light.

From the Log

"Distressed by swordfish cavorting around the boat for some time. Immense one—Passed some seaweed and something that looked like trunk of old tree, but no birds —beginning to be afraid Islands not there. Today it was said to the Capt., and in the hearing of all, that some of the men would not shrink, when a man was dead, from using the flesh, though they would not kill. Horrible! God give us all full use of our reason and spare us from such things! . . ."

CHAPTER V

A Grim Voyage to New York

Mark Twain found himself more at sea in San Francisco than during those ocean days of drifting calm. He was uncertain which way to turn. His literary ventures were neither satisfactory nor profitable. A lecture on the islands which his friends urged him to deliver was much more successful and he toured the coast with it that winter. With considerable ready money in hand, he decided now to return home—after an absence of five and a half years. In the back of his head was a plan for a trip around the world, including a visit to Anson Burlingame, who had invited him to Peking. He would begin his travels by sailing for New York, via the Isthmus of Nicaragua. He bought a new notebook which he labeled:

From San Francisco to New York by way of San Juan and Grey Town-Isthmus.

Sailed from San Francisco in Opposition steamer, *America,* Capt. Wakeman, at noon 15th Dec. 1866.

Pleasant sunny day, hills brightly clad with green grass and shrubbery.

Runaway match—boarded by irate father and bogus policeman—Repulsed by passengers—Love victorious.

First night a tempest—the greatest seen on this coast for many years—though occupying an outside berth on upper deck it yet did not seem so rough to us as it did to those below and we remained in bed all night, while the other passengers realizing the great danger all got up and dressed.

The ship was down too much by the head, and just doggedly fought the seas, instead of climbing over them.

Nearly everybody seasick. Happily I escaped—Had something worse—lay in bed and received passengers' reports.

A sea that broke over the ship about midnight carried away 20 ft. of the bulwarks forward. The forward cabin was drenched with water and the steerage fairly flooded—a case of claret floated into a stateroom in the forward cabin. The water must have been 6 in. deep if a case of claret float, or wash, at all. A man's boots were washed to farther end of the room. Various things were afloat.

They prepared the boats for emergency.

Old ship captain of 28 years' experience said he had never seen the equal of this storm. He instructed a friend to stay by him till all but the ship's officers were adrift and he and they would make a raft—"Curse the boats in such a sea and such a lot of passengers." Men were praying all about the cabin on their knees. Brown went to one and said: "What's the matter?" and he said: "O, don't talk to me. Oh my!" Passenger said he had served 14 years at sea, but considered his time had come now, but added: "If anybody can save her it's old Wakeman." [1] I perceive by these things that we might have gone to the bottom unaware that we were in danger—why the Ajax cut up worse in a dead calm.

Sunday 16th. This is a long, long night. I occupy lower berth and read and smoke by ship's lantern, borrowed from the steward. I won the middle berth, but gave it

[1] Captain Ned Wakeman, later to figure in *Roughing It* as "Captain Ned Oakley," and as "Captain Stormfield" in the *Visit to Heaven*. Capt. Wakeman also appears as Capt. Hurricane Jones, in "Rambling Notes of an Idle Excursion."

to Smith because he is seasick and we have piled our wines, books and small traps in the upper one.

I don't know what time it is—my watch is run down—I think it is 7 bells in the 3rd watch but I am not certain, the wind may have blown away one tap of the bell—we hear it very faintly away up here, anyway.

Thursday 20th. At noon, 5 days out from San Francisco abreast a high stretch of land at foot of Magdalena Bay. Capt. came and said: "Come out here" (we had just got into warm weather and covered the whole after part of the vessel with awnings, making it extremely cool and shady). "I want to show you something"—Took the marine glass—Whaleship at anchor under the bluffs—one listed and hoisting vast mass of blubber aboard. Capt. said: "Now tonight they'll try it out on deck and it will look like a whole ship on fire. The first time I ever saw it was in '50s—I came along here just after dark—saw a ship on fire, apparently—I didn't know the country—didn't dare to go in there with the ship, so I sent a boat crew and said, 'Pull for your lives, d'n you, and tell the captain I'll lay here for a week and send him all the assistance I can and then carry his people to San Francisco.' Well, we laid to, and waited and waited—all the passengers on deck and anxious for boat to come back and report,—but 10 o'clock no boat,—11 o'clock no boat—passengers began to get tired and sidle off to bed,—12 o'clock no boat—every passenger gave up and went below except one old woman, she stuck it out and never took her eyes off the fire.

"By and by, at 12:30, back the boat come, and I and the old woman crowded to the lee rail to see and hear it all—couldn't see any extra men. The officer of the boat stepped on deck and lifted his hat and says: 'The captain of the ship sends great gratification—great obligations and thanks you for your trouble and good intention, but he ain't in trouble, but quite the reverse—is full of oil and ready to up anchor tomorrow and is giving his crew a big blow-out on deck and is illuminating. Sends his good wishes for success, and hopes you will accept this boatload of A-1 sea turtles.' The old woman leaned over the rail and shaded her eyes from the lantern, and she saw them varmints flapping their flippers about in the boat and she says 'For the land's sake, I sot here and sot here all this blessed night calculating to see a whole boatload of sorrowful roasted corpses and now it ain't nothin' after all but a lot of nasty turtles.' "

22nd December midnight. Smooth sea—or rather just rippled with a pleasant breeze—perfectly fair wind—yards squared—splendid full moon—ship riding along placidly in full view of Mexican shore—all in bed but me—night is magnificent—temperature, too, soft—balmy, delicious.

From the next entry it is clear that Captain Ned Wakeman was beginning to take shape in Mark Twain's imagination as literary material.

I'd rather travel with that old portly, hearty, jolly, boisterous, good-natured sailor, Capt. Ned Wakeman, than with any other man I ever came across. He never drinks and never plays cards; he never swears except in the privacy of his own quarters, with a friend or so, and then his feats of fancy blasphemy are calculated to fill the hearer with awe and admiration. His yarns—just as I got that far Capt. W. came in, sweating and puffing, for we are off the far southern coast of Mexico and the weather is a little sultry, and he said:

"Speaking of rats, once in Honolulu me and old Josephus—he was a Jew, and got rich as Crœsus in San F. afterwards—we were going home as passengers from the S. I. in a brand-new brig on her 3rd voyage—and our trunks were down below. He went with me—laid over one vessel to do it—because he warn't no sailor and he liked to be with a man that was—and the brig was sliding out between the buoys and her head-line was paying out ashore. There was a wood-pile right where the line was made fast to the pier, and up come the damndest biggest rat—as big as an ordinary cat he was—and darted out on that line and cantered for the shore—and up came another—and another—and another—and away they galloped over that hawser—each one treading on t'other's tail till they were so thick that you couldn't see a thread of the cable, and there was a procession of 'em 200 yards long over the levee like a streak of ants—and the Kanakas, some throwing sticks from that wood-pile and chunks of lava and coral at 'em and knocking 'em endways and every which way. But do you s'pose it made any difference to them rats? Not a particle—not a particle, bless your soul—they never let up till the last rat was ashore out of that brand-new beautiful brig. I called a Kanaka with his boat, and he hove alongside and shinned up a rope and says I: 'Do you see that trunk down there?' 'Ai.' 'Clatter it ashore as quick as God'll let you.'

"Josephus, the Jew, says: 'What are you doing, Captain?' and I says: 'Doing? Why I'm a-taking my trunk ashore, that's what I'm a-doing!'

" 'Taking your trunk ashore? Why bless us what is that for?'

" 'What is it for?' says I—'Do you see them rats? Do you notice them rats a-leaving this ship? She's doomed, Sir—she's doomed! Burnt brandy wouldn't save her, Sir! She'll never finish this voyage. She'll never be heard of again, Sir.'

"Josephus says: 'Boy, take that other trunk ashore too.'

"And don't you know, Sir, that brig sailed out of Honolulu without a rat aboard and was never seen again by mortal man, Sir. We went in an old tub, so rotten that you had to walk easy on the main deck to keep from going through—so crazy that in our berths when there was sea on, the timbers over our heads worked backwards and forwards 11 inches in their sockets—just like an old basket, Sir—and the rats were as big as greyhounds and as lean, Sir, and they bit the buttons off of our overcoats and there were so many of them that in a gale once they all scampered to the starboard side when we were going about and put her down the wrong way, so that she'd come monstrous near foundering! But she went through safe, I tell you, because she had rats aboard."

Christmas Eve—9 P.M. Myself, the Captain and Kingman out forward. Capt. said—"Don't like the looks of that point, with the mist outside of it." Quartermaster, touching his cap: "The child is dead, Sir." [Had been sick 2 days] "What are your orders?"

Capt.: "Tell Ben to send the Dr. for the Parson to speak to the grandmother, and the Mate to speak to the young mother—bury at sea at daylight."

It was the first death of that tragic journey.

On the San Juan River

In that day eastern-bound passengers landed, crossed the Nicaragua Isthmus by river, lake, and overland, to Grey Town, to take the Atlantic-bound steamer. The next entry is made on the river steamer.

While gazing up a little narrow avenue, carpeted with greenest grass and walled with the thickest growth of bright ferns and quaint broad-leaved trees whose verdant sprays sprang upward and outward like the curving sprays of a fountain—an avenue that is fit for the royal road to Fairyland that is closed with a gate of trellised vines stretching their charming maze of festoons bright with their beautiful blossoms, some scoundrel interrupts with:

"You'd oughter gone ashore, there where we wooded—bananner trees till you couldn't rest—leaves 7 ft. long and 1½ ft. wide, and natives doing something or other with coffee trees—what is it—and what were they doing it for?"

I got up and left.

San Juan Bay—Neat little semicircle shut in by wooded hills. Fine breeze. Must remain this afternoon and leave early in A.M. on account of cholera—brought by Santiago—300 soldiers and several hundred passengers—26 deaths among former and 9 of latter and 40 of natives—all in past 11 days—all subsided now.

Dec. 28. Left San Juan in carriages—native drivers armed with long knives—native soldiers barefooted, with muskets. Threatened war between 2 candidates for Presidency of Republic of Nicaragua—case of a contested election—present President going to hold his posish and whip both parties.

Long procession of horsemen and hacks—beautiful road and cool, rainy atmosphere. All on lookout for wild monkeys.

Orange, banana, aguardiente, coffee, hot corn, carved cups—stands, pretty native women, ruffles around bottom of dress.

Snake cactus clasping trees. Calabash trees. One hack broke down. Threatened bloodshed between passengers and drivers.

Beautiful breezy lake—2 circus tent mountains—cloud-capped—wooded densely to summits, save where lava passed—One 4200 ft.—other 5400 ft. look higher—very beautiful with their solid crown of clouds and rising abruptly from water—coffee, cattle, tobacco, corn—all sorts of ranches on them—raise everything with no trouble—splendid temperature.

Changed boats and started down lovely San Juan River, at 4 A.M. saluting old Fort San Carlos with 3 whistles—Bank full—spots of grass—trees like cypress—blossoming trees—trees so festooned with vines that they look like vine-clad towers of ancient fortresses—great tree-ferns and tall graceful clumps of bamboo—all manner of trees and bushes and all so woven together with a charming lacework of vines that a monkey can't climb through.

On first San Juan River steamer man at companionway said: "None but first cabin allowed up here—you first cabin?" with a most offensive emphasis—and let a whole sluice of steerage pass unchallenged—quite a compliment to my personal appearance.

On the second river boat challenged me faithfully and passed the other first cabin unchallenged.

> Mark Twain had been ranked as a "dresser" on the River, but apparently did not consider it worth while to array himself for travel.

Town of Castillo where we walked 300 yards and changed boats below rapids—old romantic doby castle of a fort on top of steep grass dome, 200 ft. high—14 houses under hill and dense vine-clad foliage appearing beyond.

Native thatched houses—coffee, eggs, bread, cigars, and

fruit for sale—delicious—10c buys pretty much anything and in great quantity. Californians can't understand how 10 or 25c can buy a sumptuous lunch of coffee, eggs and bread.

Vine-festooned terrace concealed hills like a web—couldn't believe they were hills, except that upper trees towered too high to be on the bank level.

Dark grottos, fairy harbors—tunnels, temples—columns, pillars, towers, pilasters, terraces, pyramids, mounds, domes, walls in endless confusion of vine-work—no shape, no architecture, unimitated—and all so webbed together with vines that short distances within are only gained by glimpses—monkeys here and there—birds warbling—gorgeous-plumaged birds on the wing—paradise itself—the imperial realm of beauty, nothing to wish for to make it perfect.

The changing vistas of the river—corners and points folding backward, retreating and unveiling new wonders beyond, of towering walls of verdure, gleaming cataracts of vines—wonderful waterfalls of glittering leaves as deftly overlapping each other as the scales of a fish—a vast green wall—solid a moment, then as we advance changing and opening into Gothic windows, colonnades—all manner of quaint and charming shapes (damn the blackguard with the damaged plug hat on who is looking over my shoulder as I make these notes on the boiler deck).

"Mrs. Grundy" (all in brown) damned old meddling, moralizing fool—said I was no better than I ought to be.

"The choir sang the damnedest, oldest, vilest songs, such as 'Marching through Georgia,' 'When Johnnie comes Marching Home,' 'Old Dog Tray,' 'Just before the Battle Mother,' etc. When they sang hymns they did well and made good music but damn their other efforts—and besides they never invited me to sing, anyhow."

Many great lazy alligators on bank, sleeping in the sun—bright-plumaged parrots flying above the trees—birds with gay plumage and great hooked villainous bills such as we see in the menagerie—long-legged, long-necked birds that rise awkwardly from the edge of the jungle, crook their necks like an S, shove their long bills forward and throw their long legs out behind like a steering oar when they are flying—and monkeys capering among the trees—these are the signs of the tropics.

At first everybody apologized for coming this way and said it must be done merely to see the country and get it off his mind—a sort of compulsory sense of duty—never should come this way again, of course—but now on the San Juan River with all this enchantment around us and after coming over what we have passed through and decided that it has been nothing but a comfortable, cheerful, satisfactory, pleasure trip, we all begin to confess that if we were already through our business in the States and ready to return we should be uncommonly apt to come this way after all.

New Year's Eve 1866. Slept on the floor and hammocks at Woodyard first night out from Castillo. Started at 2 A.M. and got to Grey Town at daylight. Found vessel San Francisco there—took them all day to transfer baggage and to remove the 2 sets of steerage passengers. Kingman told them in joke uptown our steerage and second cabin had small-pox and they anchored 'em out. Much crowded all night and wouldn't let any come ashore during day. We stayed aboard most of the day, anchored out and slept uptown—had to come to boat at 6 A.M. At 7 Capt. Merrey sent us in surf boats in rainstorm—our boat had to go to the Nicaragua and finish her complement with second-cabin passengers—a dozen—and came near being swamped by them. Took 3 hrs. to disembark the New York passengers and then we got under way.

Everlasting curses on the man who invented the villainous little lamp they put in a man's stateroom on shipboard. That is as honest a prayer as I ever uttered.

Jan. 2. All right now on this ship, got plenty of ice and ice-water, no more melting here in the tropics.

That infernal monkey is having a perfect carnival all to himself. Smith and Kingman gave him a good square drink of brandy and now he feels it—one moment he is in the quarter boat abreast my room and the next he is at the top-gallant crosstrees and scampering wildly from rope to rope, capering out on the yards like a lunatic—the dizzy height, the blowing of the gale and the plunging of the ship have no terrors for him.

A sailor scared the monkey awhile ago and he jumped from the top-gallant yard arm and caught a back stay or something away down 20 or 30 ft. below.

The next note is brief, but ominous:

Jan. 2, 1867. Two cases of cholera reported in the steerage today.

Kingman's report of small-pox kept the steerage from getting ashore at Grey Town, and now I don't more than half believe his report that there are 2 cases yellow fever (cholera!) belowdecks.

Got captain's permission to have a safety lantern in my room.

4 P.M. Jan. 2. The surgeon of the ship has just reported to the captain in my hearing that 2 of the cases are "mighty bad" and the third "awful bad."

This is neither cholera nor yellow fever, I suspect—these men have been eating green tropical fruit and washing it down with villainous aguardiente.

A ship is precisely a little village where gossips abound and where every man's business is his neighbor's.

The prospect of going into quarantine for 30 days is worrying the passengers like everything.

7 P.M. Neither of the sick men quite dead yet—the ship has stopped her wheels.

Passengers growl less this trip than any I ever saw, but they will growl some on all trips, no matter how favorable everything is.

Custom-house list must be made up by purser, who makes it up according to his own notion, thus:

"Miss Smith, 45, milliner, Ireland (and she young and wealthy)

Mark Twain, barkeeper,—Terra del Fuego."

One of the sick men is bad. This calls for Rev. Fackler again (10 P.M.).

It was cholera of a malignant type.

The man was buried overboard at a little past 10 P.M.

Jan. 2. Midnight, another patient at the point of death. They are filling him up with brandy.

2 bells—the man is dead. 4 bells—he is cast overboard—expedition is the word in these crowded steerages.

Jan. 3. Our tropic drink:

¾ lb. of sugar, 1½ lbs. of ice, 1 doz. limes, 1 lemon, 1 orange, half a bottle of brandy. Put in a ¾-gallon ice pitcher and fill up with water.

Jan. 3, 9:30 P.M. Astonished to hear 3 bells—been sitting here reading so long I never thought of its meaning anything else than half past one—went to get ship time—find it is only 3 bells in the first watch. It is so stormy tonight that most of the passengers have gone to bed seasick, long ago.

We are to be off the coast of Cuba tomorrow, they say—I cannot believe it.

Folded his hands after his stormy life and slept in serenest repose under the peaceful sighing of the summer wind among the grasses over his grave.

A captain who came aboard at Grey Town, where in 3 years he had worn out his constitution and destroyed his health, lingered until 10 this morning and then died and was shoved overboard half an hour afterward, sewed up in a blanket with 6 lbs. of iron. He leaves a wife at Rochester, N. Y. This makes the 4th death on shipboard since we left San Francisco.

Mrs. Grundy seems to be still on his mind. He even composes some poetry about her:

She talketh scandal all day long
With false malicious tongue.
She'd blast the brightest character
That ever poet sung.

Jan. 5. We are to put in at Key West, Florida, today for coal, for ballast—so they say—but rather for medicines, perhaps—the physic locker is about pumped dry.

7 cases sickness yesterday—didn't amount to anything.

Col. Kinney pretty sick all night with cholera or cholera morbus.

Shape is said to be dying of cholera, this morning.

There are half a dozen on the sick list today. The cussed fools let the diarrhea run 2 or 3 days, and then getting scared they run to the surgeon and hope to be cured. And they lie like blazes—swear they have just been taken and the doctor of course knows better. He asked a patient the other day if he had any money to get some brandy with—said no—the ship had to furnish it—when the man died they found a 20-dollar piece in his pocket.

Shape has been walking the deck in stocking feet getting wet—exposing himself—is going to die.

The disease has gotten into the second cabin at last and one case in first cabin. The consternation is so great that several are going to get off at Key West, if quarantine regulations permit it, and go North, overland.

The captain visits every corner of the ship daily to see that it is kept in a state of perfect cleanliness.

Jan. 5, continued. 10 A.M. The Episcopal clergyman, Rev. Mr. Fackler is taken—bad diarrhea and griping.

All hands looking anxiously forward to the cool weather we shall strike, 24 hrs. hence, and drive away the sickness.

Shape dead—fifth death—Shape, barber, only sick about 12 hrs., usually ate rations for 4.

Rev. Fackler has made himself sick with sorrow for the poor fellows that died.

12:30 P.M. The minister has got a fit, convulsion of some kind—so they are burying poor Shape without benefit of clergy. They don't wait many minutes after breath is out of the body.

There is no use in discussing it—I really believe the ship is out of medicines—we have a good surgeon but nothing to work with.

Just heard the captain say: "Purser, put up an immense sign that all can read: no charge for medical attendance whatever—put it so all can read it."

I told the captain this morning that the fear of doctor's bills was one chief reason why the steerage passengers were concealing their illness till the last moment.

Jan. 5, 2 P.M. As the boys come to my room, one after another (I am abed), I observe a marked change in their demeanor during the last half hour—they report that the minister, only sick an hour, or maybe two, is already very low—that a hospital has been fitted up in the steerage and he has been removed thither.

Verily the ship is fast becoming a floating hospital herself—not an hour passes but brings its fresh sensation, its new disaster—its melancholy tidings.

When I think of poor Shape and the preacher, both so well when I saw them yesterday evening, I realize that I myself may be dead tomorrow.

Since the last two hours all laughter, all levity, has ceased in the ship—a settled gloom is upon the faces of the passengers.

Jan. 5, 4 P.M. The unfortunate minister is dying—he has bidden us all good-bye and now lies barely breathing. His name is Rev. J. G. Fackler, and he was on his way to the States to get his wife and family.

The passengers are fearfully exercised, and well they may be, poor devils, for we are about to see our fifth death in five days, and the sixth of the voyage. The surgeon, a most excellent young man, a Mason and a first-rate physician and one of considerable practice, has done all he could to allay their fear by telling them he has all the medicines he wants, that the disease is only a virulent sort of diarrhea, cholera morbus, etc.

Discovering that he was a Mason, I took him aside and asked him a plain statement for myself *alone,* and told him I thought I was man enough to stand the truth, in its worst form.

He then said the disease was *cholera* and of the most virulent type—that he had done all a man could do, but *he had no medicines* to work with—that he shipped the first time this trip and found the locker empty, and no time to make a requisition for more medicines.

To add to the gloom of the situation there occurred now a break-down in the engine-room.

Jan. 5, 5 P.M. That bolt-head broke day before yesterday and we lost 2 hours. It broke again yesterday and we lost 3 or 4 hours. It broke again this afternoon, and again we lay like a log on the water (head wind) for 3 or 4 hours more.

These things distress the passengers beyond measure. They are scared about the epidemic, and so impatient to get along—and now they have lost confidence in the ship and fear she may break again in the rough weather that is to come. I did not take any interest in the matter until just now I found the cursed little bolt was a sort of king-pin and that the engine must stop without it.

The passengers say that we are out of luck and that it is a doomed voyage.

It appears, though it is kept from the passengers, that there are seven or eight patients in the hospital down below.

Mem. Get names of the dead from the F. O. [First Officer], to telegraph.

Some misgivings, some distress as to whether the authorities of Key West will let our pestilence-stricken ship land there—but the captain says we are in sore distress, in desperate straits, and we must land; we will land in spite of orders, cannon or anything else—we cannot go on in this way.

If we do land, some of our people are going to leave—among them the doctor, who is afraid of the crazy machinery.

Sea in storm—caps crawling and squirming like white worms in the midst of ink.

The Dead

(1) (Baby) Harlan, Sacramento, baptized day it died—died 24th, buried 25th.

(2) Jerome Shields, aged about 34, buried at sea Jan. 2. His friend Patrick Burns took charge of his effects, consisting of $55 in coin, a carpet bag containing clothing, letters, a navy pistol and other small articles, photographs, etc. His friends reside in Waverly, Ia. His brother-in-law, John Clark, lives at Pine Grove, Sierra Co., Calif.

(3) Martin Sherlock, of Irish descent, aged about 30, died and was buried at sea, Jan. 3. He had no friends or acquaintances on board ship. His effects, consisting of carpet sack of clothing, $20 piece and letters from Mary Ann Sherlock, his mother, residing at Port Byron, Ill., are in possession of first officer.

(4) Capt. Chas. Mahoney, aged 40, late employee of Central American Transit Co. Died Jan. 4 and was buried at sea. Has a family somewhere about Rochester, N. Y.

(5) Andrew Nolan, about 20 or 21 (Shape), barber by trade, died Jan. 5 and was buried at sea. Funds $77. He belonged in Jersey City.

(6) At 2:20 A.M. (this morning, Jan. 6) Rev. J. G. Fackler, Episcopal clergyman of San Francisco. At 2:30 we anchored at Key West, Florida—and he will

be buried on shore. Was bound for the States to get his family.

Sunday, Jan. 6, 1867. We are out 22 days from San Francisco.

This Key West looks like a mere open roadstead, but they call it one of the best harbors in the world—they say that the 100 little keys scattered all around keep off the sea and storm. It seems to be a very pretty little tropical-looking town with plenty of handsome shade trees. It is very cool and pleasant. The great frowning fortification is Fort Taylor, and is very strong.

We don't calculate to find any Key West folks in Heaven.

Sunday, Jan. 6 continued. Rev. J. G. Fackler was buried here at Key West at noon by Episcopal minister.

Our doctor told me it was Asiatic cholera, but they must have deceived the port surgeon, else they wouldn't have let us land.

I attended Episcopal service—heap of style—fashionably dressed women—350 of them, and children, and 25 men.

Don't see where so much dress comes from in a town made altogether of 1 and 2 story frame houses, some crazy, unpainted and with only thick board shutters for windows—no carpet, no mats—bare floors—cheap prints on walls.

Only about 10 or 12 houses with any pretension of style and one-half of these are military officers' quarters.

The contribution box fooled me—I heard no money dropping in it, and the paper currency never occurred to me.

Men stylishly dressed with yellow ribbon cravats.

Townful of cocoanut trees of the many-leaved low-branching pattern, very pretty.

Girls singing in most houses.

Got up a dinner party in town—our own claret and champagne good, and there was nothing else good about the dinner except the fried eggs—and they didn't hold out.

This is really a big town, big enough to hold over 2000, though many houses seem deserted. Business mostly gin-mills—that is for soldiers.

Brandy here (good article) costs $15 a quart—$40 a gallon.

Key West, 7th. 21 passengers left the ship here, scared. Some of them gave dinner and berth tickets to remaining friends in the steerage. I am glad they are gone, d'n them.

Jan. 7th. Capt. Behm has just poked his head in at the window to say how lucky we were not to be quarantined at Key West (we are off—have just turned the pilot boat adrift). Lucky! Damnation! If I have got Key West sized up right they would receive War, Famine, Pestilence and Death without a question—call them all by some fancy name, and then rope in the survivors and sell them good cigars and brandies at easy prices and horrible dinners at infamous rates. They wouldn't quarantine anybody; they'd say "come," and say it gladly if you brought destruction and hell in your wake. They rely upon the salubrity of their climate and its famous healthfulness, for immunity from disease.

More cheerfulness at table this morning than ever before.

Key West prices: putting coal aboard $2 a ton—in N. Y. 25c. Pilotage $108. Making a bolt $50. They say it was the first Cal. steamer that has touched there in 2 years, so they scorched us.

Oliver tried to get the captain, for $100, to contract not to bury him at sea in case he died—Capt. refused, so Oliver went ashore Key West at 9 P.M.—the last man.

Sewing society for the monkey.

18 invalids yesterday and 13 today—only 2 really dangerous—one of them was getting along handsomely, but got drunk and took a relapse.

The noblest cigars in the world at Key West for $6 per hundred—smuggled from Havana.

The sewing society have dressed the monkey up in black pants and vest and a roundabout and cuffs of bright red and yellow, curtain-calico pattern, and paper collar—and he looks gay scampering around among the rigging.

Oliver had 380 cholera articles cut out.

Kingman found his long girl sitting by the taffrail alone. He is in love with her.

Belmayne died Jan. 8 and was buried at sea abreast of Florida.

The temperature of the Gulf Stream here (they try it every 2 hrs. for information for Navy Dept.) is 76—atmosphere 72. We are comfortable enough now while we are in this fluid stove, but when we leave it at Cape Hatteras, Lord, it will be cold.

The speed of the stream varies from 1/3 to 3½ knots an hour. We have been making 200, 210, 220 miles a day, but now in this current we can turn off 250 to 275.

Soaked banana and plantain in brandy, and got the monkey tight.

Jan. 10, 1867. 26 days out from San Francisco today—at noon we shall be off Cape Hatteras and less than 400 miles south of N. Y.—a day and a half's run.

We shall be leaving this warming-pan of a Gulf Stream today, and then it will cease to be genial summer weather and become wintry cold. We already see the signs. They have put feather mattresses and blankets on our berths this morning.

It is raining—warm.

Jan. 10. Rainy. At 11 A.M. 18 miles from Cape Hatteras. Distance to N. Y. 320 miles.

8 sick, 5 diarrhea, 3 convalescent—2 better.

Jan. 10. Passing out of the Gulf Stream rapidly. At 2 P.M. the temperature of the water had fallen 7 degrees in half an hour. Already the day is turning cold and overcoats coming into vogue.

Jan. 10, 11:30 P.M. Dark and stormy, and the ship plunging considerably. It is villainously cold. Have just come forward from the purser's room and felt something blow in my face like snow. Think it was, but too dark to tell.

Jan. 11, 7 P.M. Been in bed all day to keep warm—fearfully cold.

We are off Barnegat—passed a pilot boat a while ago.

We shall get to N. Y. before morning.

The d'd crowd in the smoking-room are as wildly singing now as they were capering childishly about the deck day before yesterday when we first struck the cold weather.

Friday night 11th, 2 bells. P. Peterson has just died, "dropsy"—the Highland light, the lightship and several other lights at entrance to N. Y. harbor in full view. This is the 8th death this voyage. Bury him ashore, as we are now on soundings.

N. Y. Jan. 12. Arrived today, 27½ days out.

> There is no mention of quarantine at New York, so we can only assume that there was none. Imagine a "cholera ship" docking in New York today! But then, of course, the last man died of "dropsy."

That Whining Puppy

Scared at the storm that first night out from San Francisco—his little wife out observing the signs of the weather.

He whined all the way down and was nursed by her.

He'd lay and whine on the lake boat and she sat up all night and fanned him. The sofa in the social hall was coolest place and she wanted it—he wouldn't give it up. She tried the stateroom—too hot—came back and fanned him all night. On the last boat on the San Juan she slept in a grass hammock without blankets and he lay on the deck on the blankets and whined as usual.

At Grey Town he went ashore and wouldn't let her go.

In the Gulf he was scared to death about the cholera—she sat by his bedside and fanned him two whole days and he whining with a headache which he feared was the cholera—yet he went to his meals regularly.

Took ⅛ share in the $40 worth of brandy at Key West and has not paid his $5.

Gives his waiter old clothes instead of money.

Where are all those people today? Where is the little doctor who had to work without medicines? Where is the whining man? The family that was waiting for the Rev. Mr. Fackler? Ah, but that was far back in another century. Few if any remain of that shipload, or of those who waited for them, and with the single exception of Mark Twain himself, have left little trace behind.

CHAPTER VI

Beginning a Literary Epoch

He seems to have made no notes in New York, but we know that he found there an old California friend, Charles Henry Webb, who had collected a number of Mark Twain sketches, including the "Jumping Frog" story, with the idea of making a book of them. When a publisher, Carleton, rejected the book, Webb decided to bring it out on his own account.

After a trip to St. Louis, to see his mother and sister, and to Hannibal, where he lectured, Mark Twain returned to New York, watched his book through the press, lectured at the Cooper Institute, and as correspondent for the *Alta California,* of San Francisco, and the *New York Tribune,* joined the Quaker City Holy Land Excursion, which had replaced his earlier dream of a trip around the world.

The notes of that first Mediterranean pleasure cruise, begun before the ship left the harbor, were set down in the very midst of the picturesque band of "innocents" and "pilgrims" that gypsied through France and Italy and trod the arid hills of Palestine. Solid little volumes stiffly bound in tan sheep—the pencilings sometimes hurried, sometimes deliberate, and nearly all legible—how close they seem to bring us to

"Dan" and "Jack" and "the Doctor" in that far day before they became immortal as "innocents abroad."

The first entry, recording as it does the beginning of this historic voyage, is perhaps as notable as any memorandum in literary history.

> Holy Land Pleasure Excursion
>
> Steamer Quaker City
>
> Capt. C. C. Duncan
>
> Left N. Y. at 2 P.M., June 8, '67.
>
> Rough weather—anchored within the harbor to lay all night.

Lying in the harbor he has a chance to look over the passengers and make a few comments, such as:

The Frenchy-looking woman with a dog—small mongrel, black-and-tan brute, with long sharp ears that stick up like a donkey's and give him an exceedingly wild and excited expression, even in his mildest moods. When he is skirmishing about the cabin she follows him anxiously about and interrupts his enterprises, and meanwhile keeps up an interminable biography of him to the passengers, embellished with anecdotes illustrative of his general disposition and with stories of some of his most remarkable performances. The dog is noisy and in the way.

The long-legged, simple, green, wide-mouthed horse-laughing young fellow who once made a sea voyage to

Fortress Monroe in the Oceanica and quotes eternally from his experiences upon that voyage. I am satisfied that we shall never hear the last of that voyage. He will harp on it from here to Palestine and back again. He wears a monstrous compass slung to his watch-guard, and consults it from time to time, keeping a wary eye on the binnacle compass to see that it does not vary from his and so endanger the ship. He says the most witless things and then laughs uproariously at them and he has a vile notion that everything everybody else says is meant for a witticism, and so laughs loudly when very often the speaker had spoken seriously or even had meant to say something full of pathos. But this fellow doesn't know. He laughs dreadfully at everything and swears it's good, dam' good, by George. I wish he would fall in the harbor.

The innocent young man—who is good, accommodating, pleasant and well-meaning, but fearfully green and is fearfully slow. He wished to know how long seasickness lasted. He is the other extreme from "Legs"—doesn't know anything at all. Came confidentially to me in a private place and seemed almost bursting with an idea—a new and dangerous guest to have about his premises. He said:

"If you had a panorama—any kind of a panorama—one of them old ones would do—why, by gracious you could pay your way on the ship—any old panorama you know—but I don't think likely you could without a lecture—because them *Italians* and A-rabs wouldn't go much, maybe, except for the novelty, because they wouldn't understand. But if you had an old panorama I should think likely you'd fetch 'em."

The "Interrogation Point" of the *Innocents Abroad* would seem to be a combination of these two young men.

Sunday morning, June 9. Still lying at anchor in N. Y. harbor—rained all night and all morning like the devil—some sea on—lady had to leave church in the cabin—seasick.

Tableau—in the midst of sermon Capt. Duncan rushed madly out with one of those damned dogs, but didn't throw him overboard.

But speaking of seasickness, there certainly are more seasick people on the ship than there ought to be. I am more than ever satisfied now that we ought to have put to sea in the storm of Saturday. The ship is strong and could have weathered it easily and everybody would have had a fearful 4 hours siege of seasickness and then been over and done with it.

Diaries

Most of the passengers being unaccustomed to voyaging are diligently keeping diaries.

He furnishes a supposed example.

Of a Lady

First Day—the ships rolls and pitches, and O, I am *so* sick.

Second Day—We met an immigrant ship today, full of Irish people. From Ireland, doubtless. Our captain got on the paddle-box and shouted: "Ship wo'haw!" or something like that, and the other captain shouted back through a horn and said he had been out 30 days. Then we started away and gave the immigrants 3 cheers and waved our handkerchiefs and they gave us 3 cheers also, but did not wave their handkerchiefs, but we thought nothing of it, because as they had been out 30 days their handkerchiefs were all dirty, likely. Still, I am so seasick.

Third Day—Mrs. S. who has got her face so sunburned since we left N. Y. made a conundrum on the promenade deck last night. She said: "Why is my face like a bird that is just about to fly?" Ans. "Because both are to soar." Ah me I am so sick.

Fourth Day—I am tired being at sea, and tired keeping journal, and very tired of being seasick. I do wonder where those Azores Islands are hidden away in this boundless expanse of heaving water? I do so want to see the land and the green trees again.

Fifth Day—Chicken soup for dinner, but my heart is not in chicken soup. I care not for poetry, or for things to eat or for dress. I have taken off hoops and put away my waterfall, and all I take an interest in is being squalmish and getting to shore again. It is funny, but somehow I don't seem to care how I look.

Sixth Day—At last I am over it! I am not a bit sick any more. And how different everything looks today. Why, the sea is beautiful, actually beautiful! The soft south wind is balmy and gentle, and I almost imagine it has lost its nauseous odor of salt. I am like a new person. I take an interest in everything now. Ah, yonder is that scrimp-nosed little doll trying to make herself so agreeable to Mr. ——. I will just happen along there as if I were not noticing and see if I don't spoil your schemes, Miss.

Here we are introduced to the now immortal "Poet Lariat."

Bloodgood H. Cutter

He is 50 years old, and small of his age. He dresses in homespun, and is a simple-minded, honest, old-fashioned [Long Island] farmer with a strange proclivity for writing rhymes. He writes them on all possible subjects and gets them printed on slips of paper with his portrait at the head. These he will give to any man that comes along, whether he has anything against him or not. He has already written interminable poems on "The Good Ship Quaker City" and an "Ode to the Ocean" and "Recollections of the Pleasant Time on Deck Last Night," which pleasant time consisting in his reciting some 75 stanzas of his poetry to a large party of passengers convened on the upper deck.

Dan said to him in a private conversation:

"It must be a great happiness to you to be able to sit down at the close of the day and put its events all down in rhymes and poetry, like a Byron and a Shakespeare and those fellows."

"O, yes, it is—it is. There is no pleasure like it in the world."

"Yes—and I should think that when a man was gifted in that way, more would be expected of him than from common people—from people who ain't poets. You'd be expected, you know, to keep that talent going at all reasonable times, and never lose an opportunity. It's a duty you owe to your countrymen and your race, you know."

"I know. I appreciate it. I do keep it a-going. Why, bless your soul, many and many a time when everybody else is asleep you'll find me writing poetry. And when I feel it coming on, there's no let-up to me."

"That's it! That's it! Often, no doubt, when you're talking to people or looking at anything, or eating dinner, it comes on you, and every thought that clatters through your head fetches up with a rhyme at the end of it—pure, honest, natural-born poetry—ain't it so!"

"Bless your soul, yes. Many's the time I've had to leave my dinner and many's the time I've had to get up in the night when it came on me. At such times as that, I can't any more talk without rhyming than you could put fire to powder and it not go off. Why bless me, this ship may go to the bottom any moment and drown us all but what of that?

Whether we're on the sea or the land
We've all got to go at the word of command—

Hey!—how's that?"

Thursday, June 13, 1867. On board steamer Quaker City at sea. 12 N.—lat. 40, long. 62—560 miles from N. Y., 1/4 of the way to the Azores—just 3 days out—in last 24 hrs. made 205 miles. Will make more in next 24, because the wind is fair and we are under sail and steam both, burning 30 tons of coal a day and fast lightening up the ship.

Friday. Shipped a sea through the open dead-light; damaged cigars, books and etc.—comes of being careless when room is on the weather side of the ship.

Prayer-meetings every night.

The Quaker City Mirror is not issued very regularly.

Heavy gale down among Azores; threw Capt. Duncan across cabin from dinner table, swept dishes away and fetched away iron water-cooler, which smashed seat just vacated by Mr. Church. Most folks in bed sick—tremendous sea running all afternoon—fierce gale. Shall I never see lightning and thunder any more?

June 21st, Azores. Daylight. Arrived at the port of Horta, Island of Fayal—Island of Pico, where the fruits are, is opposite and looks beautiful, with its green slopes and snow white houses.

Rode jackass, on mattress, with sawbuck for a saddle, 10 miles among the hills, caverns and beautiful scenery of the suburbs, with a troop of barefooted, noisy, young patched-and-ragged devils following with gads. Paid 30c an hour for the jack.

Everything calculated by reys—takes about a million of them to make 6 bits—a thousand reys make one dollar.

Brown having heard that prices were very moderate here, opened his heart and ordered dinner for 8 of us. Here is the bill. It knocked him senseless.

dinner for 8 at 3000 equal	24,000
wine, 10 bottles, at 1200 equal	12,000
cigars	2,000
	38,000

That is, $38. This is the dinner accredited to "Blucher" in the *Innocents*.

Fayal, June 22, '67.

Mules and family live all together in one small room—five in center—no escape for smoke save through small passages built in walls. Hardly a chimney in the city.

Saw no graveyards. They say they do not reverence their dead very highly; only a few graves are well cared for.

Wheat is threshed by oxen in the old Scriptural way—"Ye shall not muzzle the ox that treadeth out the grain." Wheat is worth 70c a bushel, but flour $12 a barrel because of their slow methods of threshing and grinding. Corn is ground in private houses with a stone mortar, and in a windmill. Near by they have a mule-mill to go, when the wind doesn't blow.

Their plow is a wooden board shod with iron. Their harrow is drawn by hand and has teeth as small as a finger. Their cart is a basket hauled by cows, and the axle and the wooden slab of a wheel both turn.

Friday, June 27. Sat up all night, playing dominoes in the smoking-room with the purser, and saw the sun rise—woke up Dan and the Doctor and called everybody to see it. Don't feel very bright.

Sailing along through the Straits with Africa (bold, sand-spotted hills) and Spain, a good deal like it, on either hand, 13 miles apart. Water green, not blue—splendid morning, spring like.

Passed close to the little heavily walled town of Tarifa, Spain; houses with pink-tiled roofs.

> Those who read *The Innocents Abroad* will remember the character the Oracle who was always overflowing with doubtful information. We come to a note here that identifies his origin.

Dr. Andrews at breakfast said: "Which side was the pillars of Hercules on?"

"Both."

"Some think different—Gibbon does. (The old fool had been smelling in a guide-book, and was trying to play it for old information that had been festering in his brain.) He said: "I suppose them old ancients really believed the Goddess Hercules lived there some time or other."

Tangier

Going through Spain or not going through Spain? What is the time to Paris? Sixty hours? Can we visit the Alhambra, Seville, Valladolid and 50 other places? Damned glad when I knew it was too late and we couldn't go.

Now as to Tangier there should be no pulling and hauling—we will go. I shall answer no questions and *not listen* to any damn fears, surmizes or anything else.

Buying gloves of the seductive Spanish wench in the main street who said *I* knew how to put a glove on and few did—when I was tearing the worthless thing to pieces with my awkwardness and taking this fearful sarcasm for a compliment. I paid the price (50c) for a torn pair of Spanish kid gloves.

Faithfully recorded in his book—Chapter VII of *The Innocents Abroad.*

Kings Arms and Club House. Hotels keep no registers and never know who is in the house—send me to find my friends, instead of a servant.

Dan told to gather all manner of statistics, reports that brandy is 8c a drink and cigars 3c apiece.

More barber shops here than shoe shops in Fayal.

Many beautiful English and Spanish girls.

In Morocco for theft of cattle they cut off right hand and left foot—cut round the joint and break it off.

When a poor Moor sees one of the scarce silver dollars he asks permission to kiss it.

Governor of Tangier used to have salary of 5 or 6 pounds a month—keeps 25 or 30 wives.

Koran allows 4 wives and many concubines. In the interior Jews marry several wives.

Snatched Major Barry out of the Moorish mosque—would have been sacrilege. Couldn't pray in there for a long time till it was purified. Would have got a shoe over his head—years ago would have got a knife—they are very fanatical.

English officer stepped in and the Moors chased him out and upstreet, with shoes.

Clock in mosque out of order. No Moroccan clock-mender so they engaged a Portuguese. They said:
"You know we permit donkeys when building to enter—we let the Portuguese take off his shoes and go in and come out as a donkey."

Moorish women cover their faces with their coarse white robes—to cover their inhuman damned ugliness, no doubt.

Emperor doesn't know how many wives he has—thinks it is 500.

Many of the blacks are slaves to the Moors:—when they can read first chapter of Koran, can no longer be slaves;—would have been well to adopt educational test for nigger vote in America.
Relation of master with female slave frees her.

Hercules is the representative of a real character;—that man landed at Cadiz with his lion skin on his shoulders and big club in his hand and founded it—came here and conquered Anitus—king of this country, who lived also at the Garden of Hesperides, 70 miles down coast from here—Hercules met and killed him in these streets. These were savages who lived in little huts and ate only the natural fruits of the land. Canaanites came here when driven out by Joshua and set up a pillar on which they inscribed:

> We are the Canaanites, driven out of the
> Holy Land by the Jewish robber Joshua

This inscription was seen by Roman historians within 2000 years, in these streets.

Cape Spartel near here—cave of Hercules—full of inscriptions—Hercules took refuge in that cave.

Game of checkers in ancient Treasury of Moorish Emperor's palace—turbans and hoods, and a negro with shaven head and a topknot—lost their temper.

Moorish woman who knows she is handsome will glance around, and if no Moor in sight unconsciously uncover the face.

Moor won't look a woman in the face, nor she him. Marriage is contracted by parents—man never sees her before he is married.

Consul McMeth has no society—keeps plenty of games—first week, his wife and her sister cried all the time.

Mrs. McMeth's little 4-year-old Katie, born in Tangier, fluently speaks Spanish and Arabic but knows no English—when very earnest talks broken English and uses figurative language of the Arabs and says "By the beard of my father—by the good health of my mamma," etc.

Questions for Debate

Is or is not Capt. Duncan responsible for the head winds? Is a tail absolutely necessary to the comfort and convenience of a dog? And if so would not a multiplicity of tails augment the dog's comfort and convenience?

Found a nation who refused to take a drink—wonderful—wonderful—will wonders never cease?

Got back to Quaker City Monday evening, July 1, 1867.

Left Gibraltar just as the sun was setting. The sunset was soft and rich and beautiful beyond description. I shall never forget what a dreamy haze hung about the silver-striped dome of the African pillar—the city and headland of Sudah and the hills beyond the neutral ground, and how the noble precipice of Gibraltar stood out with every point and edge cut sharply against the mellow sky. Nor how like a child's toy the full canvased ship looked that sailed in under the tremendous wall and was lost to sight in the shadows.

Beautiful starlit night on the Mediterranean.

All we left behind (on the ship) are in snowy Gibraltar shoes, and our African party are gorgeous with yellow Moorish slippers.

Midnight July 1.

After all this racing and bustling and rollicking excitement in Africa it seems good to get back to the old ship once more. It is so like *home*. After all our weary time we shall sleep peacefully tonight.

"Sleep makes us all pashas." (Moorish proverb.)

"Sleep joins the parted lovers' hands."

> Following this is a memorandum of a hotel bill in Morocco on which food for 8 is set down at $12.50 and liquors $18.50, by which one may suppose that the Tangier stay ended pleasantly.

July 2, 1867. The Mediterranean this morning is a paler blue than any other sea, perhaps, but the richest and most lustrous and beautiful color imaginable. 20 ships in sight all the time.

What a good thing Adam had—when he said a good thing he knew nobody had said it before.

Chapters VIII and IX of *The Innocents*

Abroad, expanded from his Tangier notes, reveal a remarkable and rather sudden development in Mark Twain's literary style. Cultured association on the ship had something to do with it, and then his imagination responded readily to the picturesque, and to the poetic association that clings to crumbling historic landmarks.

CHAPTER VII

Athens, Constantinople, Ephesus

Readers of *The Innocents Abroad* may recall that the *Quaker City* landed at Marseilles and that Mark Twain and his special little group went to Paris, later to Genoa, then by rail through Italy to Milan, Venice, Florence and the rest, joining the ship again at Naples. Unhappily, the notes of this period are lost. We shall never know just what memoranda he made on the spot of the doings of Dan and Jack, and of the guide-baiting "Doctor" whose eternal and devastating inquiry, "Is—is he dead?" made eager guides lose heart and shrivel, and caused him to be remembered the length of the Peninsula during many years.

The next existing notebook begins with Seba Smith's stately "Burial of Moses," a poem whose lofty wording and majestic imagery had no small influence on Mark Twain's work. He frequently recited two stanzas from it, and now in view of the coming Holy Land trip set them down in full.

> By Nebo's lonely mountain,
> On this side Jordan's wave,
> In a vale in the land of Moab,
> There lies a lonely grave.
> And no man knows that sepulchre,
> And no man saw it e'er,
> For the angels of God upturned the sod
> And laid the dead man there.

. . .

And had he not high honor—
  The hillside for a pall,
To lie in state while angels wait,
  With stars for tapers tall;
And the dark rock-pines, like tossing plumes,
  Over his bier to wave,
And God's own hand in that lonely land
  To lay him in his grave?

From Naples

Sailed from Naples Aug. 11, at 6 A.M.

7 P.M., with the western horizon all golden from the sunken sun and specked with the distant ships the bright full moon shining like a silver shield high overhead, the deep, dark blue of the Mediterranean underfoot and a strange sort of twilight affected by all these different lights and colors all around us and about us.

Sighted old Stromboli. How grand it looms up out of the lonely sea, and how symmetrical. It is beautiful now with its dark blue just veiled under a pearly mist that half conceals and half discloses.

The two jets of smoke have turned into one, 100 feet broad—can't see how high—can't see it after it gets above the black background of the farther rim of the crater.

In Rome saw Peter's footprints.

Peter's Prison (Mamertine)—Print of face—miraculous spring he made to baptize the soldiers—hole where he broke through.

Man on this ship as hard a case as Paul—got to knock him endwise with a streak of lightning before he could get religion.

Aug. 14. Approaching Athens. The town extends most

of the way around the deep circular basin, and has the cleanest, neatest two- and three-story square cream-colored buildings we have seen. [Sketch of small sailing-craft.]

Boats are not pretty but how they fly, and how exquisitely skillful these Greeks are in handling them. I would like to stay with them a while.

> Bad news. They had touched at infected ports —all ports were likely to be that—and were not allowed to land.

Athens

Thursday Aug. 15, '67.

We were put into quarantine at once, yesterday, and rather than be cooped up at anchor remote from shore for 11 days the captain decided to lie still 24 hrs., then sail direct for Constantinople.

It was remarked by the Commandant of the port (at Piræus) that guards would be set, and a watch kept upon us, and anyone found breaking the quarantine by stealing ashore would be severely dealt with—and quarantine laws in these countries are usually harsh, and even unnecessarily cruel, sometimes.

It was a bitter disappointment to the whole ship's company, to be so near to famous Athens and not be permitted to visit it. We could see the city vaguely defined in the distant valley, with the glass. With the naked eye we could see the grand ruins on the Acropolis, and with the telescope could count the columns of the Parthenon.

We imagined we could trace out Mars Hill (the Areopagus where Paul preached, where the highest court was held 3 days in a year, and where Demosthenes thundered his Philippics into the ears of the disheartened Athenians); we believed we could see the Museum Hill and the Pnyx. We cared little for Hymettus and Pentelicus.

At 11 o'clock at night Dr. Jackson, Col. Denny, Dr. Birch and I left the ship in a boat and got set on shore outside the quarantine lines—then straggled over the hills, serenaded by 100 dogs, skirted the town under a clouded moon, and in half an hour were safe beyond any chance of capture and fairly away for Athens. We could not find a road that seemed to lead in the right direction, and so, taking the tall steep mountain to the left of the Acropolis for a mark, we steered at it industriously over hills through valleys, over stony, desert places, plowed fields and vineyards, and walked fast, too, for there was little time to spare if we would get back to the ship before the treacherous day should dawn.

We made the trip (stopped occasionally by savages armed with guns who rose mysteriously up out of shadows and darkness and said "Ha!" when we happened casually to be stealing grapes, and stood under the towering massive walls of the ancient citadel of Athens—walls that had loomed above the heads of better men than we 1000 years before the Son of God was born in Bethlehem.

It was between 1 and 2 o'clock—the place was silent—the gates were shut—the devil to pay. Denny tried to climb over a ruined wall—knocked down a stone—somebody shouted from within and Denny dropped! We soon roused that fellow out (the guard) and entered the majestic ruin.

The Propylæa, gateway to the temples of the Acropolis, is of lovely fluted columns, of white marble.

All about us fragments, marble-armed chairs, bas-relief and tablatures, statues, etc.

Grim marble faces, glancing up so suddenly out of the grass at our feet.

Temple of Minerva small.

Temple of Hercules with the 6 noble Caryatides supporting the portico.

Old ruined arches in the valley below on the right.

The narrow rocky ridge and flights of steps and square rostrum on the Areopagus or Mars Hill, sacred to the memories of St. Paul and Demosthenes, Aristides, Themistocles, etc.

But Athens by moonlight from the bastions! The King's white palace and shrubberied garden flecked with mellow gaslights! The sharply defined windows, chimneys, shingles, of almost every single house in Athens, in the splendid lustre that was pouring out of the heavens, even paling the scattering gaslights. Athens spread out right underneath our feet, 200 ft. below us, and the grand white ruin of the Parthenon towering over our heads. Athens by moonlight! When I forget it I shall be dead—not before.

> Upon these notes he built that wonderful chapter in *The Innocents*—a prose poem, though hardly more vivid than these hasty jottings.

We made the trip, undisturbed save by the armed grape-guards and 17,000,000 dogs that followed us through Piræus, and reached the ship at 4:30, this morning just as the day was dawning. I sat up an hour or two and saw a very beautiful sunrise, a rich flush that suffused all the heavens behind the Acropolis like a blush.

At 6:30, after I had gone to bed, Mr. Griswold came and got my Moorish fez and he and James and Crocker went ashore, intending to steal away to Athens, but the guards discovered them before they went 1000 yards and chased them—they say it was a close race but they won the boat and escaped to the ship.

Aug. 16. Troy.

We are now—11 A.M.—right abreast the plains of Troy

—a little rock 200 yards long with a light on it was the anchorage of the Greek vessels. The plain of Troy is wide and low—8 or 10 miles back is a range of undulating hills. Half the plain is covered with what seems to be green underbrush, and the other half is sand. We are making a straight break for Dardanelles and shall enter in an hour—Mt. Ida in the distance.

Noon. Passed abreast of ancient Troy and not long afterward entered the Dardanelles (or Hellespont) and after this passed the harbor whence Agamemnon's fleet sailed to the siege of Troy.

Farther along the tomb of Hecuba on one side and Ajax on the other.

First architects of Xerxes' bridge of boats over the Hellespont were beheaded because the bridge broke away —the hint was not lost on the second lot—Xerxes' host 2,600,000 men and 2,500,000 camp-followers crossed it.

Just entering the Hellespont 3 or 4 miles wide—guarded on either side by Turkish castles, flying the crescent flag. We are gaining fast on a French steamer since we have hoisted main and main-top sails and jib—we'll catch him in an hour. See a camel train on shore with the glass. [Sketches and crude drawings of maps—entrance to the Hellespont, etc.]

Aug. 16. Entered the Sea of Marmora at 5 in the afternoon, if I remember rightly.

The Viceroy of Egypt passed us in his lightning yacht as if we were standing still, waved his hand to us. He looks a good deal like his uncle (or his brother—which?) the Sultan of Turkey.

Night—Rev. Mr. Bullard lectured on Athens, and I said a few words—same subject.

Constantinople

Aug. 17 reached Constantinople at daylight and anchored in the mouth of the Golden Horn.

Visited the celebrated mosque of St. Sophia near the Grand Seraglio Gardens, but found nothing there to go into ecstasies over. It is an immense structure and its dome is very peculiar, being as great in diameter as St. Peter's, perhaps, but enough flatter to be remarkable.

It seemed curious to see these Eastern devotees going through their extravagant ceremonies in a church that was built for Christian worship; this strikes one more than anything else.

The painted bronze open work of the capitols of the columns and the filigree inlaying above them are curious but not fascinating. The numerous pillars in one piece, precious marbles, are not lovely because they are so chipped and dented and rusty and unattractive.

The gaudy mosaics in the dome and their grotesque Turkish writing are not pretty.

The vast gilt circular wooden signs at the corners are not handsome.

Neither are the numberless coarse oil-mugs for tapers, suspended everywhere. I had to enter in stocking feet, and caught cold and got my feet stuck up with the abominations that besmeared the paved floors everywhere.

It was not bewitching to see a number of dirty varlets in all manner of absurd costume, sitting tailor-fashion on the floor, reciting their lessons.

I don't think much of St. Sophia.

1000 columns underground—curious—nothing more.

The fact that he caught cold there had something to do with the temper of these notes, of course, but in the book written months later he still had little good to say of St. Sophia. Other aspects of the city he found more pleasing:

Women rather pretty with their veiled faces and flowing Oriental robes—but flitting about in the magnificent distances of the dim arches of the great bazaars, look horribly like the shrouded dead abroad in the earth.

The bazaars of Stamboul—wonderful.

The dogs of Constantinople more so.

Embroidered jackets of gold and purple, blue and crimson—splendid. Persian shawls and fabrics—and Turkish—gorgeous.

Turkish Father Recommends His Son

"Can recommend my son as a smart boy and terrific liar—can cheat deftly."

New palace on the Asiatic side of the beautiful Bosphorus (3 miles wide) is built on spot where Constantine erected a gold cross to commemorate his conversion. When Turks took the place and began to build, many thought he would declare himself Christian when finished, and waited to baptize their children then. They are waiting yet.

Russia

Spent a day at Sebastopol. Melancholy place—wilderness of battered down houses—look like forest of broken chimneys. Not 3 dozen habitable dwellings—*they* all new.

Visited Redan, Malakoff, etc. and picked up cannon balls and other light relics.

Russia claimed exclusive right to put a new dome on the Church of the Holy Sepulcher at Jerusalem, and France claimed the same—England wanted a chance at Russia—hence, the war. Sounds as absurd as the crusades.

A large number of handsome young English and Russian young ladies visited the ship and spent the afternoon. They were delighted at her fine appointments and great size.[1] If we could have brought them back we might have taken them to Odessa. It was pleasant to hear our own language again.

Several gentlemen insisted on our visiting the Emperor with the ship—said they would insure us a superb reception by him and would not only telegraph but send a courier to notify him we were coming. He is spending the heated months at a little watering-place 30 miles from here.

For certain reasons we declined, and everybody was sorry enough, very naturally.

This has been the pleasantest afternoon we have had for a good while.

Everywhere the prints of cannon balls are in the stone walls—some as neat as if cut. Some balls still stick in the walls, and from them iron stains run.

It (Sebastopol) is a completely destroyed town—not one of its old houses was left standing in that fearful 18 months' siege.[2]

[1] She had a register of eighteen hundred tons!

[2] Surrendered Sept. 9, 1855. The Russian loss (defenders) 102,670.

They sell Circassian girls yet in Constantinople, but the markets are private.

Aug. 25.—On our way back to Yalta to call on the Emperor of Russia, who has telegraphed the Governor General of Odessa concerning the matter, and the thing is all right.

O, geeminy, what a stir there is! What a calling of meetings! What an appointing of committees! What a furbishing up of swallow-tail coats!

A committee was appointed to draft an address to the Emperor. Mark Twain was elected chairman and instructed to prepare the address; which here follows, as originally set down in his note-book.

Your Imperial Majesty:

We are a handful of private citizens of America, travelling simply for recreation, & unostentatiously, as becomes our unofficial state, & therefore we have no excuse to tender for presenting ourselves before your Majesty, save the desire of offering our grateful acknowledgments to the lord of a realm which, through good & through evil report has been the fast friend of the land we love so well.

We could not presume to take a step like this did we not know well that the words we speak here, & sentiments wherewith they are freighted, are but the reflex of the thoughts & the feelings of all our countrymen, from the green hills of New England to the shores of the far Pacific. We are few in number, but we utter the voice of a nation!

One of the brightest pages that has graced the world's history since written history had birth, was recorded by your Majesty's hand when it loosed the bonds of twenty million serfs; and

Americans can but esteem it a privilege to do honor to a ruler who has wrought so great a deed. The lesson that was taught us then, we have profited by, & are free in truth, to-day, even as we were before in name. America owes much to Russia—is indebted to her in many ways—and chiefly for her unwavering friendship in seasons of our greatest need. That that friendship may still be hers in time to come, we confidently pray; that she is & will be grateful to Russia & to her Sovereign for it, we know full well; that she will ever forfeit it by any premeditated, unjust act, or unfair course, it were treason to believe.

(Signed) Sam. L. Clemens, Ch'n

D. Crocker)
A. N. Sandford) Committee
Col. Kinney)
Wm. Gibson)

On behalf of the passengers of the U. S. Steamer Quaker City, C. C. Duncan commanding.

Yalta, Russia—Aug. 25, 1867

That job is over. Writing addresses to Emperors is not my strong suit. However, if it is not as good as it might be, it doesn't signify—the other committeemen ought to have helped write it—they had nothing else to do, and I had my hands full. But for bothering with this matter I would have caught up entirely with my N. Y. Tribune correspondence, and nearly with the San Francisco cor.

The reception of our party by the Emperor is to come off at the summer palace at noon to-morrow.

Aug. 26. The imperial carriages were in waiting at 11, and at 12 we were at the palace.

In 5 minutes the Emperor and Empress, the Grand Duchess Marie and the little Grand Duke appeared and welcomed the party pleasantly.

The consul for Odessa read the address and the Czar

said frequently, "Good, very good indeed" and at the close, "I am very, very grateful."

After talking half an hour the Imperial party conducted us all through the palace and then all through the young crown prince's beautiful palace.

By this time it was after 1, and an invitation came from the Grand Duke Michael to visit his gardens, park and palace and breakfast with him, which we did.

Prince Dalgorouki went along, and so did that jolly Count Festetics who is to marry the Governor-General's daughter. So also the Lord High Admiral of Russia and a number of the nobility of both sexes connected with the Emperor's household.

But the Grand Duke Michael is a rare brick!—and his wife is one of the very pleasantest of all these pleasant people, and both are sociable.

What happened in the park—and again in the court of the palace, where the fountain was, and the flowers—and above all the occurrence under the porch which has the Caryatides in imitation of the Temple of Erechtheus at Athens—these were rich—they must never be trusted to treacherous paper—memory will do—I guess no one in the world who could appreciate a joke would be likely to forget them.

> What really happened in the park was that one of the Quaker City "pilgrims" said to the Grand Duke, in a voice subdued in quality, but not in carrying power,
>
> "Say, Dook, where's the water-closet?"
>
> The "under the porch" joke was, as he confessed years afterward, on himself. He had noticed that a number of the foreign guests had a bit of red ribbon in their buttonholes—an ornament, as he supposed. He thought it attractive, and discovering a bit of red ribbon—from a cigar,

> perhaps—tied it in his own buttonhole. Presently Count Festetics, Grand Master of Ceremonies, inquired as to his Legion of Honor decoration. He realized then, and was embarrassed, but not entirely floored. He said hastily that his ribbon was merely a symbol of a club of journalists to which he belonged.

We had not been at the Grand Duke's long when the Empress and the Grand Duchess Marie came, and shortly afterward the Emperor himself. He looked much nobler than the Emperor Napoleon, and a hundred times more so than the Sultan of Turkey. Remained half a day, nearly.

Aug. 27. Carpets were spread over the pier and the Governor-General and family came on board the ship (we saluted with 9 guns) and afterward [here follows a list of dignitaries, including Gen. Todtleben, the honored defender of Sebastopol all during the siege. And a large number of army and navy officers and titled and untitled ladies and gentlemen].

Champagne blow-out.

Aug. 28. Sailed for Constantinople last night, saluting as we left—and fireworks. That beautiful little devil I danced with at the ball in that impossible Russian dance still runs in my head. Ah, me! if I had only known how to talk Russian! However, she must have known I was saying *some*thing with all that absurd English which she couldn't understand.

All day ladies bathe naked in full view of the ship. They don't consider it any harm, I suppose. At Odessa all ages and sexes bathe together.

Aug. 29. Passed through the beautiful Bosphorus just

after daylight and anchored away up in the Golden Horn, nearly to the lower bridge. Been on shore and found Dan and Foster, Jack Van Nostrand and Col. Haldeman.

The American minister (Mr. Morris) is to drink wine on board tonight.

Our imperial visit has had a good effect. It worries the Sublime Porte a good deal. It is well, for the offensive resolutions of Congress concerning the Cretan insurrection have just been received and it may prevent an offensive reply—may even avert a war—who knows.

Sept. 2. Went over to Scutari—took horse and went on top of mountain back of city—beautiful view of Con.—Bosphorus Islands in sea of Marmora—saw most of Black Sea, etc.

Found a gold mine—good live quartz—the gold in snuff colored sulphurettes—ought to be very valuable here, where the labor is so cheap. Its presence is unsuspected.

> This is an interesting item, but we hear no more of it. Perhaps the mine still waits for an active discoverer.

Sea of Marmora

Sept. 3. Tried to leave Constantinople at 7 P.M., but in dodging a schooner, whose mainsail we tore with our bowsprit, we fouled a buoy just abreast of the Grand Seraglio (but within the Golden Horn) and drifted down on the bowsprit of a Beuctra boat—which cut our starboard quarter boat clear in two. We got clear at 11 o'clock, and in a few moments we saw nothing but 5 miles of lights, elevated in pyramids, lines and semicircles—arches—the last of Constantinople.

CHAPTER VIII

Syria and the Holy Land

Smyrna

Field—villages of scattered houses or tents that look like sugar-loaves through the glasses.

Smyrna Bay is very deep—Country low hills and rolling.

Afternoon—officers of gunboat Swatora came aboard.

Ascended Citadel Hill (Mt. Pagus of Scripture). Went to Caravan Bridge to see the camel-trains come in.

Ephesus

Sept. 6. All hands took train and went to ruins of ancient Ephesus, 45 miles hence.

Another of the 7 churches of Asia was here.

Apollo and Diana were born here. Here the god Pan lurked in the Coressus and the Prion hills; here Bacchus and Hercules fought against the Amazons; here Hannibal, Scipio, Lysander, Alexander the Great and many another man great in ancient history tarried. Here Homer was born; here Brutus and Cassius lay in refuge in the temple, and Anthony and Cleopatra held their gorgeous revels. Here stood the splendid temple of Diana of Ephesus, one of the Seven Wonders of the World.

Here Paul and John preached; here the Virgin Mary lived with John, and here both died and were buried. Here is the tomb of St. Luke the Disciple. Here Mary

Magdalene lies buried. Here John the Baptist labored. From these noble ruins many a church in Christendom and many a mosque has been supplied with its grandest, its costliest and most enduring columns.

Syria

Sept. 11. Left Beyrut for Jerusalem at 3 P.M.
Our company is composed of 8 persons:
Church, of Ohio
W. R. Denny, Va.
Jack Van Nostrand, N. J.
Davis, Staten Island
Dan Slote, N. Y.
Moulton, Missouri
Dr. Birch
Sam Clemens, Cal.

all mounted on horses. Abraham of Malta is chief dragoman, and Mohammed of Alexandria, Egypt, is first assistant.

Camp equipage: 3 sleeping-tents; 1 kitchen tent, and 1 eating-tent all large, finely furnished and handsome.

Our caravan numbers 24 mules and horses and 14 serving-men—28 men all told.

Camped that night on high ground of the Lebanon foothills 10 or 12 miles from Beyrut.

They were off on "the long trip" through Syria and the entire length of Palestine, in summertime. Three or four weeks later those who survived would join the ship at Joppa. In the *Innocents* we read,

> . . . terms five dollars a day apiece, in gold, and everything to be furnished by the dragoman. They said we would live as well as at a hotel. I had read something like that before, and did not

shame my judgment by believing a word of it. I said nothing, however, but packed up a blanket and a shawl to sleep in, pipes and tobacco, two or three woolen shirts, a portfolio, a guide-book, and a Bible. I also took along a towel and a cake of soap, to inspire respect in the Arabs, who would take me for a king in disguise.

But it all turned out as promised. If their livestock was not very sightly, the comforts were beyond belief. The finishing touch that night was when their serving-men spread carpets in their tents.

I simply said: "If you call this camping out, all right—but it isn't the style *I* am used to; my little baggage that I brought along is at a discount."

It grew dark and they put candles on the tables—candles set in bright, new, brazen candlesticks. And soon the bell—a genuine, simon-pure bell—rang, and we were invited to "the saloon." I had thought before that we had a tent or so too many, but now here was one, at least, provided for; it was to be used for nothing but an "eating-saloon." Like the others, it was high enough for a family of giraffes to live in, and was very handsome and clean and bright-colored within. It was a gem of a place. A table for eight, and eight canvas chairs; a tablecloth and napkins whose whiteness and whose fineness laughed to scorn the things we were used to in the great excursion steamer; knives and forks, soup plates, dinner plates—everything in the handsomest kind of style. It was wonderful! And they call *this* camping out. Those stately fellows in baggy trousers and turbaned fezes brought in a dinner which consisted

> of roast mutton, roast chicken, roast goose, potatoes, bread, tea, pudding, apples, and delicious grapes; the viands were better cooked than any we had eaten for weeks and the table made a finer appearance, with its large German-silver candlesticks and other finery than any table we had sat down to for a good while, and yet that polite dragoman, Abraham, came bowing in and apologizing for the whole affair, on account of the unavoidable confusion of getting under way for a very long trip, and promising to do a great deal better in future!
>
> It is midnight now, and we break camp at six in the morning!
>
> They call this camping out. At this rate it is a glorious privilege to be a pilgrim to the Holy Land.

It would not all be a "glorious privilege," but not many things in this world could be more inspiring than their start. To be young (he was not yet 32), starting with boon companions on a trip into historic Syria and the Holy Land—days of it, weeks of it, no hurry—and then, next morning:

> The saloon tent had been stripped of its sides, and had nothing left but its roof; so when we sat down to table we could look out over a noble panorama of mountain, sea, and hazy valley. And sitting thus, the sun rose slowly up and suffused the picture with a world of rich coloring.

Sept. 12. Broke camp at 7 A.M. just as Col. Foster and Col. Hyde went by in the diligence bound for Damascus. We passed the Leary party and the Bond party during the day.

Came down into the great Lebanon valley at noon and rested and lunched at an old kahn. Far away on the right the snow-spotted peak of Mt. Hermon.

Passed up the valley and camped on the lower side under the dews of Hermon—first passing through a dirty Arab village and visiting the tomb of Noah, of Deluge notoriety.

Ruins of Baalbec

Broke camp at 6:30 A.M., crossed the valley and at 11 reached the magnificent ruins of Baalbec. Marched about the ruined temples and the quarries 3 or 4 hours. Found Bullard, Mrs. Fairbanks, James, and Beach and daughter there; met Jackson and party, and the Leary and Bond parties arrived afterward, fagged out—then departed.

> One of the fine chapters of *The Innocents* is the one describing Baalbec, yet these, apparently, are his only notes of the ancient city. Very likely he carried the picture in his head and set it forth that night in an *Alta* letter. He was writing an average of three letters a week for the *Alta* and the *New York Tribune*—long letters. When did he find the time? In later life he classified himself as "lazy"; the earlier facts do not bear him out.

Rode seven hours, partly through wild, rocky scenery and camped at ten-thirty on the banks of a pretty stream, near a Syrian village. Two horses lame, and the others worn out.

Sept. 14. Broke camp at 7 A.M. and made a fearful trip through the Zeb Dana valley and the rough mountains (temples carved in them) and finally along a beautiful stream in a chasm, lined thick with pomegranate, fig, olive and quince orchards, and nooned an hour at 1

P.M. at the celebrated fountain of Figia, second in size in Syria, and the coldest water in the world. Bathed in it. It is the principle source of the Abana River and is only half mile long to where it joins.

Beautiful place, giant trees all around—vast stream gushes from under the mountain in a torrent. Over it is a very ancient ruin, with no known history—supposed to have been for the worship of the fountain.

Where Baalam's ass lived, holy ground.

Damascus

Left the fountain at 1 P.M. and reached Mohammed's lookout place over the wonderful garden and plain of Damascus and the beautiful city in time to get a good long look and descend into the city before the gates were closed.

Sept. 15. Taken very sick at 4 A.M.

Sept. 16. Abed all day yesterday—got enough of Damascus. Don't want to see any more of it. Took a jackass and an Arab to drive it and visited the "Street called Straight." Judas's house where St. Paul lay blind after his adventure—house and well of Ananias (these are genuine, at any rate) the disciple who went and invested Paul with the sacred office as commanded by the Saviour—the house of Naaman the leper, whom the prophet Elijah (or Elisha) ordered to wash 7 times in Jordan and so cured him—the place in the city wall (evidently old Roman wall) where Paul was let down in the basket and made his escape toward Jerusalem when a Jew sought his life—outside the wall the tomb (red chicken-coop) of St. George, a gate-keeper beheaded for conniving at Paul's escape. Further out the hole (genuine and ancient) where Paul lay hid till he got a chance to get away—and the great tomb of the 5000 Christians massacred in Damascus 7 years ago.

Enough of Damascus.

Sept. 16. Left Damascus about 10 or 11—4 hours out saw the spot where Paul was miraculously converted.

Nimrod's tomb. 4000 years old. The first king.

Camped at an Arab village where Nimrod, the mighty hunter, the builder of Babylon and the Tower of Babel, lies buried. He was a fine old sport and a great linguist.

In his book Mark Twain writes:

> The last twenty-four hours we stayed in Damascus I lay prostrate with a violent attack of the cholera, or cholera morbus, and therefore had a good chance and a good excuse to lie there on that wide divan and take an honest rest.

He was better next day, able to go on, but at a village a few days later Dan was taken violently. He might never go any farther. The pilgrims were anxious to get on; they might miss the boat. Besides, it was very uncomfortable there—a hot, infected, squalid place. The pilgrims passed resolutions: they would make Dan as comfortable as possible, and leave him. Mark Twain said:

"Gentlemen, I understand that you are going to leave Dan Slote here alone. I'll be God-damned if I do."

With a few attendants he remained behind, with Dan, who presently recovered. They overtook the others without much delay. Neither in his book nor in his notes does Mark Twain mention anything of this. It was told later by Deacon

William F. Church, a member of the party—a man of orthodox views, who did not approve of Mark Twain, his language, or his habits.

"He was the worst man I ever knew," Church said; then added, "And the best."[1]

Holy Land

Sept. 17. Edged into the Holy Land proper, today.

After noonday lunch, climbed a great cone 1000 ft. high which overlooks the ancient ruined city of Cæsarea Phillippi, Dan, and the great plain wherein are visible some little streams—sources of the Jordan.

This place where we are encamped is beautiful with olive groves and the fountain which is the main source of the Jordan—we washed in it and drank of its waters. The fountain comes from a great grotto, where the Greeks (and the Romans afterward) worshiped the God Pan (hence the name, Panias) and niches are carved in the rocks still, and the Greek inscriptions. At the same place Herod the Great erected a marble temple to commemorate the visit of Cæsar Augustus to the city and changed the city's name to Cæsarea Phillippi also.

Cæsarea Phillippi

A great massive ruined citadel of 4 acres. Ruined arches, waterways, bridges, columns, capitols etc. everywhere. Hoofprints deep in old rocks.

This is the first place we have ever seen whose pavements were trodden by Jesus Christ. Here he asked the disciples who the people took him to be, and asked Peter who *he* took him to be and Peter's confident answer elicited that famous sentence upon which all the vast power and importance the Church of Rome arrogates to itself is founded: "Thou art Peter and upon this rock

[1] Letter from George H. Warner (brother of Charles Dudley Warner) to the writer, March 14, 1911.

etc.—and what thou shalt bind upon the earth shall be bound in Heaven" etc.

Here Christ cured a woman who had had an issue of blood for years (nowadays there would have been an affidavit published) and near here, possibly on the castle hill, some claim that the Saviour's ascension took place.

Dan

Sept. 18.

It was first, ages ago the Phœnician Laish—a lot of Danites from Sodom, 600, came over like a pack of adventurers, as they were, and captured the place and lived there, as sort of luxurious agriculturists, till Abraham hazed them in after times.

We traveled a long stretch (4 miles) of miserable rocky road, overrun by water, and finally turned and followed down the other side of the valley, over a half green, half rusty country full of fine sheep, bulls of Bashan and Bedouin shepherds. The Bedouins are descended from Esau, and scorn to live in houses. Saw their tents. Then through several large Arab villages made of coarse matting houses, shaped like an omnibus, and finally after nooning and riding 2 hrs. along a vast green swamp that occupies the whole width of the valley we camped at last at a fountain and mill well down abreast of Lake Hula, or the Waters of Merom, of Bible fame.

Sept. 19. Left our camp by the Waters of Merom, at 7 A.M.

The Arabs threw stones into the camp last night and tried to stampede the horses.

Rode 2 hrs. over tolerably arable land (fast) and came in sight of the Sea of Galilee—shortly came to an old kahn, and in it examined the arched pit called Joseph's well, where his brethren threw him. Then over a horrible, rocky, barren desert (like Nevada) with scattering goats and shepherds (with pipes) and passed Safed, and close to that Bethsaida, from which Christ sent his disciples in a boat, after the miracle of 5 loaves and 2 fishes performed at the other Bethsaida, which is above the mouth of the Jordan 2 miles and a little to the eastward, where Andrew and several other disciples hailed from. One mile from Bethsaida we descended to the Sea at Capurnaum, Christ's dwelling-place, where he performed a great many miracles. Some old crumbling ruins there, a ruined kahn and a fig tree and fountain, Arabs and camels.

Near here was the marvelous draught of fishes.

Tried to get a boat, and didn't.

This is the brief note that Mark Twain enlarged later in Chapter XLVII of *The Innocents Abroad*. The pilgrims, he says, had been in a semi-rhapsody ever since they had arrived near the Sea of Galilee. The thought of actually sailing on the waters that had borne the Saviour and the Apostles almost overcame them. As to the cost in money of this precious privilege it was not even considered. Then they heard the price and lost enthusiasm.

Something of the sort happened. As related, it may be mixed with imagination a little, but at any rate the pilgrims did not get the boat.

A brief note follows:

"Took a bath"—(to cool themselves off, perhaps).

Crossed a long, rich, oleander plain along the sea to Magdala, the birthplace of Mary Magdalene—the rattiest, rustiest, dirtiest little collection of mud hovels, tattooed women and sore-eyed children in Palestine.

Thence along the edge of a mountain, to Tiberius, another nasty mud-hovel village, full of Arabs, Jews and Negroes.

It was built by Herod Antipas, the murderer of John the Baptist, and named after his friend, the Emperor Tiberius, so it is only mentioned in the New Testament.

The Sanhedrim met here last, and for 300 years it was the metropolis of the Jews in Palestine. It has been the abiding-place of many famous and learned Jewish rabbis. They are here buried.

Opposite Tiberius on the east side of the lake the swine ran down to the sea.

We have seen no country between here and Damascus capable of supporting any such population as one gathers from the Bible.

The people of this region in the Bible were just as they are now—ignorant, depraved, superstitious, dirty, lousy, thieving vagabonds.

Sept. 20. Bathed in Galilee before breakfast. Passed through the strange old town (beautiful porphyry columns with paintings almost worn away.) Had a wretched-looking scalliwag imposed upon us as a guard by the sheik—a beat with a long harmless silver-mounted gun and 2 pistols.

Mount Tabor

Transfiguration.

It is mentioned all through the Bible. New convent, and ruins of an old one built by the crusaders. Also ruins of Joshua's time.

Saw from its summit, Galilee, Hermon, Little Hermon, Gilboa, where Saul and Jonathan fell, Nain, Endor, Fountain of Jezreel, the Plain of Ezbraelon, where Napoleon, the Crusaders, the ancient Jews and all the nations of the earth have fought at different times.

Then came to Nazareth where Christ lived and carpentered till 30 years of age (not allowed by Jewish law to teach sooner).

Imagine Christ's 30 years of life in the slow village of Nazareth.

> If Mark Twain had not been previously familiar with Bible history he was to become reasonably familiar with it now. He had bought a little Bible at Constantinople, and he read it diligently. That he was deeply impressed is certain—his writing shows that, and in a way which perhaps he did not at the moment realize. Something of the stately simplicity of the King James version crept into his style, and remained there. If, as has been said, Mark Twain "wrote the purest English of any modern writer," the reason for it, in some measure at least, is to be found here.

Sept. 21. Left Nazareth and its chalk hills at 7.30 and galloped across the Plain of Esdraelon to Endor, the rustiest of all of them, almost—a few nasty mud cabins—many caves and holes in the hill from which the fierce, ragged, dirty inhabitants swarmed. Pop. 250.

The Witch's Cave

Has a fig tree before it and a spring within. Endor is a fit place for a witch. Camel dung on the roofs and caked against the houses to dry.

Nain

An hour further—still small towns. Little moss over spot once occupied by the widow's house. Graveyard—very old and ratty—exists yet, and place shown where corpse was passing through city wall when Christ resurrected it.

City of Jezreel

On the hill where Ahab, King of Judah, lived in splendor with his awful heifer, Jezebel, who swore away a fellow's life who would not sell his valley vineyard to her, and then took possession—on account of which she fell under a curse. Jehu, the mighty rider, "rode furiously" (couldn't have done it anywhere but in this plain) captured the city, threw Jez. over the walls and she was eaten by the dogs.

Fountain of Jezreel

Where Gideon slipped up on the Midianites and Amalekites with his 300 who lapped like dogs and with candles, pitchers and trumpets made a great host slay themselves.

Here Saul camped, while the Philistines lay at Shunam (big advantage of slope all the way). In the night he passed over left shoulder of Little Hermon to Endor where witch called up Samuel who prophesied Saul's defeat. Next day he and Jonathan and 2 other sons fled over Mount Gilboa (over our heads) and the 3 were killed and Saul fell on his sword thus making the throne to David. Esdraelon is what stands for the Armageddon of Scripture—Megiddo.

This Esdraelon is called the battlefield of the nations. 11 separate and distinct nations have fought in it. Think of all these marshaled at once in this great level plain, 25 miles long and 8 broad—the Assyrians and Persians, the Jews and Gentiles, Crusaders and Saracens, Egyptians, Turks, Arabs and Franks, in divers costumes, a splendid array. Call up the shadowy warriors and deploy them again on the great plain under the moon! 5,000,000!

Next to El Genin, where we are camped. Dr. Jackson and Payne are here and the Pasha of Akka with a great retinue of many camels. Crocker party have gone to Shechem.

Sept. 22. Left Genin at 1 A.M. Some time before daylight passed near another place where Joseph's brethren pitted him.

Samaria

About noon, after passing over a succession of mountain tops (saw the Mediterranean Sea 40 miles distant) and many biblical cities in which the inhabitants looked savage and would have liked to throw stones (women and babies with elaborate coin head-dresses).

We came to the singularly terraced hills which showed that we were out of Galilee and into Samaria.

Climbed a hill to visit the ruin of the city where the woman of Samaria conversed with Christ and gave him to drink—where the good Samaritan (the only one that ever lived there) dwelt, and where Elisha brought Naaman to be cured of his leprosy.

It is rough stone mud hovels and camel dung as usual—and a hundred limestone columns 2 ft. in diameter, 20 ft. high and no capitols or bases—lowest grade of architecture—and I suppose that *this* is all that remains of Herod's boasted beautifying of the city.

Ruins of a Christian church of the Crusades and the tomb of St. John the Evangelist—remains transferred to the Church of the Annunciation, Genoa.

The Arabs stoned Mr. James here, and 2 stones hit Miss Brown—our party was not molested except that a small boy threw a stone at the doctor.

Nablus or Shechem. Luncheon there at 3 P.M. The Crocker and Beach party on the hill. Ebal on the left (hill of cursing) and Gerezim on the right (hill of blessing). Ebal is cultivated with grapes—scattering olives on the other—disproves the enthusiasts who say the accursed mountain is barren and the other blooming.

On the hill is the oldest manuscript in existence—Jewish law.[1] Here Jacob (and I believe Abraham, Isaac, Joseph etc.) lived, and here Joshua gave the people his dying injunctions.

Camped at 7 P.M. at an Arab village Lubia (Libonia of the Bible) tents behind. Slept on the ground in front of an Arab house. Lice, fleas, horses, jackasses, chickens and, worse than all, Arabs for company all night.

Sept. 22. Broke camp at 2.30 A.M. and passed the Severance party in the foot of the valley—lights burning in their tents.

After daylight passed somewhere in the neighborhood of Shiloh, where the Ark of Covenant rested 300 years—Ark taken to battle and lost—Eli fell and broke his neck.

Jerusalem

Loafed all the afternoon at the Mediterranean Hotel. We entered by the Damascus Gate, part of which is very old and part was repaired by the Crusaders.

Sept. 23. Visited the Mosque of Omar.

Footprint of Abraham, I suppose when he was going to sacrifice Isaac. Great rock of Abraham's sacrifice (authentic).

Down below is a place where Mohammed shoved rock up with his head. The rock is suspended between Heaven and earth. Hole in middle which leads down to Mohammedan Hell. Souls stand there and Mohammed lifts them up by the hair of the head, so they leave a scalplock—if they lose it they will go to Hell sure.

[1] "Written on vellum and is some four or five thousand years old" (*The Innocents*).

Calvary

Church of the Holy Sepulcher.
Organ and chanting of the monks.
Dim cathedral lights of many smoking tapers.
Place where Helena found the cross and her chapel where she sat.
Pillar of Flagellation.
Place where soldier was beheaded who said, "Truly this was the son of God."
Place where John and Mary stood looking at Christ on the cross when he said "Woman, behold thy son."
Place where Jesus appeared to Mary in the Garden.
Place where the women came at early dawn and saw the angel at the sepulcher.
The rent rock and the holes where the 3 crosses stood.
Navel of the world in the Greek chapel, where Adam's dust came from. Sword and spurs of Godfrey of Bouillon, first King of Jerusalem (genuine).
Adam's grave.
Crown of thorns.

The fact that he notes parenthetically that the sword and spurs of Godfrey of Bouillon are "genuine" casts a doubt on the other relics and landmarks. His chapter on the Church of the Holy Sepulcher, including his reflections at Adam's grave, is one of the best in the book.

With Jerusalem as their headquarters, they now made excursions to near-by localities of sacred interest.

Sept. 24. Left Jerusalem at 8 A.M. Passed out at St. Stephen's Gate, along base of Olivet in Valley of Jehosaphat by Jewish graveyard and tomb of Absalom—Jews throw stones at it to this day.

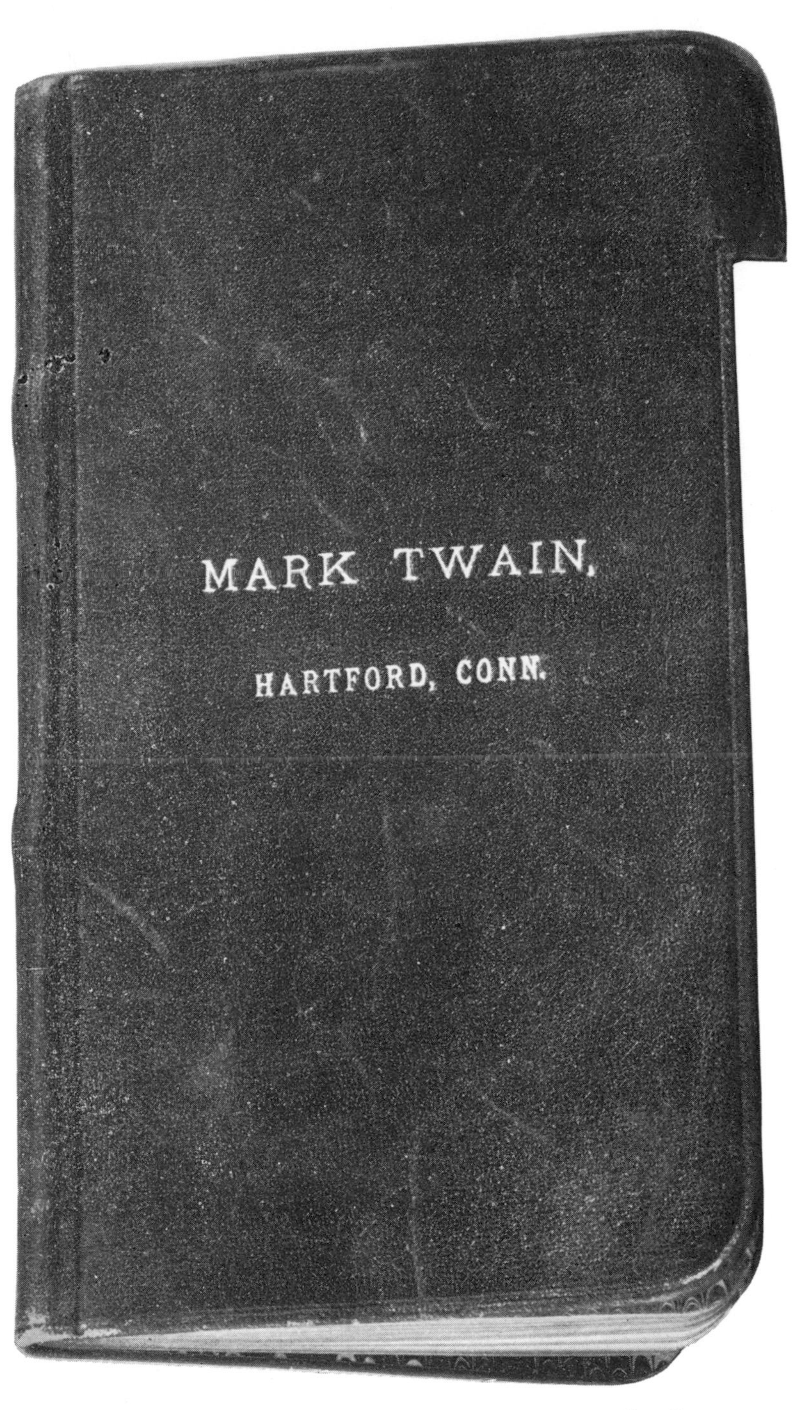

NOTEBOOK INVENTED BY MARK TWAIN. EACH PAGE HAD AN "EAR" AT THE TOP, TO BE TORN OFF WHEN THE PAGE WAS FILLED. THE BOOK THEN OPENED AT THE NEXT BLANK PAGE

Village of Bethany. It is fearfully ratty—some houses—mud—6 ft. square, and others holes in the ground—all windowless.

House and tomb of Lazarus and his 2 sisters.

Ancient Jericho

Where Joshua marched around 7 times and blew down the walls. Many ruins still there—arches, of course, and mosaics in the brook. Precipice perforated with holes.

This is the Plain of Jericho, noted as the most fertile spot in Palestine—they used to irrigate it.

Camped near old square tower (Middle Ages, no doubt) and modern mud Jericho—garrisoned by 12 men—Bedouin war.

Priest only entered Holy of Holies once a year, and then sent scapegoat through Golden Gate to the wilderness—some rascal gobbled him up, sins and all, before he got a hundred yards.

No Second Advent—Christ been here once, will never come again.

Dead Sea

Sept. 25. Visited ancient Jericho and the Fountain of Elisha. Found mosaics in the pool.

Abraham had a row with the Arabs about pitching tents in a hot valley among the fig trees.

As usual, got up 2 hrs. too soon (at 2 A.M.) and at 4 had traversed the Plain of Jericho and arrived at the River Jordan—the ford where the 12 stones were taken out.

Lay down in the bushes and slept 2 hours and caught cold. Got up and crossed the Jordan. Then rode 2 hours to the Dead Sea, and took a long bath. Face blistered and hair filled with crystallized salt.

After providing so many sheiks and guides, never saw a Bedouin.

Sept. 26. Got up at 3 A.M. and traveled 2½ hours over mountains and got to the enclosure of olive trees in a plain where the angels announced the birth of the Saviour to the shepherds. Then ¼ hour to Bethlehem and to the Milk Grotto. Then to the Convent of the Nativity built by St. Helena in 326.

Place where 20,000 children beheaded by Herod were buried.

Lunched there and left—2 hours to Jerusalem. On the way visited Rachel's tomb (authentic).

In Jerusalem breakfasted at noon at the Mediterranean Hotel and then went to the Hill of Offense where Solomon built a temple for his Egyptian wife. Tree there that Judas Iscariot hanged himself from.

Went to the Jews' wailing-place along the old wall of Solomon's Temple—Cyclopean masonry—many Pharisees with a curl forward of the ear.

Another part of the Temple Wall where Dr. Robinson discovered the spring of the arch which Solomon built to connect Zion Hill with the temple. The prophecy that 2 stones should not remain 1 upon the other not strictly fulfilled.

The ravens could hardly make their own living, let alone board Elijah.

Jerusalem, cont.

Sept. 27. Left camp outside the city walls between the Damascus and Jaffa gates (in head of Hinnom valley which carried the waters of Gihon) and passed Jaffa Gate on west of the city and crossed Hinnom valley, between upper and lower Gihon pools where an aqueduct built by Solomon crosses. Then went south and climbed the Hill of Evil Council and stood on the house of Caiaphas where the priests conspired against Christ, and where Judas went to receive his 30 pieces of silver—and sat under the tree whereon he hanged himself. To the south was the Plain of Ephraim and the Hill.

Proceeded to the Garden of Gethsemane with its Garden of Flowers and 8 holy olive trees.

Outside saw little lane where Judas betrayed Christ and, just above, the rock on which the disciples slept.

Turned up to the left, passed St. Agnes' and Virgin Mary's tombs and ascended to top of Mount of Olives, by road which David ascended when Absalom drove him out and members of the house of Saul threw stones at him. By convent where Catholics say Jesus ascended to Heaven.

To the southwest saw another hill between Olivet and Bethany where Bible says he ascended.

Sept. 28. Went all through the Holy Sepulcher again.

Saw the rock faces in a wall on Via Dolorosa that cried "Hosanna" when Jesus passed.

Visited the Fountain of Hezekiah where David saw the mother of Solomon bathing.

Went to the Pool of Bethesda again for water.

Got a branch from the Cedar of Lebanon planted by Godfrey de Bouillon, first King of Jerusalem, about 1085 to 1099.

Went out by the Damascus Gate, and 3 P.M. left for Ramleh—reached there at 8 P.M. or 9. Tall, handsome Crusaders' Tower. This is the Valley of Ajalon where the moon stood still.

Next morning, Sept. 30, rode 3 hours in a gallop to Joppa—where timbers for Solomon's Temple were landed. Jonah sailed from here on his mission. Visited house of Simon the Tanner where Peter had the vision of unclean beasts. Napoleon took this place once.

October 1st, 1867. Sailed for Egypt.

CHAPTER IX

Supplementary Holy Land Notes

Apparently Made on the Vessel, En Route for Egypt

Nazareth

Joseph of Arimathea, carpenter.

The synagogue where Christ read the Scriptures now a Christian church.

The hill where the multitude intended to cut him down.

The hill in the rear of the town whence an extensive view can be had—Tabor—Hermon—Carmel—Esdraelon—he saw all these—one's thoughts run on the boyhood of Christ so connected with these scenes. Here his mother marked the sayings of the Christ and pondered them in her heart.

Mount Tabor

Tabor is in the distance—an isolated town in the Plain of Esdraelon—on top, ruins since Joshua and Crusades. Here Deborah, by direction of God, gathered 10000 men under command of Barak (Judges V).

Bonaparte, Kleber with 3000 men engaged 27000. Napoleon from Tabor drove them back upon Murat's cavalry. Jesus took Peter, James and John—while praying his garment became white and shining, and there appeared Moses and Elisha, talking with him.

Joseph's Tomb

Joseph came to this field where is his tomb, in search of his brother.

Josh. 24-32

Joseph when closing his eyes in death said "God will assuredly visit you and bring you out of this land, unto the land which he sweared to Abraham, Isaac and Jacob. There and then he exacted of them an oath that they would carry up his bones with them when they went out of Egypt.

"And the bones of Joseph which the children of Israel brought up out of Egypt buried they in Shechem in a parcel of ground which Jacob bought of the sons of Hamor the Father of Shechem for 100 pieces of silver."

At the base of Ebal is a little square area enclosed by light stone wall neatly whitewashed—across one end of this enclosure is a Moslem tomb, the Tomb of Joseph.

Samaritan and Jew, Moslem and Christian alike, revere it, and honor it with their visits. The Tomb of Joseph, the dutiful son, the affectionate forgiving brother, the virtuous man, the wise prince and ruler. Egypt felt his influence—the world knows his history.

Jacob's Well

How many historic associations cluster around it! Here patriarchs watered their flocks—here Jesus rested and refreshed himself. It is just at the opening of the valley between Gerizim and Ebal—it is 9 by 90 ft.—an excavation in the solid limestone rock—it is hewn smooth and regular. An excavation 10 by 10 deep has been made about the mouth, walled up and arched over, making a vault or chamber over the mouth of the well. Here Christ talked with the woman (John iv-10). This renowned parcel of ground was bought by Jacob of the children of Hamor near 800 years before Christ, for a hundred pieces of money. It has lately been bought by the Greeks (had its value increased—had real estate advanced?) and they have begun to make improvements around it.

This is an interesting spot. Jesus rested here on his journey from Jerusalem to Galilee while his disciples went to the city to buy meat. 2000 years have not changed the scenery and the customs of the inhabitants remain the same—women with water-pots on their heads. This well, these mountains, yonder city were looked upon by the Saviour.

The old manuscript of the Samaritan in the synagogue here done up in the form of a scroll, kept in an elegant silver case and rolled in cloth of blue, purple and scarlet interwoven with threads of gold. The transcriber's imprint is wrought in one portion of the scroll into the text in the form of an acrostic and reads, "Written by Abishua son of Phineas, son of Eleazar, son of Aaron."

Bethel

House of God—so called by Jacob—visited yearly by Saul. Here Jeroboam set up his idol calf.

It is a long low ridge, covered with great piles of stone —about 3 or 4 acres of ground are covered with ruins. A few miserable huts—20 in all—constructed from fragments of the ruins constitute the village.

In the valley, a little west, is a huge cistern, built of massive stone—one side in good preservation, the other much dilapidated by the ravages of time. Its bottom is now a beautiful grass plot. Near by are 2 small fountains of pure clear water from which this great tank was originally supplied.

Originally it was called Luz. Abraham, in his first journey through the land, built an altar and worshiped God. On his return from Egypt he could not forget the rich pastures and their refreshing springs of water. Rich in cattle, in silver and gold, he returned to this altar and again called on the name of the Lord. Here his flocks roamed, here the maidens of Sarah came to fill their pitchers.

Here in these pasture grounds began the strife between Abraham and Lot's herdsmen and here the old patriarch made that munificent offer to Lot.

"Let there be no strife, I pray thee, between thee and me, and between my herdsmen and thy herdsmen, for we be brethren. Is not the whole land before thee? Separate thyself, I pray thee, from me. If thou wilt take to the left hand I will take to the right, or if thou wilt depart to the right hand I will go to the left."

Lot looked down upon the beautiful plain of the Jordan and chose himself a residence among those cities which now lie buried in the bitter waters of the Dead Sea.

Here the Lord promised this land: "Lift up now thine eyes, and look from the place where thou art, northward, and southward, and eastward, and westward: for all the land which thou seest, to thee will I give it and to thy seed forever." So the old man went in and preëmpted a county or two.

Time passed on—Abe rested in the cave Machpelah, and Isaac saw his sons growing up around him. A lone traveler is seen passing along this valley, his staff in his hand. (There was no style about Jacob.) He has made a long journey from Beersheba, 40 miles, and was necessarily pretty well fagged out. Night gathers around him—he takes a stone for a pillow (Jacob was not particular)—the hard earth for his bed, hard but roomy and the broad canopy of the heavens for his covering, with a good deal of wind under it for comfort on a cold night. Why was he traveling in that sort of style, and his grandfather so rich? He had a long journey of nearly 500 miles before him. He was in the vigor of life and though his fare was scanty, and his pillow hard, he had a stout heart and was favored with pleasant dreams. He saw a ladder set upon the earth, and the top of it reached to heaven! And behold the angels of God ascending and descending upon it! Above that ladder he saw the vision of the Holy One and heard a voice: "I am the Lord God of Abraham, thy father, and the God of Isaac; the land wherein thou liest, to thee will I give it, and to thy seed." And here the promise was made him that he should be kept in all his ways, and brought again in safety to this land. He awoke from this strange vision. "Surely," said he, "the Lord is in this place, and I knew it not. . . . How dreadful is this place! This is none other but the house of God and the gate of heaven."

Early in the morning Jacob rose up, took a stone he had used for his pillow, set it up for a memorial and dedicated it to the Lord,—and he called the name of that place Bethel, house of God.

Time passed on—Jacob returned with his wife, children, servants, flocks and herds. Again the Lord appeared unto him: "Arise, go up to Bethel and make there an altar unto God." Again Jacob and all his household dwelt upon this ground—again he built an altar and worshiped God.

And he called the place El Bethel—God, the house of God.

So when Jacob wanted a farm he only had to dream.

Here Deborah, Rebecca's nurse, died and they buried her beneath Bethel, under an oak.

What a history this place has! How strange to stand here on the camping-grounds of the patriarchs.

Bethel in Joshua's time was a royal city, governed by a king. Here Samuel held one of his circuit courts (was he a circuit judge?) when he traveled the circuit and judged Israel. The Ark (of the Covenant, not Noah's) seems to have been kept here at one time.

In the separation of the kingdom, after the death of Solomon, Jeroboam, fearing to have the people go up to Jerusalem to worship, lest they should go back to their old allegiance, established idolatrous worship, made 2 golden calves, set one up in Dan, the other in Bethel. Here he built a *magnificent* temple after an Egyptian model, intending to *rival* the *one at Jerusalem*. Such was the idolatrous worship that the name was changed to Bethavan, House of Idols.

It was at one of these idolatrous festivals that Jeroboam attempted to lay hold of the prophet of God who rebuked his abominable worship, and his arm was paralyzed and withered. These iniquities drew down the wrath of God upon the place, and 2500 years ago the prophet Amos was inspired to say: "Seek not Bethel, nor enter into Gilgal, for Gilgal shall surely go into captivity and Bethel shall come to naught."

Look upon these heaps of ruins, these broken cisterns, these neglected valleys—has the prophecy been fulfilled? Whose handwriting is here?

And with the same propriety you might point to the site of *any* city of that day and say the very same—only Jerusalem and Damascus have survived—and even the Jerusalem and Damascus of that day are desolate enough, for they lie 30 ft. under the ground! All the other cities are gone! There is a good deal of humbug about proving prophecies by this sort of evidence.

It is easy to prove a prophecy that promised destruction to a city—and it is impossible to prove one that promised *any*thing else—more particularly life and prosperity. It seems to me that the prophets fooled away their time when they prophesied the destruction of the cities—old Time would have fixed that, easy enough. Solomon's Temple was not to have one stone resting upon another, but infatuated travelers of the present day are determined to believe in spite of prophets, Holy Writ and everything else, that they have found the foundations of Solomon's doomed temple! Possibly they can reconcile this with the prophecy by saying it is only the ground there they have found.

I can go as far as the next man in genuine reverence of holy things, but this thing of stretching the narrow garment of belief to fit the broad shoulders of a wish, 'tis too much for me.

Gibeon or El Gib

This place is spoken of in the Old Testament as a great city—"one of the royal cities." Here lived the people when the Israelites invaded the land, gathered their old tattered garments and worn out shoes, packed their sacks with musty bread, and came with their jaded hungry animals and beguiled Joshua and the others into a treaty of peace. It is a small village now, but great in historic interest. In the plain below the 5 kings of the Amorites assembled together to punish Gibeon. Toward Gilgal eastward Joshua and his host encamped. The Amorites are defeated, the day is not long enough for Israel to continue the conquest, and Joshua gives the ever-memorable command: "Sun, stand thou still over Gibeon, and thou moon in the valley of Ajalon." And the sun stood still and the moon also until Israel was avenged.

On the east side is a pool or spring. There is first a natural cavity or grotto in the rock—then an inner chamber has been excavated which is entered by a long narrow opening down several steps of stone. Here a copious fountain gushes apparently from the rock—a little below it on the hillside are the ruins of a large reservoir. It was here that a remarkable meeting took place between Abner and Joab—they were gencrals of the armies of Israel and Judah—12 men of Judah were charged to fight 12 men of Israel. The whole 24 were slain. "For they caught every one his fellow by the head (got him in chancery) and thrust his sword in his fellow's side, so that they fell down together." And on that plain the subsequent battle took place. Abner was defeated and the swift-footed Usahel slain.

At this city also David's nephew, Amasa, was slain by his cousin Joab.

Here too on Gibeon Solomon offered up his 1000 funeral offerings and here the Lord appeared to him and gave him the desire of his heart—"Wisdom and Understanding."

> Some idea of the care which Mark Twain took in the matter of Biblical references and reading is shown in this notebook by his having set down no less than 20 pages of reference—specifications of chapter and verse.

It is so long now that I do not remember what we did after the morning that Dr. Birch and I went to the Pool of Bethsaida to get a flask of the water. We visited the Baths of Hezekiah where David fell in love with Uriah's wife while she was bathing—also, occasionally, the church of the Holy Sepulcher and around about the traditional houses of Pilate, Caiaphas, Dives and Lazarus, and poked through the Via Dolorosa etc. and so on—and got a most infernal Turkish bath one night—nothing to the baths of Damascus and Constantinople. These thieves don't like to wash Christians, I think. X took his wife to dinner at the Mediterranean Hotel one night when we were there (they still lived in their tents outside the Damascus Gate) and came in himself after all the courses were served but dessert and coffee and tried to get off from paying because he hadn't eaten a full meal. The old Dutchman made him pay, though.

Major Barry, Griswold and party have been down to Jericho, the ford of the Jordan and the Dead Sea, and were attacked by a gang of Bedouins. A shot or two was fired—nobody hurt, but Griswold scared a good deal.

Leary's party was threatened with raid one night, somewhere down there by the Fountain where the ravens fed

Elisha, and had to decamp. We are the crowd, so far, that have gone to these localities unmolested—weren't worth robbing, maybe.

Curse their accursed carelessness to leave that deadlight open; spoiled the cushions and everything—all the cigars in the water and tobacco. It never seems to occur to them that ours is the weather side of the ship, *sometimes!*

CHAPTER X

Egypt and Home

MARK TWAIN's Egyptian notes were few and brief. The ship remained less than a week at Alexandria, which gave them hardly more than enough time for Cairo, with the Sphinx and Pyramids.

Oct. 3. Landed at Alexandria. Fine streets and dwellings. Fine shade-tree avenues.

Oct. 4. To Cairo, by rail—7 hours—arrived after night.

Oct. 5. Donkeys to Pyramids of Ghizeh—passed old Cairo, Island of Rhodes.

Crossed the Nile from old Cairo to Ghizeh. Splendid atmosphere. Beautiful Oriental scenery. Naked girls in the streets.

Ascent of Pyramid of Cheops.

The Sphinx.

Went into the Pyramid.

Newly opened tomb behind the Sphinx.

Theater of old red granite open near it.

The whole place round about is rich in art—under the sand.

Dr. Gibson at the Sphinx.

Citadel and lofty wall where the last Mameluke Bey jumped down.

View of Cairo and Memphis.

Heliopolis and the petrified forest.

Projecting lattices.

Shepheard's infamous hotel.

Splendid avenue of sycamores and acacias, 3 or 4 miles to the Pasha's great garden.

Oct. 7. Returned to Alexandria—Pyramids in the distance.

Cultivation—vast oceans of corn etc.

Queer villages.

Soft scenery.

No more than that, yet the Egyptian chapter with its lofty prose poem of the Sphinx, beginning, "After years of waiting it was before me at last," is probably the high spot of his book. That and the one of Palestine, beginning: "Palestine sits in sackcloth and ashes." Readers who have been wont to think of Mark Twain chiefly as a funmaker will do well to turn to Chapters LVI and LVIII of *The Innocents* and consider those particular extracts.

After Egypt the notebook contains just five items.

Oct. 7. Left Dan, and sailed for Africa.

Oct. 11. At sea somewhere in the neighborhood of Malta. Very stormy.

Terrible death to be talked to death.

The storm has blown 2 small land birds and a hawk to sea and they came on board.

Sea full of flying fish.

That is all. The ship put in at Gibraltar for coal, and with three others Mark Twain spent a delightful week through Andalusia, "the garden of old Spain." But he did not try to write about it. How could he? After Palestine and Egypt, even Andalusia must have been tame enough—restful, but tepid. His book really ends with the

Egyptian chapter, and it is easy to see that he could not take up Spain after writing of the land

> . . . that built temples which mock at destroying time and smile grimly upon our lauded little prodigies of architecture; that old land that knew all which we know now, perchance, and more; that walked in the broad highway of civilization in the gray dawn of creation, ages and ages before we were born; that left the impress of exalted, cultivated Mind upon the eternal front of the Sphinx, to confound all scoffers who, when all the other proofs had passed away, might seek to persuade the world that imperial Egypt, in the days of her high renown, had groped in darkness.

Washington

Mark Twain returned to America to find himself scarcely less than famous. His *Alta* and *Tribune* letters had been widely copied and were universally known. Not many Americans had traveled in those days, and they eagerly read about ancient lands. They had even read the sanctimonious drivel of certain doctors of theology who had been sent abroad by their "flocks" to see and report—what they carried with them, rather than what they found in fact. Mark Twain's letters had struck a new note. They had the ring of sincerity, truth. They destroyed sham where they found it, and they were sinfully readable. A big Hartford publisher wanted to make a subscription book of them—the book which would be named *The Innocents Abroad, or the New Pilgrim's Progress,* and make his fame secure.

He went to Washington, ostensibly as Secretary to Senator Stewart, really to write Washington letters for New York papers. His next notebook begins:

Fame is a vapor; popularity an accident; the only earthly certainty is oblivion.

Didn't drink much on that ship—was like Congress—prohibit it save in committee rooms—carry it in demijohns and carry it out in demagogues.

Acquainted with General Grant—said I was glad to see him—he said I had the advantage of him.

Brief Impressions of Washington, Senators and Congressmen

Washburn of Ill.—gray, unshaved, fleshy a little.

Fernando Wood—iron-gray hair—white moustache.

Jas. Brooks—gray and spectacles.

Woodward (Dem.) of Pa.—bald, specs, unshaved.

Eldridge of Wis.—leading and malignant copperhead.

Alison of Iowa—sack-coat, light-blue pants—looks like a village law student—plays for handsome looks—30—hands in pockets—excessively ordinary-looking man—large flat foot—light handsome brown hair—youngest-looking member—essentially ornamental—stands around where women can see him.

John Buckland (O.)—large bald, never says anything—clothes ungainly on his shapeless body.

Thad. Stevens—very deep eyes, sunken unshaven

cheeks, thin lips, long and strong mouth, long, large, sharp nose—whole face sunken and sharp, full of inequalities—dark wavy hair—Indian—club-footed—ablest man.

Logan—black eyebrows—long black implacable straight hair, without a merciful curve in it—big black moustache—pleasant-looking eye often—even makes bad jokes sometimes, but tigers play in a ponderous sort of way. Splendid war record—15th army corps and Army of Tenn.—1 of Sherman's generals—better suited to war than making jokes.

Thomas of Md.—belongs to another age—Whig—old style—hermit in every way—woman-hater—lives up in mountains alone in N.W. Maryland—one of the oldest Reps.—is a radical—white hair laid in folds—hair comes washing forward over his forehead in 2 white converging waves over a bare worn rock.

Judge Shellabarger—able.

Bingham, Ohio—nervous, severe and ready debater.

Garfield—young, able and scholarly—was chief of Rosencranz staff—preacher.

Carey of Ohio (8 hour) witty speech—large face—a little full—Indian—long iron-gray hair tuned back and not parted—heavy, large, portly man—shaven—long, thin, strong mouth—slow of movement—ponderous every way—his strong suit his persistence, no doubt.

Bingham, Conn.—eloquent—commands attention of House—silky very light hair, just touched with gray—kinky or rather curvy—turned back loosely so as to suggest, apparently, with a harrow—large, high, broad forehead, slightly wrinkled—little gray side whiskers—eyes that have a drawn appearance of having been strained to the focus of glasses—a sharp beak of a nose—chews nervously, and when gets fagged out poking around, sits down —is generally around elsewhere than in his seat.

Horace Maynard, Tenn.—one of purest men in Congress—Union from first—very gentlemanly, talented and fine speaker. Remarkable-looking man—very tall and very slim—long black hair, combed flat and behind ears gives him a trim, shrewd, "cleared for action" old-style look. Indian. Pleasant look in face. Very little black moustache.

John D. Baldwin (of Mass.)—Prop. Worcester Spy—unblemished character—one of the best read men—very large—specs gold—light gray hair—dark goatee and moustache—patriarchal look.

Ben Butler—forward part of his bald skull looks raised like a water-blister—its boundaries at the sides and at its base in front is marked by deep creases—fat face—small dark moustache—considerable hair behind and on the sides—one reliable eye. Is short and pursy—fond of standing up with hands in pants pockets and looking around to each speaker with the air of a man who has half a mind to crush them and yet is rather too indifferent. Butler is dismally and drearily homely, and when he smiles it is like the breaking up of a hard winter.

Robinson, Brooklyn—hair kinky, thick, pretty long—in odd stripes of rich brown and silver—glossy.

One wishes these notes might continue—thumb-nail sketches—vivid likenesses. They break off short. Complications over the *Alta* letters (their book use) seemed to make it advisable for their author to return to San Francisco. He decided to do his book there. If he made any notes of the outward voyage they are lost. He left early in 1868, arranged all matters with the *Alta,* finished his book, at top speed, lectured in San Francisco on the Quaker City trip, covered his old Nevada circuit and returned triumphantly with his manuscript by midsummer.

CHAPTER XI

Notes San Francisco to New York

LEFT San Fran. for N. Y. in P.M. S.S. Co.'s Steamer, Montana, July 6, 1868.

July 13. Arrived at Acapulco.
Only 150 passengers on board.

Montana fine ship—stateroom ought to have craft over berths.

In Aspinwall, all it is necessary to do is to cry Viva Revolucion! at head of street, and instantly it is in commotion. Doors slam to, 50 soldiers march forth and cripple half a dozen niggers in their shirt-tails, a new President is elevated, and then for 6 months (till next rev.) the proud and happy survivors inquire eagerly of newcomers what was said about it in America and Europe.

Trip of a man in a balloon from Paris over India, China, Pacific Ocean, the plains to a prairie in Illinois.

> This was a preliminary memorandum of a story he had in mind to write. Some pages farther along the story is begun, but by the time he was well started he learned that Jules Verne had published a story with a similar idea which brought his own to a sudden end. His final memorandum reads:

While this was being written, Jules Verne's "Five

Weeks in a Balloon" came out and consequently this sketch wasn't finished.

> It seems too bad now that it should have been dropped. Its resemblance to Verne's tale would probably not have been striking, and the interest and atmosphere of the beginning makes us wish to see more.
>
> The reader may consider a few paragraphs:

John L. Morgan of Ill., a farmer and a man of good reputation, told me the following a few weeks ago while I was visiting at his house. I give it as he gave it to me. He said:

"In January, 3 winters ago, we had a heavy snowstorm. It lasted the best part of 3 days, and at the end of that time it lay on the ground 15 inches deep. The prairie in front of my house, as far as the eye could reach, was a level plain of snow. The roads were covered up. There was no sign of hoof or track or road. About noon 2 days after the snow had ceased falling, I walked out, intending to go to a grove of large timber which stood, a solitary landmark on the prairie, some 400 or 500 yards from my house. When I had proceeded halfway, I suddenly came upon a man lying on the snow. He was insensible. The snow was broken as if he had fallen there and then rolled over once. He had on heavy brogan shoes, somewhat worn, a sort of gray striped knit nightcap, on his head, and wore a shirt and pantaloons of grayish striped stuff. He did not look like an American. He seemed to be an invalid, for he was very much emaciated. This is a runaway scrape, I thought. He was too weak to hold his horse and has been thrown from a wagon or from a saddle. I knelt down and placed my hand on his heart to see if it were still beating, and very naturally glanced around, half expecting my eye to fall upon the horse or the wagon, but neither was in sight. His body was warm and his heart still throbbed faintly.

"I rose up to run for assistance, when an odd circumstance attracted my attention: he could not have lain there the last two cold days and nights, in his feeble condition, without dying—no snow had fallen during that time to obliterate the tracks and yet there was no sign of wheel, hoof or boot anywhere around, except my own clearly marked footprints, winding away toward my house! Here was a living man, lying on the snow in the open prairie, with the smoothness of the snow around him, totally unmarred except where he had turned over in it. How did he get there without making a track? That was the question. It was as startling as it was unaccountable."

> The man is carried to the farmer's house and restored to consciousness. The neighbors assemble with many surmises as to how he came there —among them the suggestion that he had been brought there by spirits. When the waif is able to speak they eagerly assemble to hear his story, but then it is found that he speaks only in a foreign tongue. The schoolmaster, known to be familiar with some of the modern languages, was sent for and in due time arrived. He at once pronounced the man to be French.

"Can you understand him?"

"Perfectly," said the schoolmaster, who was now lion number two.

"Then ask him how in the mischief he got there where he was in the snow."

The Frenchman said that he would explain that cheerfully, but he said that the explanation would necessitate another, and maybe he had better begin at the beginning and tell the whole story, and let the schoolmaster translate as he went along. Everybody said that would answer and the stranger began.

"I am Jean Pierre Marteau, aged 34. I was born in the little village of Sous-Saône in the south of France. My parents cultivated a little patch of ground on the estates of the Marquis La Bordonnais. Our good priest taught me to read and write and my parents looked upon me with much pride for they thought I was going to amount to something, some day."

> But he read books of adventure and grew up with a restless longing to go to sea. At sixteen he ran away and at Marseilles went as ship's boy on a coasting vessel. He was a good sailor and in time became first officer, but his habit of going on a spree at the end of a voyage got him into trouble. One night in a row a sailor was shot and killed.

"There were several circumstances which cast strong suspicion upon me, and I was arrested. I was tried and condemned to the galleys for 12 years."

> He made several attempts to escape but each time was captured.

"At last one day when I was at work in Paris, a week ago—a week before you found me——"

"How? In Paris a week ago?"

"It is incredible—it is impossible!"

"Let me tell my story, messieurs. I shall not falsify—we were in Paris, I and many of my fellow galley slaves. We had been taken there to labor on some government work. It was 10 in the morning. An officer was sent for some tools of various kinds—some chisels, files, augers and a hatchet. I was sent with the officer to bring the things. I had them all in my arms except the hatchet. The officer had that. In a great open space we saw a crowd of people gathered together. The officer locked his arm in mine and pressed through the crowd to see what the matter was. We could see an immense balloon swaying about, above the people's heads. We elbowed our way through and stood beside the car. It was made fast to the ground by a rope. A man was making a little speech. He begged the multitude to be patient. He said he was only waiting a minute or two for his assistant to come and make a line fast to something—a valve, I think he said, and then he would be off. The balloon was distended with gas and struggling to get away. An idea flashed like lightning through my brain. I tore loose from the guard, snatched the hatchet from his hand, threw my tools into the car, jumped in and cut the anchoring rope with a single stroke!

"Whiz! I was a thousand feet in the air in an instant."

That is all. We shall never know the rest of that story. We should like to, for it has movement and possibilities.

CHAPTER XII

A Trip to Bermuda

Now comes a long break, during which Mark Twain either kept no notes or they have disappeared. He was so busy, now, perhaps he had little time for notes. Following success of *The Innocents Abroad* he married Olivia Langdon, of Elmira, New York; took up residence in Buffalo, where he had become one of the owners and editors of the *Buffalo Express*; wrote *Roughing It*; lectured; sold out in Buffalo and removed to Hartford; wrote (with Charles Dudley Warner) *The Gilded Age*; wrote a play ("Colonel Sellers"), based on that book; wrote and published *The Adventures of Tom Sawyer*; began the *Adventures of Huckleberry Finn*; built a house; made trips to London and lectured an entire season there, besides doing a quantity of short stories, articles, etc., the story of all of which has been elsewhere set down.[1]

It was not until the spring of 1877 a new notebook begins—a record of a trip he made with his dear Hartford friend, Joseph H. Twichell, a minister who had helped to marry him to "Livy" Langdon seven years before. The book is labeled:

Trip to Bermuda with Twichell

May 16 (1877). Gobbled a youth's place in the line—

[1] In *Mark Twain—a Biography*, chapters LXVII to CX.

(for seats in the dining-saloon) and was proud of my manly assertion of my rights. When he yielded and looked so meek and abashed, I felt infinitely ashamed of myself. Did not get through blushing for an hour.

In a Bermuda Boarding House

Read self to sleep with the Ladies Book of 44 years ago—such pieces as the "Broken Vow" (Mrs. Norton), "The Lone Indian," etc. They were a sad and sentimental lot in those days. Then I woke Joe up with my snoring, and he came in and after a world of row and trouble got me awake. I apologized.

Drove alongshore—one horse and intelligent young colored man. The seaview always enchanting—light green water striped here and there with brown where rocks lying near surface. Sailboats flying over the rippled water, distant glimpses of brilliant green water through narrow gaps between many little islands.

> Here and there his notebook is illustrated with sketches—palm tree, bamboo, etc.

The whitest, loveliest chimneys with soft shade on the shady side. They don't look like marble but something whiter, daintier, richer—white sugar is the nearest to it. No sign of mortar joints or any joints of any kind in house or chimney—just solid seamless white sugar, carved out of a single cake—then the windows sawed out and the green Venetian blinds put on.

There is a painful and constant sense of a great undefinable lack here—at last it burst upon us what it was—*Tramps!*

Living is very cheap and there are potatoes and onions for all. Nobody can starve. Plenty of schools—everybody can read.

Rent a cottage for $5 a month; heavy farm work wages

5 shillings per day—lighter work 4 shillings per day—pretty high wages—don't see how living can be so cheap. Yet we were shown a lovely new house, white as the driven snow, situated on a lovely rocky point running out into the sea—said the house and grounds only cost $900, which was probably a lie. In New England or New York that house would cost $10,000, without the ground, that is, if the inside work is at all in keeping with the outside. There are not twelve houses in Hartford as picturesque and as beautiful and captivating to the eye as this $900 affair.

A good deal of change during the half-century or so since then.

Hamilton is the place for pretty outsides.

Saw one outcrop of hard limestone—all the rest of the island is coral. By the queer and abrupt dip it has in a thousand places, suppose it was hove up from below surface by earthquake.

Our darky said that here everybody knows everybody. Presently (away on a country road) Twichell said, "There's a little dog—seems lost and is worn out."

"He belongs to an old man named Yokes." So the driver is acquainted with all the dogs too.

Well, he doesn't need to know many, for dogs are very scarce. However, they make it up in cats.

Cedar is a pretty enough tree except when it is the prevailing tree, then it is not so pleasant. In fact the cedar is so everywhere that you almost get the impression that it is the only tree here.

Pretty little bird on wall—had to stir him up with whip handle to make him move—so he moved a foot and grumbled about it—and we left him there.

A country cottage here with its cozy comfort bedded in among a wealth of brilliant scarlet geraniums and other flowers, and the pink oleander, is a might pretty thing. In other countries you'd know the cottage was worm eaten and rotten—here you know it is as sound as if brand new.

Started with basket of lunch to go yachting—turned back to get soft hats—took a back street to avoid passing a second time the negro man who is building the fence and to whom we talked yesterday. What might he think—though he said nothing. We were not brave enough to have his secret and depreciatory thoughts about us. Got the hats and took another back street.

Couldn't get a yacht so returned home with the basket, and this time boldly passed the negro—arguing inwardly: "There has been time enough now for him to imagine we have done the thing we set out to do."

That is it. You are a coward when you even *seem* to have backed down from a thing you openly set out to do.

Saw a tree wholly naked of leaves, but with brilliant red flowers, of a shape that rather more suggested a star than anything else—the flowers were wide apart so the tree was a sort of constellation.

Cat-poisoning case, where chickens got some of the poison (after warning) and one whose cat got some, egged on the negro woman to bring suit. Magistrate gets half the fines—decides against the client who is ablest to pay the fine. That's the dimensions of the country.

One can't imagine where the poor live in these bewitching cottages.

We said to our driver, referring to a man in front of us, "Drive ahead of him."

"He'll turn out in a minute."

I wondered how the driver knew. But he did know, because he knew the man and where he lived. He knows everybody. The man did turn out.

The houses and roofs are like the white frosting or icing on a cake.

At Sea

Went to sea at 4 P.M. A doctor aboard has an infallible remedy for seasickness—is going from lady to lady on upper deck administering it and saying it never fails. This as we go out over a reef.

7 P.M. All the ladies are seasick and gone to bed, except a Scotchman's wife.

7:30. The Scotchman's wife has "caved."

8 P.M. The doctor is emptying himself over the side. So much for infallible preventives of seasickness.

> Mark Twain went to Bermuda, as he declared later, purely for pleasure, but he wrote three articles about it: "Rambling Notes of an Idle Excursion," published in the *Atlantic,* and today in his collected works. He always loved Bermuda, and during his later years made frequent trips there, his final visit ending a little more than a week before his death in 1910.

Indians at dinner with whites. One ate spoonful of mustard; another one said: "What crying about?"

"Thinking about the good old chief that died."

Number two ate a spoonful of mustard—number one asked:

"What you crying about?"

"Thinking what a pity you didn't die when the old chief did."

Political parties who accuse the one in power of gobbling the spoils etc. are like the wolf who looked in at the door and saw the shepherds eating mutton, and said: "Oh, certainly—it's all right as long as it's you—but there'd be hell to pay if I was to do that."

Adam was the author of sin, and I wish he had taken out an international copyright on it. For international copyright could have won, then. But when there came to be two men, it was too late, because there was one to oppose it, and experience shows that that fellow would have had the most influence.

The old man said: "When I think of the suffering which I see around me, and how it wrings my heart; and then remember what a drop in the ocean this is, compared with the measureless Atlantics of misery which God has to see every day, my resentment is roused against those thoughtless people who are so glib to glorify God, yet never have a word of pity for him."

CHAPTER XIII

Notes, Literary and Otherwise

Nov. 23, 1877. First note made of *The Prince and the Pauper.*

Edward VI and a little pauper exchange places by accident a day or so before Henry VIII's death. The Prince wanders in rags and hardships and the pauper suffers the (to him) horrible miseries of princedom, up to the moment of crowning in Westminster Abbey, when proof is brought and the mistake rectified.

A man sent to superintend a private madhouse takes charge of a sane household by mistake. It is in England and when they call him the "keeper" they do so because they think he is the new gamekeeper, who by mistake is now in charge of the maniacs in the other house, and vastly perplexed too.

Dion Boucicualt, the dramatist, gave me this idea and told me to use it.

Publish scraps from my autobiography occasionally.

March 20, Twichell, at the farewell Pentecost meeting yesterday, urged people to keep on going to church—"We can't give you such preaching, but you can come, nevertheless, and take what God can give you through us (the local preachers), remembering that half a loaf is better than no bread. You know that the ravens brought food to Elijah, and when he got it, it was as nutritious as if it had been brought by a finer bird."

He was preparing at this time to rewrite *Captain Ned Wakeman's Visit to Heaven,* based, as he always said, on a dream told him by Capt. Wakeman, whom he had first met on the ship on which he sailed from San Francisco to Nicaragua in 1866. He had met Wakeman again in 1868, on the way to San Francisco, and had written then a rough draught of story.

Have all sorts of heavens—have a gate for each sort. One gate where they receive a barkeeper with artillery salutes, swarms of angels in the sky and a noble torchlight procession. *He* thinks he is *the* lion of Heaven. Procession over, he drops at once into awful obscurity, but the roughest part of it is that he has to do 3 weeks penance—day and night he must carry a torch and shout himself hoarse, to do honor to some poor scrub that he wishes had gone to hell.

Wakeman is years and years in darkness *between* solar systems.

Noble system, truly, where a man like R. H. Dana can't be confirmed, and where a person like Jones, whose proper place is shyster in a Tombs court, is sent to the U. S. Senate; where it is impossible to reward the most illustrious and fittest citizens with the presidency.

Look at the list:

Polk, Tyler, Pierce, etc. and *almost* Tilden, with the suit pending for swindling the revenue. Half the nation voted for him.

This beggarly congress of ignorance and frauds. The back-pay gang of thieves.

Congregational singing reminds one of nothing but the dental chair.

As sure to do you ultimate insult and injury as a supplicating sufferer whom you have helped out of his distress.

The Congregational graveyard at Washington—stones even for ex-members of Congress buried elsewhere. Chuckle-headed vanity of brief grandeur can no further go. Congressman is the trivialest distinction for full-grown man.

To go abroad has something of the same sense that death brings. I am no longer of ye—what ye say of me is now of no consequence—but of how much consequence when I am with ye and of ye. I know you will refrain from saying harsh things *because* they can't hurt me, since I am out of reach and cannot hear them. This is why we say no harsh things of the dead.

Going abroad we let up on the weight and wear and responsibility of housekeeping—we go and board with somebody, who is suffering it but it troubles us not. Here we are helping the *nation* keep house—we go abroad and become another nation's guests—we don't have to feel any responsibility about his housekeeping, nor about our nation's that we've left behind. So, to go abroad is the true rest—you cease wholly to keep house, then, both national and domestic.

How insignificant a Senator or an M. C. is in N. Y.—and how great a personage he is in Washington!

We should have a much better sort of legislation if we had these swollen country jakes in N. Y. as their capital. Congress *ought* to sit in a big city.

I remember how those pigmy Congressmen used to come into the Arlington breakfast room with a bundle of papers and letters—you could see by their affection for it and their delight in this sort of display that out in the woods where they came from they weren't used to much mail matter.

They always occupied their seats at table a level hour after breakfast, to be looked at, though they wore a weak pretense of settling the affairs of empires, over their mail —contracting brows, etc.

How N. Y. would squeeze the conceit out of those poor little Congressmen.

There's a cherk and natty something about N. Y. dress and carriage male and female which can't be imitated by the outsider. On a railway, steamboat or elsewhere there can always be a question as to where a lady or gentleman hails from, unless from N. Y.—then there is no question. Getting your millinery made by the N. Y. milliner doesn't help—you can't fool anybody—you're a provincial in disguise and any blind man can see it.

CHAPTER XIV

Notes for a New Book

"A Tramp Abroad"

MARK TWAIN and his family—Mrs. Clemens, and their two little girls, Clara and Susy—accompanied by Miss Clara Spaulding of Elmira, N. Y. (later Mrs. John B. Stanchfield) sailed on the *Holsatia* for Hamburg, April 11, 1878.

An exceedingly steady ship in an ordinary sea is the *Holsatia*—rolls very little.

The ship, however, did not prove entirely satisfactory. In one of his notes, partly in German, he writes:

Noisy cabin—shrieking children—the ceaseless metallic clatter of that old cracked kettle of a piano and the thunder and pounding of the screw, with an occasional avalanche of crashing crockery as the ship lurches, this is the afternoon hell in this ship daily. But the piano is the special hell—how it racks one's head.

Until it stops—then you think the scream-voiced boy is it.

There goes the B's crying baby. Now a guffaw of beastly laughter. Now the little Spanish boy is hurled headlong down into our gangway by a lurch of the ship and fetches up with a heavy bang and pile of books and rubbish tumble down.

20th April. Three days of heavy sea now and the above is my first attempt to get an afternoon nap.

It is a marvel that never loses its surprise by repetition, this aiming a ship at a mark 3000 miles away and hitting the bull's-eye in a fog—as we did. When the fog fell on us the captain said we ought to be at such and such a spot (it had been 18 hours since an observation was taken) with the Scilly Islands bearing so and so, and about so many miles away. Hove the lead and got 48 fathoms—looked on the chart and sure enough this depth of water showed that we were right where the captain said we were. Another idea. For ages man probably did not know why God carpeted the ocean bottom with sand in one place, shells in another etc. But we see, now; the kind of bottom the lead brings up shows where a ship is when the soundings don't—and also it confirms the soundings.

Lying story books which make boys fall in love with the sea. Capt. Brandt's experience and that of young Cooper in the English paper and a million other instances show 2 things (Dana's and that of the young Canadian of the Astor expedition)—that a common sailor's life is often a hell, and that there are probably more brutes in command of little ships than in any other occupation of life.

Hamburg

Church St. Nicholai very beautiful, openwork stone spire (said to be next highest in the world) set upon a huge brick edifice. One account says this spire is the highest in the world. Well, no matter, the church can claim one preeminence I think which cannot successfully be disputed—that the inside of it is the dismalest, barrenest, ugliest barn that exists in the boundless universe of God.

200 people present (forenoon) commoners of the commoners, not a gentleman or lady—what they seem to need at St. N. is more congregation and not quite so much steeple.

The German Stove

"Who is buried here?"

"Nobody."

"Then why the monument?"

"It is not a monument. It is a stove."

We had reverently removed our hats. We now put them on again. Stove 8 ft. high—female bust in a circle in the side midway—3½ ft. by 2¼—very ornamental, around the top.

Huge parlor and bedroom. Silk quilts and top beds. Parlor vast—looks out on great paved space before the stately railroad station. Two red silk sofas; 4 tables; writing desk; 12 chairs. Polished floor with rugs.

Three large windows; 2 large mirrors; 2 candelabra with 3 candles each against the walls; 2 with 4 each before the mirrors.

In Europe they use safety matches and then entrust candles to drunken men, children, idiots, etc., and yet suffer little from fires, apparently. The idea of an open light in one of our houses makes us shudder.

Heard cuckoo in woods at W. May 2. Heinrich said: "How long shall I live?" The cuckoo went on cuckooing for the next 20 minutes—wherefore H. is a Methuselah, each yell meaning a year. First cuckoo I ever heard outside of a clock. Was surprised how closely it imitated the clock—and yet of course it could never have heard a clock. The hatefulest thing in the world is a cuckoo clock.

German cleanliness reaches an altitude to which we may not aspire. These peasants are as cleanly in their houses as the Yankee of romance, and more cleanly than the reality.

Even in the narrow crooked lanes of the old parts of the cities where the poor dwell, the children are neat and clean—much white stockings on the little girls.

Legend that Charlemagne arrived at the Main with his army, chasing the Saxons, or chased by them—early in the morning—fog and could not see well—saw a deer taking her young along, judged she would seek a ford. So she did—C. crossed there and resolved to build a city which he named the ford of the Franks—Frankfort—there's an old bridge there with C's statue on it.

In Frankfort, hotel chandelier with 9 burners but you had to light 8 of them in order to see the other 1. Bad gas has no nationality.

Students in Göttingen with dreadfully scarred faces. Here you can't tell whether a man is a Franco-Prussian war hero or merely has a university education.

Street-car conductor wears bright new uniform and is as polite as—but there is nobody at home to compare his politeness with—and politeness costs so little. Our national impoliteness is not natural but acquired. It would be a curious study, *how* and from whom we acquired it.

The bank in Hamburg was up a stable yard, apparently. If ours were as modest, they wouldn't fail so often, maybe.

Bought good cigar for 2c, though my friends say I don't know a good cigar when I see one.

The lower-class women, however nicely dressed, wear nothing on the head in this hot sunshine.

They look surprised here when I order a second armful of wood for the monument. Proper enough, for I find that one small armful, if it be good brisk burning wood, heats the entire monument, and it stays hot for 6 hours—a more economical stove than exists elsewhere in the world, perhaps. No wonder it has held its own for several hundred years.

A fire was made in our monument at 11:30 this morning. It is now 7 P.M. and I cannot bear my hand on the lower part of it. The room has been uncomfortably warm all the time, and is yet. It is not cold weather, but with *no* fire the room is quite uncomfortable—chilly.

A little later, however, he was out of sympathy with the monument, and wrote,

How we miss our big wood fires, these raw cold days in the end of May. In all this region, I suppose they've nothing but their close stoves, which warm gradually and then stink and swelter for hours. It is the same vile atmosphere which a furnace has which has no cold air box and so heats and reheats the same air.

John Hay, attempting German with a stranger all day, on a diligence—finally stranger, after trying for 20 minutes to form a sentence, said, "Oh, God damn the language!" Hay—embracing him, "Bless my soul you speak English!"

Some of the German words are so long that they have a perspective. When one casts his glance along down one of these it gradually tapers to a point, like the receding lines of a railway track.

Clara (Spaulding) reading in the sun in the castle grounds:—fine old gentleman hesitated, passed on, came back and said he *must* tell her she was injuring her eyes.

Students send 2 to Berlin and 2 come here from Berlin, to fight.

This morning Mar. 17, 8 couples fought—2 spectators fainted. One student had a piece of his scalp taken. The others' faces so gashed up and floor all covered with blood. They only wear protecting spectacles.

Mr. Pfaff had a 6-inch piece of sword that had been broken in the fight. It was two edged and wonderfully whetted up and sharp.

They fight twice a week—in a Wirtschaft up a little road, opposite hotel on the other side of river.

Told 2 German gentlemen the way to the Wolfsbrunen, in elaborate German—one put up his hands and solemnly said, "Gott im Himmel."

Dreamed all bad foreigners went to German heaven, couldn't speak the language, and wished they'd gone to the other place.

To make a German sentence complete and beautiful you have only to add: "Wollen haben sollen werden," after you have got through with what you wanted to say.

May 24, theater, Mannheim. King Lear—performance began at 6 sharp. Never understood a word—by and by a terrific and perfectly natural peal of thunder and vivid lightning. G. said. "Thank heaven it thunders in English anyway." Afterwards, at home, said, "Sat three hours—never understood a word but the thunder and lightning."

May 25. Not a star tonight—consequently the display of lights is particularly plentiful and vivid—strong reflections in water from the lights on both bridges.

And the Bahnhof! What to liken it to!

But nothing in the world so overpoweringly beautiful as a tree in an ice-storm, in sun and gentle wind. It is worth crossing three oceans to see.

The Grand Duchess of Baden passed through today—streets and Bahnhof decked with bunting, and cannon fired. She is the Emperor's daughter and was in the carriage with him last week when that communist fired on him.

A coin, sleeve-button or a collar-button dropped in a bedroom will hide itself and be hard to find. A handkerchief in bed *can't* be found.

A dog is "der Hund"; a woman is "die Frau"; a horse is "das Pferd"; now you put that dog in the genitive case, and is he the same dog he was before? No, sir; he is "des Hundes"; put him in the dative case and what is he? Why, he is "dem Hund." Now you snatch him into the accusative case and how is it with him? Why, he is "den Hunden." But suppose he happened to be twins and you have to pluralize him—what then? Why, they'll swat that twin dog around through the 4 cases until he'll tnink he's an entire inter-national dog-show all in his own person. I don't like dogs, but I wouldn't treat a dog like that—I wouldn't even treat a borrowed dog that way. Well, it's just the same with a cat. They start her in at the nominative singular in good health and fair to look upon, and they sweat her through all the 4 cases and the 16 the's and when she limps out through the accusative plural you wouldn't recognize her for the same being. Yes, sir, once the German language gets hold of a cat it's good-bye cat. That's about the amount of it.

May 28. Bought a couple of gorgeously dressed horrors in castle museum to start a portrait gallery of my ancestors with. Paid $1.25 for the male portrait and $2.50 for the lady. The gentleman has a most self-satisfied smirk, but if he had known he would be sold to a base untitled

Republican a hundred years later for $1.25 would it have taken some of the tuck out of that smirk?

And this fair young creature with her lavish finery and her hair in a druggist's mortar shape with a bed of roses on top—what has become of her graces in these hundred years? Very likely the gallants praised this picture and said it was destined to grow in value and fame with the century like the works of the old masters, and by and by be within the purse-reach of none but kings and successful brewers. And now she goes for $2.50.

June 2, '78, ten days ago a socialist fired 4 shots at the emperor, in Berlin, without effect. He was captured. The emperor was driving out with his daughter, the Grand Duchess of Baden.

Today he was fired upon again, this time by an under officer of the government, it was said. Wounded in cheek and arm he lost a good deal of blood. He is so old the shock may kill him. A crowd rushed at the house and were received with a shot from the assassin which hit a landlord. The assassin wounded himself, but not fatally.

June 10, Emperor to leave his bed again—this is wonderful. 8 days after receiving such lacerating wounds in arm, shoulder and side—with buckshot—and at his age.[1]

The best English characteristic is its plucky and persistent and individual standing up for its rights. No other people approaches England in this admirable, this manliest of all traits. It makes every man in the whole nation a policeman—the administration of law can never go lax where every individual sees to it that it grows not lax in his own case, or in cases which fall under his eyes.

June 19. Dreamed Rosa (nurse) complained in German of Fräulein—good, fluent German—I could not under-

[1] William I, then 81 years old.

stand at all, but got the sense of it—could hardly scare up words enough to reply in, and *they* were in very bad grammar. Very curious.

In early times some sufferer had to sit up with a toothache, and he put in the time inventing the German language.

Antique oak chair and table, bought very cheap in Heidelberg. Made last year of pine and stained this year in water-color black which rubs off. Rubbed off all the antiquity in 6 weeks.

They work the cows in wagons—maybe they *can't* give good milk—would like to put one in a hydraulic press and squeeze her.

German laundry could not have acquired this perfect ignorance of how to do up a shirt without able instruction—one easily sees England in it. Your collar is like a horse-collar; your shirt can stand alone and when you get into it you feel ready for crime. It is a wonder they do not have more crime here, but it is increasing as adoption of clean shirts spreads among the social democrats.

June 29. Six students entered the Schloss grounds this afternoon in single file, each solemnly towing a big dog.

German hotels and houses are as brilliantly lighted as English ones are dark.

The Children

Clara, age 4: "I brang you some flowers—no I bringed 'em."

Clara: "Why mustn't I?"
"Because I said *not*."

"But that is no *why*."

Mr. Albert: "Why, your papa would let you have one."

Susie: "Yes—but we do as mamma says."

At Venice

October 14, 1878. This, to all Americans and Englishmen who have read my books and been made wiser and better thereby:

I hardly ever venture to recommend anybody to a stranger, lest I do that stranger an unintentional harm, but in this case I do not feel afraid. If you employ Dittura Agostino you will find that you have done wisely and well.

Venetian oysters the size of beans—half a dollar a dozen—tasted 4 dozen.

Close to the end of a red stone bench, where a strip of embedded iron clamps a new corner, the shape of a brick, to the rest of the bench, I discovered a mottled surface, polished by the loiterers of several centuries, another antique, one which made the hoary mosaic of St. Mark's but novelties born of yesterday—an antique which was already an antique when these fables pictured over my head were invented—an antique which was already an antique a hundred thousand years or so before—it was a fossil shell, nearly as large as the crown of my hat. It had been polished down until it was of the appearance of the section of a periwinkle (for its form was a spiral).

> New acquaintances and old were always recommending to him remedies for ailments and accidents.

Crude petroleum is an infallible cure of rheumatism, applied externally.

A man dreadfully poisoned by poison oak (poison ivy) was urged to eat the leaves of it and was thoroughly cured. Since then he rubs his hands and face, or eats the leaves with impunity—never gets poisoned.

> It is to be hoped he did not employ these remedies. Possibly the crude petroleum might help his rheumatism, but eating the leaves of the poisoned ivy, as the writer knows by experience, could only have resulted in his having a very badly poisoned mouth. It is difficult to say how that old fallacy became current.

The Old Masters' horses always rear after the fashion of kangaroos.

About 1440-45, a Candian named Staminato in the suite of a prince of the House of Este was permitted to view the treasure collection of St. Mark, and concealed himself behind an altar in the body of the cathedral, but was discovered by a priest. Then he entered by false keys. After numerous difficulties and the labor of many nights he removed a block of this marble paneling which walled the lower part of the treasure. This panel he fixed so as to be removable at will. Then night after night he visited this magnificent mine, inspected it at his own sweet pleasure and carried away jewels and gold worth 2,000,000 golden ducats, or $8,000,000, say at present valuation $50,000,000. He even carried off a unicorn's horn (a mere curiosity) and had to saw it in two with great patience and difficulty. It shows how perfectly secure and undisturbed he was. He could have gone home the richest private citizen of his country, and it might have been years before the plunder was missed. But he could not enjoy his delight alone. So he exacted a solemn oath from a Candian nobleman named Crioni, then took him to an obscure lodging and astounded his eyes. Great carbuncle—(afterwards on Ducal cap). He detected a look on C's face which excited his suspicion, and was about to slip a stiletto into him when C saved himself by saying the display so astonished him. He excused himself for a moment, went and showed the carbuncle at the palace and denounced the criminal, who was hanged with a gilded rope (he having such a fancy for gold) between the columns. All the booty was recovered.

October 17, 1878. Left for Florence. Good-bye Ditturo Agostino.

It is wonderful how many celebrated men this little town of Florence has produced. In niches in the arcades of the Uffizzi they have life-sized statues of 24 of them—20 of them being names familiar to every schoolboy in the Christian world—Buonarroti, Benvenuto, Machiavelli, Giotto, Dante, Petrarch, etc.

Swell turnout with 12 beautiful bay horses—never saw anything like this outside the circus.

That most entertaining of books, Benvenuto's. It will last as long as his beautiful Perseus.

October 23. In Santa Croce today a well-dressed young man followed us, begging for centimes.

An old frowsy woman watched where I laid my cigar, then approached us with it as we came out and said she rescued it from some boys and wanted five centimes for her trouble. She followed us into the street and finally cursed us and called down sudden deaths upon us.

Hall of Mars, Pitti Palace, No. 92, Titian portrait of A Man—half length, dressed in black robe, a trifle of lace at neck and wrists, short brown hair, thin, handsome, manly features, full of character and firmness; blue eyes, oval face, thin hair making fence around upper lip and chin—and along his jaw—full of a most noble dignity. This person is so human—you recognize in him at once the very highest type of man—he is a person who commands instantly your respect and your homage—and lord how sappy and gushy and chuckle-headed and theatrical the surrounding saints and angels and Holy Families of the other Old Masters do look in his august company.

October 29. It is the most ridiculous spectacle to see a Virgin or a copper Apostle stuck on top of every stately monument of the grand old "pagan" days of Rome.

Castellani today allowed us to walk off with jewelry worth frs 1500. and never even asked our names or hotel—insisted upon our taking it home and examining it at our leisure—said "tomorrow is a festa—no shops open—bring it back Saturday no hurry."

Italians and Swiss seem to trust to the honesty of strangers readily. We have noticed this very often.

New American artist goes to little Italian squalid village, sits down to sketch on a three-legged camp stool. Peasant brings oxen and addresses him—American abuses and curses and finally appeals to his comrade (Vedder).

"What is this devil saying? Why does the scoundrel bring his oxen here?"

"He was saying that he has brought his oxen at the usual hour and place to water them, but if they are an interruption he will take them away, and wait—and he adds that your camp chair seems uncomfortable and he will go to his house and bring you a chair, if you desire it."

The Italians and French are so artistic and so kindly that their impulse is always to assist in any way possible an artist who is sketching.

November 5. Spent all day in Vedder's lofty studio, and the evening with him and another artist spinning yarns and drinking beer in a quiet saloon. Big row in the street but no bloodshed.

Visited the Catacombs. One mummy (shapeless) and one slender young girl's long hair and decaying bones—both in stone coffins and both between 1500 and 1600 years old.

The greatest charm we have found in Europe by all odds is the open fireplaces in Florence and Rome.

Of all countries America is the most comfortable. Palace cars with water, food, liquors, fruit, attendance, water-closets, space to walk about, heating apparatus, and a seat secured beforehand of which no one can deprive you. Plenty of trains, reasonably fast on great trunk lines, sleeping-cars and not obliged to start or arrive at horrid hours of the night. Clean closets in hotels—rare in Germany, Switzerland and Italy. They serve a dinner better in Europe, and outside the great cities they cook it infinitely better than in our minor cities. Their servants are politer and far more efficient than ours. They do not know what coffee is—nor cream. The former is the case with all European hotels, without exception—but in ours one finds something which at least vaguely resembles cream.

All of which of course was written a very long time ago. France and England today have some of the finest trains in the world, and French hotels especially have made great forward strides in modern conveniences, sometimes to the damage of their picturesqueness and charm.

European coffee, however, still leaves something
to be desired.

November 13, 1878. Left at 10:45 for Bologna, and tried being courier for the first time. Leave the omnibus-driver a franc to bring the conductor of the train out there to me. Made him understand I wanted a first-class compartment to myself and had five in my party—for future cash. All right. Omnibus-driver also took my luggage into waiting-room and brought the ticket taker to me. Gave *him* two francs and he flew around with many winks and brought the conductor again and both winked that all was right. The former took my five through tickets and sent a fat porter to get them viséd. Then allowed our tribe to pass through to the train without tickets. Found the conductor right outside on the quivive, who helped me carry my luggage, put us into a compartment and fastened the door. Presently the fat porter came with my tickets and I gave *him* a franc. The conductor allowed nobody to look in all the way—not even a ticket puncher. Had a mighty smooth trip of it. Gave the conductor five francs. Total cost nine francs. If I had had a courier I should have had to take care of him, pay him ten francs wages and twelve francs fare.

From Rome to Florence I paid the conductor five francs and had a heap of attention. Once he kept the train waiting for me at a station.

Am a shining success as a courier, so far, by the use of francs.

Munich, December 20, 1878

Today by telegraph in the papers comes the sad news of Bayard Taylor's death yesterday afternoon in Berlin, from dropsy. I wrote him three or four days ago, congratulating him on his recovery. He was a very lovable man.

December 21. On scores of street corners in the snow are groves of Christmas trees for sale and the toy and other shops are crowded, and driving a tremendous trade.

Reading German books shows in what a narrow groove of vocabulary authors travel—they use the same words all the time. Read a book of one and you can fluently read his others. Take up a book by another author and you have got to go for the dictionary. His vocabulary is all different.

Christmas in Germany

In the week a prodigious audience of parents and children in the big theater. A curtain hung across the middle of the stage from right to left. In front a lady with a lot of eager children around her on stools. She asks what familiar story from folklore she shall read. They clap their eager hands and name a story. She reads; they applaud, or laugh, or are grieved—all well drilled and natural—and as she finishes the curtain slowly rises and displays in tableau an exquisite picture from the story. The children in the audience get so carried away that they applaud, shout, cry and make comments aloud.

Germans comb their hair in public and have some other little peculiarities, but there is one thing which you can charge the entire nation with: ask any German a question and you will get a civil answer.

After the naked model was dressed (in Rome) she showed a touch of nature—for as she climbed down from the platform she exposed too much of her ankle and rectified it.

January 25, 1879. The mother of the king, 55 or 60, was out walking in the street today, a maid of honor walking beside her, the two talking zealously, two vast footmen in blue livery walking behind them—everybody who came along either on the street or on the sidewalk, took off hats and bowed—little boys, gentlemen, ladies, soldiers, cabmen, everybody, and the queen saw every bow and bowed in return and still kept up her end of the conversation.

I can't exactly define what it is, but there is something very cheerless and depressing about the inside of European houses, and English:—outside is another matter—beautiful England.

Europe is the hungriest place in the world for an American to live in. The food is trifling in variety (at least the tables are) and villainously cooked.

English toast! Execrable! Muffins good. In Europe they don't give you hot bread. Ah, for a hot biscuit and coffee, *real* coffee with *real* cream—and *real* potatoes, fried chicken, corn bread, *real* butter, *real* beefsteak, good roast beef with taste to it.

> His old Southern memories and appetite troubled him. He often spoke of the excellencies of French cookery, but now and again, remembering the fried chicken and corn bread and gravy of his youth, he could find no good thing outside of his native land, especially in England.

January 23. Frank Bliss wrote to inquire what progress I am making on the book. Of *course* I sat down in Munich as soon as he took up his pen in New England, and by the time he had got his brief inquiry on paper I was well under way with my long answer to it. Had not heard from him since last June.

Pontius Pilate, wandering around with heavy conscience, drowned himself in Lake Lucerne—hence, Mt. Pilatus.

A part of the plan for gathering material for the new travel book, *A Tramp Abroad,* was to have Twichell come over as his guest, and "tramp" with him. Twichell arrived August 1, and the tramping began at once, through the Black Forest and down into Switzerland. They really walked a good deal, but had taken no ironclad pledge to do so. They were likely to take a train, or a cart or a carriage, and they had long days of talk and idle loafing. In the book as published Twichell is "Harris."

The Clemens family spent the winter of 1878 and 1879 in Munich, where Mark Twain worked pretty steadily on his book. Later they went to Paris and crossed over to London, returning to America at the end of August, 1879. Details of this European sojourn are set down, somewhat illuminated, in *A Tramp Abroad,* and more literally in *Mark Twain—a Biography,* chapters CXVII to CXXI.

1879

The English ought not to patronize the Zulus, the Livingstone River Cannibals, and say piously: "We are better than thou," for it is very plain that they have been better for no more than a hundred years. They are a very fine and pure and elevated people, now, but what they were between the Roman Invasion and the time within the memory of a centenarian was but a small improvement upon the Shoshone Indians. I select the Shoshones because they have certain peculiar vices and also certain peculiar conspicuous virtues.

I disfavor capital punishment.

Sampson was a Jew—therefore not a fool. The Jews have the best average brain of any people in the world. The Jews are the only race who work wholly with their brains and never with their hands. There are no Jew beggars, no Jew tramps, no Jew ditchers, hod-carriers, day laborers or followers of toilsome, mechanical trade. They are peculiarly and conspicuously the world's intellectual aristocracy.

It depends on who writes a thing whether it is coarse or not. Rabelais. I once wrote a conversation between Elizabeth, Shakespeare, Ben Jonson, Beaumont, Sir Walter Raleigh, Lord Bacon, Sir Nicholas Throckmorton and a stupid, stupid old nobleman—this latter being cup-bearer to the queen and ostensible reporter of the talk. There were four maids of honor present, and a sweet young girl two years younger than the boy Beaumont. I built a conversation which *could* have happened—I used words such as *were* used at that time—1601—I sent it anonymously to a magazine—and how the editor abused it and the sender. But that man was a praiser of Rabelais, and had been saying "Oh, that we had a Rabelais." I judged I could furnish him one.

Then I took it to one of the greatest, best and most learned of Divines and read it to him. He came within an ace of killing himself with laughter (for between you and me the thing *was* dreadfully funny. I don't often write anything that I laugh at myself, but I can hardly think of that thing without laughing). That old Divine said that it was a piece of the finest kind of literary art—and David Gray of the Buffalo Courier said it ought to be printed privately and left behind me when I died, and then my fame as a literary artist would last.

This was the "Fireside Conversation in the Time of Queen Elizabeth." The "Divine" was Joseph H. Twichell, of Hartford, to whom it was *sent*, as a letter. Several private editions have been printed. Mark Twain's statement that he sent it to an editor is to be heavily discounted, though it is not unlikely that as a joke he showed it to Mr. Alden of Harpers or to one of the editors of the *Century Magazine*.

March 28, 1879 (Paris Salon)

Went to see pictures rushed into Palais d'Industrie, end of afternoon—last chance to get them in. Stairways crowded—street full of vans and the vans full of pictures. Every time a poor picture came in everybody groaned. Perfect howl went up sometimes when particularly poor one came—it was snatched and passed from hand to hand. Picture of wood-sawing—everybody made a sound like sawing. Picture of St. Jerome and skull—lot of students followed it, weeping on each other's shoulders. There was a row last year, so it was announced that this year only people having pictures would be admitted—so there came fifty students each carrying a ten-cent chromo, very carefully. There were acres of pictures, any artist may send two or three, but not more—I think they said two was the limit. A jury of the first artists of France (elected by the exhibitors) will examine these 6000 or 7000 pictures between now and May 11, and retain about 2000 and reject the rest. They can tell a good or a bad one at a single glance—these are at once set aside and the real work begins, the culling the best from among those that lie somewhere between the perfectly good and the perfectly bad. And a tough job it is. An artist can't vote for the jury till he has exhibited more than twice. Pictures are often rejected for want of room. These can be offered again, next year. Among the acres we saw one which had been rejected twice already. It would take a plucky man to carry his own picture up those stairs. Sometimes a fine picture is applauded.

Take a ride on the steam roller to the Bois de Boulogne from Place de la Concorde to avoid carriages.

Religion consists in a set of things which the average man thinks he believes, and wishes he was certain.

Paris May 7

I wish this eternal winter would come to an end. Snowflakes fell today, and also about a week ago. Have had rain almost without intermission for two months and one week. Have had a fire every day since September 10 and have now just lighted one.

Salon

Criticism is a queer thing. If I print "she was stark naked" and then proceed to describe her person in detail, what critic would not howl? Who would venture to leave the book on a parlor table? But the artist does this, and all ages gather around and look and talk and admire.

France has neither winter nor summer nor morals—apart from these drawbacks it is a fine country.

For 1000 years the savage nation (France) indulged itself in massacres—every now and then a big massacre, or a little one. The massacreing spirit is peculiar to France, I mean in Christendom. No other state had it. In this, France has always walked abreast, kept her end up with her brethren, the Turks and Burmese.

Afternoon of the 12th of July went to Antwerp. Thirteenth, Sunday, went on board flagship Trenton, dined that evening with Consul Stewart and some officers of the Trenton and the Alliance. Took the family and breakfasted on board the Trenton, Monday, 14th. Admiral Rowan arrived during the meal. I smoked on the Admiral's side of the deck, not knowing it was sacred, by naval etiquette.

In Brussels Cathedral heard the most majestic organ music and men's voices ever listened to. Never heard anything that rose to the sublimity of those sounds. The jingling of a little bell occasionally, the distant booming of the great bells in the steeple, the remote bowing and mumming, the faint clouds and puffs of incense rising from swinging censers, the dim distances, the picture windows, the going and coming kneelers, the high miraculously made and miracle working Virgin, the old women selling candles, were all highly impressive.

No wonder William III pined for Holland—the country is so green and lovely and quiet and pastoral and homelike. Boats sailing through the prairies and fat cows and quaint windmills everywhere.

At The Hague visited Museum and saw Rembrandt's School of Anatomy and Potter's Bull (flies visible under the hairs). This is absolute nature—in some other pictures too close a copy of nature is called a fault.

Drove out to a country palace where Motley used to visit long at a time with the Royal Family. Good portrait of him there. Also some Frescoes which can't be told from stone, high relief across the room. Drove there through about the noblest woods I ever saw.

We have been obliged to keep fires going constantly ten months steadily—from the 19th September to the 15th of July—in Italy, Bavaria, France, Holland and Belgium.

London, July 20, 1879

Arrived here at 8 A.M. Rainy and cold. Have had a rousing fire, blazing in the grate all day. A remarkable summer, truly!

Galleries of pictures where there is much splendid conflagration of color, have a curious effect upon the spectator. Turner soon makes one ill—it is partly intense admiration, partly the color.

One must have a play-book at an English play—the English accent is so different one cannot understand or follow the actors. The same in ordinary conversation which one tries to hear.

Sunday, August 17, 1879. Raw and cold and a drenching rain. Went over to the Tabernacle and heard Mr. Spurgeon. House three-quarters full—say 3000 people. First hour, lacking one minute, taken up with two prayers, two ugly hymns and Scripture reading. Sermon three-quarters of an hour long. A fluent talk. Good sonorous voice. Topic treated in the unpleasant old-fashioned way. Man a mighty bad child, God working at him in forty ways and having a world of trouble about him.

A wooden-faced congregation—just the sort to see no incongruity in the Majesty of Heaven, stooping to beg and plead and sentimentalize over such and to see in their salvation an important matter.

Spurgeon was not at his best today, I judge. He was probably even at his worst.

It was so cold I was freezing—the pouring rain made everything gloomy—the wooden congregation was not an inspiration—the music was depressing, so the man *couldn't* preach well.

Tuesday, August 19. Went up Windemere Lake in the steamer. Talked with the great Darwin.

August 31. At sea in the Gallia, approaching New York (left Liverpool 23d). Now about 9 P.M. Brilliant moon, a calm sea and a magnificent lunar rainbow—a complete arch, the colors part of the time as brilliant as if it were noonday—some said not quite as brilliant, softened with a degree of vagueness, but to me it was not different from a daylight rainbow. One cannot see this wonder twice in his life. Fifteen years ago I saw a lunar rainbow, a complete arch in California, but it was silver white—perfectly colorless.

The reader may remember that he had also once seen this phenomenon on the way from Hawaii to San Francisco.

The Colorado miner on board who hates English and won't allow them to pass things to him at the table. Loathes his three English roommates because of their effeminate affectation of wearing nightshirts.

All English individuals are kind and likable—the newspapers are snobbish, pretentious, and they scoff at America, or contemptuously ignore her. English preachers and statesmen try to draw the two nations together in friendship and mutual respect—the newspapers, with what seems a steady and calculated purpose, discourage this. The newspapers are going to win in this fight. The nations are at their friendliest now—the widening apart has begun—the separation will be complete in a generation. (1879.)

For some years a custom has been growing up in our literature to praise everything English and do it affectionately. This is not met halfway, and so it will cease. English individuals like and respect American individuals, but the English nation despises America and Americans. But this does not sting us as it did when we were smaller. We shall presently be indifferent to being looked down upon by a nation no bigger and no better than our own. We made the telegraph a practical thing. We invented the fast press, the sewing-machine, the sleeping and parlor car, the telephone, the ironclad, we have done our share for the century, we have introduced the foretelling of the weather. Nobody writes a finer and purer English than Motley, Howells, Hawthorne and Holmes.

CHAPTER XV

America Again

(*At Quarry Farm, Elmira, N. Y.*)

August 1, 1880. Talking last night about home matters, I said: "I wish I had said to George (colored butler) when we were leaving home, 'Now, George, I wish you would take advantage of these three or four months' idle time, while we are away—' 'to learn to leave my matches alone!' interrupted Livy. They were the very words I was going to use, yet George had not been mentioned before nor his peculiarities.

Several years ago I said: "Suppose I should live to be 92, and just as I was dying a messenger should enter and say"—

"You are become the Earl of Durham—"
interrupted Livy. The very words I was going to utter. Yet there had not been a word about that earl, nor had there been any conversation calculated to suggest any such subject.

> The earldom of Durham was an appanage of the English Lamptons (or Lambdons) of whom Mark Twain's mother was a descendant. Mark Twain sometimes amused himself with the remote possibility of the title shifting to his branch of the family, and his book *The American Claimant,* grew out of this idea.

In Canada November 28, 1880

Mild yesterday and sifted snow all day. That was according to Vennor's prediction made Sept. 1. This morning it is mighty cold with yesterday's one inch of snow crunching and grinding under the cart wheels in a shrill metallic way. Vennor says: "A very sudden and severe fall of temperature will occur throughout Canada in the last days of November, with but little snow, if any, on the ground."

There has been mild weather for some time before this—Vennor spotted it right.

Sir, I think I am lost, but I am not acquainted with the city, and so I cannot really tell. If you will be so kind as to give me an idea of the direction of the Windsor Hotel, God will reward you. Of course I may not be lost, after all; I cannot by any means swear that I *am,* for there is nothing here to swear by—I mean nothing I could recognize, nothing I ever saw before; but if I could see something which I have seen before, I could tell in a minute by its position whether I am lost or not: that is, I could tell by comparing its position with mine, whether *it* was lost or whether it was me; and I could then know *which* of us was lost, and act accordingly: that is to say, if it turned out to be *me* that was lost, I shouldn't do anything, at least at the moment, preferring to wait and sue the city; but if it turned out to be *it* I should of course call assistance; for I hold that a humane man ——

It is a great and beautiful city from Royal Mount—the great St. Lawrence stretching in both directions and the wide plains on the other side with groves and meadows and with mountains beyond.

So many pretty girls—never so many in one town before—beauty of girls and of little children so common as to be almost monotonous, but then one has the occasional relief of the other sort or one can look into the glass.

Girl's costume is plain, simple, graceful, shapely and topped with brimless fur cap, often a black fur cape, handsomer than sealskin; then there are often fur borders to the clothing. The dresses are short.

This nipping air is delicious and gives everybody splendid ruddy cheeks. The complexions are very fair among the girls and also darkish—half and half—English and French.

The French went to church in troops and droves, from 8 till 9 this Sunday morning, and the English from 10 to 11.

Drove halfway to Falls of Montmorency, then came back and bought a photograph. The wind down on the low ground was mighty cold. The photograph is very satisfactory.

I am so indolent, and all forms of study are so hateful to me, that although I was several years living constantly on steamboats I never learned all the parts of a steamboat. The names of parts were in my ear daily whose office and locality I was ignorant of, and I never inquired the meaning of those names. For instance, I think I never saw the day when I could describe the marks on a lead line. I never knew what "in the run" meant—I couldn't find the run in a steamboat today and be sure I was right.

After my first voyage at sea I never took any interest in knowing the parts of the ship. I cannot name two-thirds of the sails in a full-rigged ship; I do not know the names or functions of half a dozen ropes. The line "A wet sheet and a flowing sea" (wind?) has always been meaningless to me. I do not know whether a sail is meant, or the rope called a "sheet"—and I have never had energy enough to inquire.

CHAPTER XVI

Mississippi River, 1882

In preparation for the writing of the second part of *Life on the Mississippi,* he had come from St. Louis to New Orleans, and was now starting the return trip. (See *Mark Twain—a Biography*, chapter CXL.)

PEOPLE talk only about the war. Other subjects are started but they soon fade and die and the war is taken up.

Left New Orleans 5:10, May 6. Reached Natchez (300 miles) at 3:40 May 7. First time I ever went to Natchez inside of 24 hours I believe.

May 8. Got up at 4 A.M., in a roasting room—some idiot had closed the transom and I was over the boilers—and went on watch. Fog—George Ritchie steered the watch out by compass, using his and Bixby's patented chart for the crossings and occasionally blowing the whistle. The chart is a great thing—many pilots use it, now.

The Biblical absurdity of the Almighty's being only six days building the universe and then fooling away 25 years building a towhead in the Mississippi. "Towhead" means infant, an infant island, a growing island, so it is said.

Pilot said some French camped on the hills at Baton

Rouge and were massacred by the Indians, who stained a mast or stick with their blood and stuck it up as a warning to other pirates to keep away; hence the name "Baton Rouge."

The snag boats and beacons are a grand good thing, but *I think* (says Pilot) the river commission will fool away money for nothing, trying to tame and order this channel.

George Ritchie was blown up on a boat above Memphis—blown into the river from pilot wheel, and disabled—clung to cotton bale in very cold water with his teeth and floated till rescued, nearly exhausted, by deck hands on piece of wreck. They tore open the bale and put him in it and warmed the life back into him and so got him to Memphis. He will never get entirely over the effects. Bixby was blown up in Madrid Bend, and his partner lost.

All the accidents, nearly, happened near Memphis, and that generous town is heavily taxed.

Prodigious storm of rain and wind opposite Buck Island, in afternoon of May 9. It seemed the pilot house was bound to be blown away, so I went down in the hold to see what time it was. Kept up till midnight.

At the devil's elbow, above Memphis, the river now runs several miles upstream where it used to run down. This is at Fogleman's chute which is half mile wide or more and is the channel, but in my time a fallen tree would almost bridge it.

At 5 P.M. got to where Hat Island *was*. It is now gone, every vestige of it. Goose Island at the graveyard below Commerce is all gone but a piece about big enough for dinner. Lots of buzzards there on wreck of Grand Tower, fishing for drowned men, etc.

Man living above Jessup timber behind Hat Island says 29 steamboats have been lost in sight of his house.

Hannibal: Garth's coachman called for me at 10 instead of 7:30—excused himself by saying, "De time is mos' an hour and a half slower in de country en what it is in de town—you will be in plenty of time, Boss—sometimes we shoves out early for church, Sunday mawnings, and fetches up dar right plumb in de middle of de sermon—diffunce in de time—a body can't make no calculations about it."

Alas! everything was changed in Hannibal—but when I reached Third or Fourth street the tears burst forth, for I recognized the mud. It at least was the same—the same old mud—the mud that Annie Macdonald got stuck in.

The water above Dubuque is olive green, beautiful and semi-transparent with the sun on it. Upper Mississippi the home of superb sunsets.

The bluffs all along up above St. Paul are exquisitely beautiful. Where the rough broken turreted rocks stand up against a sky above the steep verdant slope, they are inexpressibly rich and mellow in color—soft dark brown mingled with dull green—the very place to make an artist worship. Remind one of the old houses in Spanish New Orleans.

Eight years ago boats like the Minneapolis used to go into St. Paul with 150 people. Men used to say, "Got 28 cars of wheat, Captain!"

"I'll take two o' them."

Now the captain inquires—"What you got for us?"
"Nuthin'!"
The railroad has done it. Used to carry loads of harvest hands; now they have invented a self-binder and don't have harvest hands any more.

Sunday, May 21, 7 A.M. Arrived per Minneapolis, at St. Paul, and put up at the Metropolitan. Cold as the very devil. Gold-band hat would give us ticket for a carriage and fetch it in 30 minutes if we paid in advance—no other way to get a carriage in St. Paul. Walked to hotel.

Wretched poor family on boat going to the frontier—man on deck with wagon; woman and several little children allowed in cabin for charity's sake. They slept on sofas and floor in glare of lamps and without covering, must have frozen last night.

This day, May 23, three inches of snow fell in Iowa.

Entering Philadelphia May 24, cut an Italian laborer's foot off. The train stopped and crowds gathered to gaze. Our tracks ought to be fenced on the principle that the majority of human beings, being fools, the laws ought to be made in the interest of the majority.

Punch's advice to persons about to marry—"Don't"—was a thousand years old when Punch was born.

"No gentleman ever swears"—the obscure person who shouts this from his pulpit, or his good goody paper, sees no immodesty in setting himself above Wellington, Washington, etc.

Speaking of duels, I think I could wipe out a dishonor

by crippling the other man, but I don't see how I could do it by letting him cripple *me*.

Emerson died while we were in New Orleans. So glad I visited him two or three weeks before.

At first he did not remember me but the voyage with his son recalled me. (Probably in 1878.)

Story of Bob Toombs who challenged an old deacon, who resigned from his church, made a will, then went to practicing with his rifle—whereupon Toombs backed out and was forever ruined in the eyes of the South.

The romance of boating is gone now. In Hannibal the steamboatman is no longer a god. The youth don't talk river slang any more. Their pride is apparently railways—which they take a peculiar vanity in reducing to initials—an affectation which prevails all over the West. They roll these initials as a sweet morsel under the tongue.

No domestic architecture twenty years ago. Now it booms in the very villages—and improves all the time. The Stewart mausoleum would not be built now.

Met a passenger who spoke good English, and who after hearing a good deal of brag about great men said his country was very small and remote, but had produced two or three pretty big men; named a couple nobody ever heard of—then offered to bet that the third had been heard of, named Jesus Christ. He was born close to the Grotto, and was familiar with it. It seemed like meeting a person who had known Him.

On this trip four great men died—Emerson and Longfellow here, and Darwin and Dr. John Brown abroad.

Had some personal acquaintance with all of them—with Brown intimate.

The physician's is the highest and worthiest of all occupations, or would be if human nature did not make superstitions and priests necessary.

Board of Foreign Missions: "We have saved a Turk's soul."

"What did it cost?"

"$2,000,000."

"Is it worth that?"

U. S. Government:

"We have killed 200 Indians."

"What did it cost?"

"$2,000,000."

"You could have given them a college education for that."

Mental Telegraphy: The things which pass through my mind when I lie awake in the morning are pretty sure to be the topics introduced by others at breakfast or dinner, that day or the next. September 20, 1882.

CHAPTER XVII

Notes 1883

MAN'S delight upon reaching an enchanted country where the rivers were all wines and liquors and water was sold and drunk as a costly luxury. He soon found himself falling into habits of watery dissipation and caring nothing for the other things—too cheap and abundant. Moral—make no Maine laws.

> A good many of his notes were written while riding on a rough train or in a carriage and are scarcely legible.
>
> As already set down (in the Foreword) Mark Twain's judgment as to the value of his own ideas was unreliable. He was likely to mistake banalities for choice humor. As an example here is a memorandum for a story he hoped to write —one of a thousand-and-one such things. Sometimes, alas, he wrote them.

Write the Second Advent, with full details—lots of Irish disciples—Paddy Ryan for Judas and other disciples. Star in the East. People want to know how wise men could see it move while sober. John interviewed.

> It was about this time that Mark Twain invented a history game—a game by which all dates, successions, etc. were to be taught as the game progressed. It was at first only a game of kings—the length of the reign—but it expanded and expanded—as his ideas were likely to do,

until it included history of every sort—of music, of art, Bible history—it could even teach geography. In one of his notes he says:

> This game can be applied to any form of memory practice—language, for instance: count a point for each word or a sentence which you get right and in the right place, and your opponent gets a point for each error-word you make.
>
> Offer a prize (fine opera glass) for the highest number of points made in a series of games, etc. etc.

He fills up page after page with details and suggestions, pausing now and then to jot down some idea for a story, even more impracticable than his proposals for games. He was also at this time working again on his Captain Stormfield story and we come upon the following note:

> Stormfield must hear of the man who worked hard all his life to acquire heaven and when he got there the first person he met was a man he had been hoping all the time was in hell—so disappointed and outraged that he inquired the way to hell and took up his satchel and left.

But these are only brief interludes. A page or two farther along he is deep in the game again, remarking in one place that it will be the best solitaire game ever invented. Then not entirely forgetting Stormfield, he writes:

> Captain Stormfield finds that hell was originally instituted in deference to an early Christian sentiment. In modern time the halls of heaven are warmed by radiators connected with hell, and the idea is greatly applauded by Jonathan Edwards, Calvin, Baxter & Co. because it adds a new pang to the sinner's suffering to know that the very

fire which tortures him is the means of making the righteous comfortable.

If you shoot at your wife in the dark for a burglar you always kill her, but you can't hit a burglar. You can always kill a relative with a gun that isn't loaded.

"What is an Englishman?"

"A person who does things because they have been done before."

"What is an American?"

"A person who does things because they haven't been done before."

Theme for Story

Life in the interior of an iceberg. Luxuriously furnished from the ship (how produce heat). Children born. Plate-glass ice windows. All found dead and frozen after 130 years. Iceberg drifts around in a vast circle, year after year, and every two or three years they come in distant sight of the remains of the ship. The berg consists of mountains, levels and valleys, and is twelve miles long by eight broad. They invent amusements. The children born reach marrying age and marry. Others try to make them comprehend life on land in the world but wholly fail. They understand life on the iceberg only. They tame great flocks of birds and animals, to eat. Perhaps they have no fire—eat raw. Children don't know what fire or coal are.

This must be a woman's diary, beginning abruptly and does not explain how they got there.

They don't know which is Sunday.

Believing they should never escape, and not wishing to curse the children with longings unsatisfiable, both families teach the young that the elders were born on the berg and know no other world.

Whence these knives and other metal things? Well, they are found in the egg of wawhawp—so the children often hunt for nests of this imaginary bird.

She must speak of one young girl who is an idiot and who is now 80 years old. She visits her husband's clear-ice grave after 30 years and finds him fresh and young, while she is old and gray.

> A typical Mark Twain idea of the more fantastic sort—too fantastic, perhaps, to be undertaken, even by him, for we hear no more of it.

People in trying to justify Eternity say we can put it in learning all the knowledge acquired by the inhabitants of the myriads of stars. We shan't need that. We could use up two Eternities in learning all that is to be learned about our own world and the thousands of nations that have arisen and flourished and vanished from it. Mathematics alone would occupy me eight million years.

August 12—I think we are only the microscopic trichina concealed in the blood of some vast creature's veins, and it is that vast creature whom God concerns Himself about and not us.

I lose my temper over a certain class of business (begging) letters, except when they come from colored (and therefore ignorant) people. Mrs. Clemens suggests that I adopt as a motto: "Consider everybody colored till he is proved white."

Jewell (of Hartford) said the church would trust me to take up a collection—with a bell punch.

On a wager I once started to ride from Virginia City to San F., in stage with several women and girls, I to play deaf and dumb. Got out early. Lost the bet.

Dream of being a knight errant in armor in the Middle Ages. Have the notions and habits of thought of the present day mixed with the necessities of that. No pockets in the armor. Can't scratch. Cold in the head—can't blow—can't get a handkerchief, can't use iron sleeve. Iron gets redhot in the sun—leaks in the rain, gets white with frost and freezes me solid in winter. Makes disagreeable clatter when I enter church. Can't dress or undress myself. Always getting struck by lightning. Fall down and can't get up.

Written across this pencil-note is another in ink, made five years later.

Fall of '84—while Cable and I were giving readings, Cable got a Morte d'Arthur and gave it to me to read. I began to make notes in my head, for a book. Nov. 11, 1886, I read the first chapter (all that was then written) at Governors Island, and closed the reading with an outline of the probable contents of the future book. Wrote a book "The Yankee at Arthur's Court" in '87 and '88, and published it in December 1889 (shall, anyway).

I have not railroaded to speak of for fifteen years but have stayed at home. This morning the usual new bride got aboard the train, and she began as usual her furtive love tappings and pettings, proud that he was hers and willing that everybody should know it and envy her, and when she wanted to ask him what time it was, or any little this-worldly trifle, she would hitch her chin on his shoulder and wall her worshiping eyes up, just in the same old soft, sweet, railroad honeymoon way which I remembered so well; and he, well he stood it in the same old patient, suffering, surfeited shame-faced martyrlike way of the railroading bridegroom of the bygone times, and wondered no doubt how he could ever have thought *he* knew anything about courting and keeping it up, for his courting before marriage must have seemed so pale and poor and lazy compared with hers after it. Yes, there was that same old gushy, sappy little drama going on before me, just in the same old soul-enchanting way without a change in any detail of the performance. But at last the bride tired herself out as usual, and then, as usual, she cushioned her dear head under his left ear and went to sleep as contentedly as if she had been in heaven—and it's a mighty trying position for the other fellow, and makes him feel bitterly conspicuous. But now a change came—the first I had ever observed in this drama—for she began to snore. It was an immense improvement and softened your hard heart toward her at once, because it showed that her sleep was honest and not gotten up for effect, as those former sleeps were. So I gratefully added that to the long list of improvements which I had noticed in these six weeks of railroading.

Lots of things have changed and all for the better. They have dry towels in the hotels now, instead of the pulpy-damp rag of former days, which shuddered you up like a cold poultice; and they have electrical buttons, now, instead of those crooked bell handles which always tore your hand and made you break a lot of the commandments—all you could think of on a sudden call that way; and at table they feed you like a man and a brother, and don't bring your dinner and spread it around your plate in a mass-meeting of soap-dishes; and you have the telephone instead of the petrified messenger boy. And then the new light. There was nothing like it when I was on the highway before. I was in Detroit last night and for the first time saw a city where the night was as beautiful as the day; saw for the first time the place of sallow twilight, bought at $3 a thousand feet, clusters of corruscating electric suns floating in the sky, without visible support and casting a mellow radiance upon the snow-covered spires and domes and roofs and far-stretching thoroughfares which gave to the spectacle the daintiness and delicacy of a picture and reminded one of airy unreal cities in the glimpses of a dream. Yes, the changes are great and marvelous and for number are past enumeration. And last night as I went to my room in the hotel when my missionary work on the platform was done, I struck the crowning blessed innovation of all, apparently—six fat green bottles in a wire frame hanging on the wall by my door. Gratis refreshment for the weary instructor in place of having to go to the bar and lie. I took that frame down and carried it into my room and got out my lemons and sugar and calculated to have a good solitary sociable time all to myself, and says I—"Here's to prohibition—for the next man that comes along the hall." But sorrow and disappointment must come to all; and thus also came it even to me, when I examined the labels to see what brand of sourmash it was, and found that those homely bottles were to put out another kind of fire.

The electric lights hung in the sky were the old arc lamps, and it is not likely that the telephone mentioned was in his room—not in 1884. Mark Twain lived to enjoy a great many innovations—those of the next 25 years: the automobile, for instance, and the phonograph, but he died too soon for the radio and the talking-pictures, and it is unlikely that he ever got a glimpse of a flying-machine.

CHAPTER XVIII

The Grant Book

> WITH Charles L. Webster, a nephew by marriage, Mark Twain by 1885 had become a publisher. A successful beginning having been made with Huckleberry Finn, the firm of Charles L. Webster & Co. was now about to undertake a venture of far greater proportions.

FEBRUARY 26, 1885. On the 21st I called on Gen. Grant and Col. Fred his son at 3 East 66th St., their home, to talk over the business details of the publication of the General's book. I was astonished to see how thin and weak he was; yet as I had just read in the papers that his bad symptoms were all gone I took it for granted that the report was true, and said I have been glad to see that news. He smiled and said—"Yes—if it had only been true." One of the physicians was present and he startled me by saying—"The General's condition was the opposite of encouraging."

Then the talk drifted to business and the General presently said, "I mean you shall have the book—I have about made up my mind to that—but I wish to write to Mr. Roswell Smith first and tell him I have so decided. I think this is due him."

From the beginning the General has shown a fine delicacy toward those people—a delicacy which is native to the character of the man who put into the Appomattox terms of surrender the words "Officers may retain their side arms," to save General Lee the humiliation of giving up his sword—a delicacy which the Century has not well deserved.

They offered him 10% royalty on his book! That was the most colossal bit of cheek the 19th century can show. Gen. Grant felt under obligations to give them the book —mainly because they suggested that he write it—a suggestion which *I* made to him three years ago. And in his modesty he didn't know that when they paid him $1500 for three articles in the Century they were exactly as just toward him as it would be to buy a dollar bill of a blind man and pay him ten cents for it. They sent him a voluntary thousand dollars the other day—after the General's first article had sprung their circulation clear away up into the clouds. They could have paid him $5000 for that article and still made that much money themselves.

Friday March 20, 1885. Gerhardt and I arrived at Gen. Grant's about half past two P.M. and I asked that the family would look at a small clay bust of the General which Gerhardt had made from the photograph. Col. Fred and Jesse were absent to receive their sister, Mrs. Sartoris, who would arrive from Europe about 4:30; but the three Mrs. Grants examined the work and expressed strong approval of it and also great gratification that Mr. Gerhardt had undertaken it. Mrs. Jesse Grant had lately dreamed that she was inquiring where the maker of my bust could be found (she had seen a picture of it in Huck Finn which was published four weeks ago) for she wanted the same artist to make one of Gen. Grant. The ladies examined the bust critically and pointed out the defects while Gerhardt made the necessary corrections. Presently Mrs. Gen. Grant suggested that Gerhardt step in and look at the General. I had been in there talking with the General, but had never thought of asking him to let a stranger come in. So Gerhardt went in with the ladies and me, and the inspection and cross fire began. "There, I was sure his nose was so-and-so," and, "I was sure his forehead was so-and-so."—"And don't you think his head is so-and-so?"[1]

And so everybody walked around and about the old hero, who lay half reclining in his big easy chair and well muffled up, and submitted to all this as serenely as if he were used to being served so. One marked feature of Gen. Grant's character is his exceeding gentleness, goodness, sweetness. Every time I have been in his presence—lately and formerly—my mind was drawn to that feature.

Presently he said—to let Gerhardt bring in his clay and work there, if Gerhardt would not mind his reclining attitude. Of course, he was glad. A table for the bust was moved up in front of him; the ladies left the room. I got a book; Gerhardt went to work, and for an hour there was perfect stillness, and for the first time during the day the General got a good sound peaceful nap. Gen. Badeau came in and probably interrupted that nap. He spoke out as strongly as the others concerning the great excellence of the likeness. He had some sheets of manuscript in his hand, and said: "I have been reading what you wrote this morning, General; and it is of the utmost value; it solves a riddle that has puzzled men's brains all these years, and makes the thing clear and rational."

I asked what the puzzle was, and he said, "It was why Grant did not immediately lay siege to Vicksburg after capturing Port Hudson." (At least that is my recollection, now toward midnight, of Gen. Badeau's answer.)

Offer Gen. Grant's family $500 a month till a year hence when first settlement due—they perhaps need it.

March 23, 1885. Drove at 11:30 A.M. to Pratt & Whitney and told Col. Woodruff to take the offensive now

[1] Karl Gerhardt was a young sculptor whose art education in Paris had been paid for by Mark Twain.

with that terra-cotta firm and require that they pay Gerhardt 65 or 70% of the profit on every bust of Gen. Grant. It is the best likeness of the General ever made in clay, oil, or any other way—in fact, much the best; and it is the last one that ever *will* be made from the living subject—therefore if they hesitate about those terms there are plenty others who will gladly take the enterprise off their hands.

Get shorthander in New York and begin my autobiography at once, and continue it straight through the summer.

Which reminds me that Susy, aged 13 (1885), had begun to write my biography, solely of her own notion—a thing about which I feel proud and gratified. At breakfast this morning I intimated that if I seemed to be talking on a pretty high key, in the way of style, it must be remembered that my biographer was present. Whereupon Susy struck upon the unique idea of having me sit up and purposely talk for the biography.

> He did, in fact, engage a stenographer at this time and begin the dictation of autobiography. He could not keep it up, however, not then. He was too busy, and he was not used to dictation. He dictated the story of the Grant book—that being the freshest and most important thing in his mind—then laid work aside for about twenty years, during which period he made no more than brief attempts to set down his memories.

Club Essay: The little man concealed in the big man. The combination of the human and the god. Victor Hugo; Carlyle; Napoleon; Mirbel; Jesus; Emerson and Washington, with a parenthesis enclosing a question mark after Washington; Grant; Mahomet—in them (including the

Saviour) was allied the infinitely grand and the infinitely little. Carlyle, whose life was one long stomach-ache, and one ceaseless wail over it. Gladstone—and out of courtesy to many here present, I add Blaine—Macaulay—Shakespeare—Burns—Scott—Richelieu—Cromwell ——

March 31. Called at Gen. Grant's and saw Mrs. Fred Grant and Mrs. Sartoris. Showed them the cover of the General's book. I took with me young Hall, who writes shorthand. I had a telegraphic paragraph from this morning's Tribune in which Gen. Jubal Early tries to take the magnanimity out of Gen. Grant's action at Appomattox in not requiring Gen. Lee to give up his sword. I hoped to find Gen. Grant well enough to tell the story of the surrender and let young Hall take it down in shorthand. I wanted to lay the suggestion before Col. Fred Grant, but he was worn out and asleep and I would not allow him to be disturbed. His wife went up to see if he might be stirring, but he was still asleep, so after waiting and talking awhile I came away. Many groups of people were distributed here and there in sight of the house, observing the visitors, and one reporter questioned me, but I was not able to tell him much. Another tried to head off the coupé, but gave it up.

Webster was up till this morning, notifying newspapers not to reproduce the stolen picture of Gen. Grant as a Lieutenant in the Mexican War.

April 4. Gen. Grant is still living this morning. Many a person between the two oceans lay hours awake, last night, listening for the booming of the fire bells that should speak to the nation in simultaneous voice and tell its calamity. The bell strokes are to be 30 seconds apart, and there will be 63, the General's age.

They will be striking in every town in the United States at the same moment—the first time in the world's history that the bells of a nation have tolled in unison beginning at the same moment, and ending at the same moment.

General Grant is still alive today and the nation holds its breath and awaits the blow.

Gerhardt wanted me to let him write a note and ask Col. Fred Grant's permission to make a death mask of his father. It is something that must be done, of course, but I could not bring myself to be a party to the request —there is something so dreadful about it. So I telegraphed him to apply through Gen. Badeau, instead of making a personal application. I had before telegraphed Col. Grant, asking that he let Gerhardt speak with him.

A telegram from Gerhardt tonight says Col. Grant has personally given him the desired permission. I am very glad indeed, for the mask must be made when the General dies and it is so much better that Gerhardt, who is honest and whom the family know, should do it than some tricky stranger.

> He was now all concerned with the manufacture of the Grant memoirs, nearly every page of the notebook bears suggestions more or less practical. As the orders were coming in for it in a real deluge the matter of finding presses and binders became very urgent.
>
> A large sum of money for manufacturing was required and this had to be borrowed for the most part. It required courage as well as credit to finance this great undertaking, but Mark Twain, impractical as he was in the matter of details, never lacked courage, and he never lacked vision as to results.

The severest censor has been the Boston Advertiser. I am sorry to impute personal motives to him but I must, he is merely taking what he imagines is legitimate revenge upon me for what was simply and solely an accident. I had the misfortune to catch him in a situation which will not bear describing. He probably thinks I have told that thing all around. It is an error. I have never told it except to one man, and he came so near absolutely dying with laughter that I judged it best to take no more chances with that narrative.

"Thrice have I been in the valley of the shadow of death, and thrice have I come out again." Rev. Dr. Newman says Gen. Grant pressed his hand and said that yesterday, April 15. Ten cents to a thousand dollars he never used that form of words. This piece of misreporting comports with what that Chinese Secretary of Legation said of Newman. Tribune version: "Thrice have I been down in the valley of death, and now I have come up." No better—gush—rot—impossible.

May 1, 1885. 60,000 sets of Gen. Grant's book (or 120,000 single volumes) which I am to publish next December are already ordered by a region comprising one fourth of the territory lying between Canada and Mason and Dixon's Line, and the Mississippi River and the Atlantic Ocean. At this rate the rest of that territory will take 180,000 sets more—240,000 sets in all, or 480,000 single volumes. The vast West and the body of Southern States ought to take together 120,000 sets, perhaps—say 600,000 single volumes. If these chickens shall really hatch, according to my account, Gen. Grant's royalties will amount to $420,000 and will make the largest single check ever paid an author in the world's history. Up to the present time the largest one ever paid was to Macaulay on his History of England, 20,000 pounds. If I pay the General in silver coin (at $12 per pound) it will weigh 17 tons.

(Note added April 15, 1889. Have just read the preceding. How curiously accurate a prophecy it was. We sold about 610,000 single volumes. We paid Mrs. Grant somewhere between $420,000, and $450,000. I do not remember the exact figure. When I talked with Gen. Grant in November 1884, 13 months before his first volume was published, I ciphered on the sales achieved by my own books and told him that by my reckoning his book must sell 600,000 volumes.)

Club Subject: The *insincerity* of man—all men are liars, partial or hiders of facts, half tellers of truths, shirks, moral sneaks. When a merely honest man appears he is a comet—his fame is eternal—needs no genius, no talent—mere honesty—Luther, Christ, etc.

Macaulay's grand edition weighed 45 tons. Our first issue (Dec. 1) ought to weigh 300 tons.

> We now for the first time begin to hear of the typesetting machine, which was to become the Frankenstein monster to destroy him. His enthusiasm concerning the book is less noticeable; the possibilities of the typesetter claim attention.

There are 11,000 papers and periodicals in America.
This typesetter does not get drunk.
He does not join the printers' union.
He does not distribute a "dirty case."
He does not set a "dirty proof."
A woman can operate him.
He can snatch up late matter, eight "takes" at a mouthful, at three in the morning, when the paper is in a hurry to get to press.

> It becomes a kind of rhapsody and breaks out in a variety of forms, often in a bewildering array of figures.

If God is what people say there can be no one in the universe so unhappy as he; for he sees unceasingly myriads of his creatures suffering unspeakable miseries—and besides this foresees how they are going to suffer during the remainder of their lives. One might well say: "As unhappy as God."

The telephone must be driven out, for it is useless—at any rate at night when the electric lights are burning.

> It was at this time that Mark Twain wrote for the *Century Magazine* his article on his experience as a Confederate soldier when this small irregular company of which he was a member was pursued by troops under the then unknown Col. U. S. Grant.

The General said he read my article, first, and all the family afterwards. (I said) I did not know that this was the future General Grant or I would have turned and attacked him. I supposed it was just some ordinary Colonel of no particular consequence, so I let him go. It was probably a great mistake.

It is curious and dreadful to sit up this way and talk cheerful nonsense to Gen. Grant and he under sentence of death with that cancer. He says he has made the book too large by 200 pages—not a bad fault—a short time ago we were afraid it would *lack* 400 of being enough. He has dictated 10,000 words at a single sitting, and he a sick man! It kills me, these days, to write half of it.

> It has been claimed by persons having no knowledge of the circumstances—having nothing indeed but a malignant desire to cheapen a great hero—that General Grant did not write his own memoirs—that Mark Twain and others wrote them. These notes are sufficiently conclusive.

May 26, 1885. This date, 1858, parted from L. (Laura Dake). Who said "We shall meet again 30 years from now."

> They did not meet in thirty years, or ever, again. During the summer of 1906, at Dublin, New Hampshire, he received a letter from her, the first in all that time. She asked a favor, which he was only too willing to grant. It has never been quite clear why their romance came to an end.

Today talked with Gen. Grant about his, and my, first Missouri campaign (in 1861, June or July). He surprised an empty camp, near Florida, Mo., on Salt River which I had been occupying a day or two before. How near he came to playing the devil with his future publisher.

Gen. Grant told me it was at Salt River his heart was in his mouth, but from that day forth he never had a tremor again in the war. He had been in war before but this was the first time he was responsible.

General Grant's first idea was to put in portraits of prominent generals, but he got so many letters from colonels and such, asking to be added that he resolved to put none in and thus avoid the creation of jealousies.

June 28. Gen. Grant telegraphed me and I went to him next day—a long trip from Elmira to Mount McGregor. Left the hilltop at Quarry Farm at 6 A.M., arrived at Gen. Grant's cottage 14 hours afterward 8:20 P.M. The business was a letter from the Century—exactions about the Century articles. I devised one method, Col. Fred another. We fixed it up.

I was ready to return next morning, but waited 24 hours for Jesse Grant to return from New York. He wanted me to furnish money for him to go to Turkey with. It appears that a year or more ago Gov. Stanford of California was dining with the Sultan when the latter offered him a franchise for a railroad from Constantinople to the Persian Gulf. Stanford came home full of the project; then his son died and he at once lost all interest in life. So he gave the chance to Jesse Grant, and offered to join Gen. Grant in furnishing Jesse letters to the Sultan.

I had to leave before Jesse could get back but I shall furnish the money for the experiment.

July 10. Gen. Grant has written the Sultan.

Write a blast against the temperance and other "pledge" folly.

Some day make a little book, call it "Picturesque incidents in history and tradition (of all countries)." For instance: Describe what England was like during the six years wherein no church bell was heard—John and his whole realm being under Papal curse and interdict.

The children's pilgrimage to Palestine.

To please Richard III a priest of Westminster invented, or allowed, the quibble that Sanctuary was a refuge for only those who were guilty of crime—and so poor little Prince Henry having committed no crime, had no right to that profession—wherefore the child was taken out of the sanctuary and delivered to his uncle, to be smothered in the tower.

I have no sense of humor. In illustration of this fact I will say this—by way of confession—that if there is a humorous passage in the Pickwick Papers I have never been able to find it.

On board train, Binghamton, July 23, 1885, 10 A.M.

The news is that Gen. Grant died about two hours ago —at five minutes past eight.

The last time I saw him was July 1 and 2, at Mt. McGregor. I then believed he would live several months. He was still adding a little, perfecting details, to his book— a preface among other things. He was entirely through a few days later. Since then a lack of any strong interest to employ his mind has enabled the tedious weariness to kill him. I think his book kept him alive several months. He was a very great man—and superlatively good.

All men in New York insult you—there seem to be no exceptions. There are exceptions of course—*have* been —but they are probably dead. I am speaking of all persons there who are clothed in a little brief authority.

August 6, 1885. Talked an hour with Gen. Sherman. He spoke in terms of prodigious praise of Gen. Grant's military genius. "Never anything like it before." I think those were his words, but he said that this talk of Grant never listening to indelicate stories was bosh. Said he had seen Grant listen and laugh by the hour at Gov. Jim Nye's yarns. They *were* indelicate, as I well remember myself.

Somebody has said "Wit is the sudden marriage of ideas which before their union were not perceived to have any relation."

The English, the arrogant nation. The Americans the material nation, the Germans the patient nation, the Russians the unclassifiable nation, the French the volatile nation, the Scotch the thrifty nation, the Italians the hot-blooded kind-hearted nation, the Irish the nation of chaste women.

The last thing after Gen. Grant's body was laid to rest

in the receiving vault, a bugler stepped out all alone in front of the tomb and blew "Taps" (put out the lights). This in the presence of a great host of war veterans who had heard it every night in the camps and on battlefields of Grant's campaign of a score of years before.

I was not there. I saw the great procession August 8, but was not at the tomb.

August 8, 1885. Witnessed the passing funeral pageant of Gen. Grant from our office windows in 14th Street, Union Square; five hours; then plowed through the sidewalk crowd up Fifth Avenue to 40th St.

CHAPTER XIX

Turbulent Years

FROM an entry made August 20, 1885, we find that to date Mark Twain has paid to Paige, the inventor of the typesetter-machine, $13,000. Most of his notes now concern The Machine. Just as humanity was going to be saved a year or two earlier by the history game, now the world's salvation lies in the typesetter. Nor was he so far wrong. He begins to estimate the returns on machines by the hundred and the thousand. Like his own Col. Sellers, he saw "millions in it." And rightly enough, if—his had only been the right machine.

JEAN (aged five) requests me to tell a story to be based on a kind of business copartnership between a "bawgun strictor and a burglar."

Cæsar's Commentaries (on the Gallic War and the Civil War) are the only books that take rank with this (Grant's). Like this they are noted for their simplicity, naturalness and purity of style.

Wit and Humor—if any difference it is in duration—lightning and electric light. Same material, apparently; but one is vivid, brief, and can do damage—the other fools along and enjoys elaboration.

The machine will not diminish the number of printers but increase composition and make it much lighter work for both body and mind.

Some of the notes are made in German—for no particular reason except that he was very much interested in the language about this time. A German class used to assemble at his house and it was during this period that he wrote the Meisterschaft sketch for the *Century Magazine*.

Printers are peculiarly well instructed men. They all know the history of the great labor-saving and speed-enhancing inventions, and they know that no hostility in the world can stop such a machine from coming into use, or even notably delay it.

He realized that his interest in his various enterprises took the form of a hobby, perhaps, for just here he makes this note:

A person should always have a hobby. Observe how a sweetheart fills every waking moment to the brim and makes life a jubilation. Observe the miser and the successful stock speculator and proprietor of vast money-making industries. Observe the student in his specialty—in bees, ants, bugs, fossils—*any* specialty that is absorbing. But the hobby must not be the *result*—no, only the pleasure of working *for* the result, and the final trial of accomplishing it.

Oct. 3, 1885. I think I have struck a good idea. It is to reduce a series of big maps to mere photographic fly-specks and sell them together with a microscope of one quarter to one inch focal distance.

Extravagant as this idea may have seemed at the moment, it came into practical use, approximately, during the World War. Maps were reduced photographically to proportions so small that they could be concealed between the glass and the rim of spectacles and in other places as inconspicuous.

October 26, 1885. Up to date 320,000 sets of Gen. Grant's book have been subscribed for—that is to say 640,000 single volumes.

Got twelve more presses to work; this makes twenty that are going night and day. If we could get 27 we could print a complete volume every second, but it is impossible to get them.

We have seven binderies at work—all large ones. One of them turns out 1500 volumes per day. This one occupies three large floors, and works upon nothing but this book. The building was rented, the machinery bought new and the hands brought from Philadelphia—all for this book. We are being well scolded by the other publishers, for they have to send their printing and binding to other cities.

November 19. Called on President Cleveland at the White House, by appointment through Johnson of the *Century Magazine* and George Walton Green, Chief of the Authors' League. By little and little I wandered into a speech, having got speedily warmed up by the first remark or two made on International Copyright—which remark or two I made myself without intending to say anything further. Then there was a four-cornered talk of an hour. The President showed great interest in our subject and will do it as good a turn as he can in his Message. I ventured to urge him to make I.C. the child of his administration, and nurse it and raise it.

December 11, 1885. Howells says "I am reading Grant's book with a delight I fail to find in novels." And again—"I think he is one of the most natural—that is, *best*—

writers I ever read. The book merits its enormous success, simply as literature."

My books are water; those of the great geniuses are wine. Everybody drinks water.

What is biography? Unadorned romance. What is romance? Adorned biography. Adorn it less and it will be better than it is.

Special Providence! That phrase nauseates me—with its implied importance of mankind and triviality of God. In my opinion these myriads of globes are merely the blood corpuscles ebbing and flowing through the arteries of God and we but animalculæ that infest them, disease them, pollute them; and God does not know we are there and would not care if He did.

> Nine-tenths of the pages of his notebooks now are filled with comments, estimates, and the like concerning the machine, but occasionally he has a diversion like this:

August 31, 1886. Revealed to Livy my project of buying the remains of Christopher Columbus and placing them in the base of the Statue of Liberty Enlightening the World in New York Harbor. No—rotunda of the Capitol at Washington.

In Wales the parson came to collect tithes. The farmer's wife said—"Parson, I have eleven children—will you take one of them? You take the tenth pig, will you have the tenth child?"

And is "tithes" a tenth of all a man's crop alive and otherwise? However, call it a tenth of the animal crop of live stock only, and think what a frightful tax it is on a poor man. It does leave a gap as if one of his family had been taken. Suppose God had levied this tax upon the incomes of the rich. How long would it have remained in force? A week? Try to imagine rich, Godly Englishmen paying from $10,000 to $800,000 to the church and making no murmur, raising no hell about it. What a pity God didn't levy the tax upon the rich alone. *I* would. However, He knew the rich couldn't be forced to pay it and the poor could. With all his brutalities and stupidities and grotesqueries that old Hebrew God always had a good business head. He always stopped talking shop (piousness, sentiment, sweetness in life) and came right down to business when there was a matter concerning shekels on hand. His commercial satisfaction in the clink of shekels runs all through his Book—that Book whose "every word" He inspired and whose ideas were all his own; among them the idea of levying a one-tenth income tax upon paupers. We hear a great deal about the interior evidences of the "Divine Origin" of that Book. Yes; and yet the tithe tax could have originated in hell if interior evidences go for anything.

April 12, 1887. Day before yesterday I encountered Mrs. Harriet Beecher Stowe on the sidewalk. She took both my hands and said with strong fervency that surprised the moisture into my eyes—"I am reading your Prince and Pauper for the fourth time, and I *know* it is the best book for young folks ever written."

May 17, 1887. Depew told this last night at the dinner at Charles A. Dana's house: "Greeley turned on the man who was collecting money 'to save millions of your fellow creatures from going to hell,' and remarked—'I won't give you a damned cent. There don't half enough of them go there now.' "

1887. Next May write Prof. Francis Wayland that I am

ready to pay the young colored man, Charles W. Johnson's, way through the Yale Law School.

> Along in the winter of 1887 and 1888 there blazed into his brain a brand-new idea:

Dress up some good actors as Apollyon, Greatheart, and the other Bunyan characters; take them to a wild gorge and photograph them—"Valley of the Shadow of Death"; to other effective places and photograph them, along with the scenery; to Paris in their curious costumes, place them near the Arc de l'Etoile and photograph them with the crowd—"Vanity Fair" to Constantinople, Cairo, Venice, 20 interesting cities, and always make them conspicuous in the curious foreign crowds by their costume. Take them to Zululand. It would take two or three years to do the photographing, and cost $10,000; but this stereoptical panorama of Bunyan's Pilgrim's Progress could be exhibited in all countries at the same time and clear a fortune in a year. By and by I will do this.

> Two things may occur to the reader in connection with this note, first, that in his idea lay a prophecy of the cinematograph and second the modest estimate of the cost of getting his enterprise under way.

October 4, 1887. If in 1891 I find myself not rich enough to carry out my scheme of buying Christopher Columbus' bones and burying them under the Statue of Liberty Enlightening the World, I will give the idea to somebody who *is* rich enough.

For Princeton Review—to be written in April, 1888: If you attempt to create a wholly imaginary incident, adventure or situation, you will go astray and the artificiality of the thing will be detectable, but if you found on a *fact* in your personal experience it is an acorn, a root, and every created adornment that grows up out of it, and spreads its foliage and blossoms to the sun will seem reality, not inventions. You will not be likely to go astray; your compass of fact is there to keep you on the right course.

Mention instances (in this article) where I think the author was imagining. Others where he built upon a solid and actually *lived* basis of *fact*.

All crimes should be punished with humiliations—public exposure in ridiculous and grotesque situations—and never in any other way. Death makes a hero of the villain, and he is envied by some spectators and by imitators.

In the note that follows there is a suggestion of the radio, or at least of its various uses, though he had in mind the phonograph, then a recent invention.

Neither printed newspapers nor books left—except as curiosities. Salacious daily news furnished in a whisper to any that want it. But the character of each sort of news is marked by signs, indicating "pure," "hellish," etc.

And now we have his prediction of television:

Portraits and pictures *transferred by light* accompany everything. The phonograph goes to church, conducts family worship, etc. teaches foreign languages. Pops the question.

Jean, age seven: "He cried *so* hard, but I gave him my little finger, and he quieted right down—though all he got was just his own juice."

To Remember

Monday Midnight, March 26, 1888. Delmonico's—supper to Irving and Miss Terry—by Daly.

MARK TWAIN

Murray Hill Hotel, New York March 14, 1888. I came down here from Hartford, Saturday the 10th, to dinner to Henry Irving, at Chas. A. Dana's, Sunday evening, and the memorable blizzard has snow-bound me here ever since. Not a train here from Hartford since early Monday morning. Mrs. Clemens was to come down today and we were going to Washington tomorrow. Of course she will not come till everything is smooth again. I can't get a telegram nor a telephone to her, nor she a message to me. A Boston friend is better off: He cabled Boston through London and got an answer back promptly over the same long road.

CHAPTER XX

Writing "The Yankee"

By the absence of an irreverent press, Europe for a thousand years has existed merely for the advantage of half a dozen seventh-rate families called Monarchs, and some hundreds of riffraff sarcastically called Nobles. Our papers have one peculiarity—it is American—it exists nowhere else—their irreverence. May they never lose and never modify it. They are irreverent toward pretty much everything, but where they laugh one good king to death, they laugh a thousand cruel and infamous shams and superstitions into the grave, and the account is squared. Irreverence is the champion of liberty and its only sure defense.

How superbly brave is the Englishman in the presence of the awfulest forms of danger and death; and how abject in the presence of any and all forms of heredity rank.

Are we asked to believe that the vote of a whole nation would voluntarily saddle upon itself any form of hereditary monarchy and hereditary nobility? Then we must also believe that it would in the same way approve the restricting, the officering of its armies and navies to persons of "noble" degree—which is on its face impossible, absurd.

Rank in the army is still restricted to the nobility—by a thing which is stronger than law—the power of ancient habit and superstition. Let a commoner become an officer—he will be snubbed by all his brethren, ostracized, driven out.

The Victoria Cross—who gets it? Intrepid commoners? Do not deceive yourself. Examine the V.C. records.

The kingly office is entitled to no respect. It was originally procured by the highwayman's methods; it remains a perpetuated crime, can never be anything but the symbol of a crime. It is no more entitled to respect than is the flag of a pirate. A monarch when good is entitled to the consideration which we accord to a pirate who keeps Sunday School between crimes; when bad he is entitled to none at all. But if you cross a king with a prostitute the resulting mongrel perfectly satisfies the English idea of nobility. The ducal houses of Great Britain of today are mainly derived from this gaudy combination.

To this day Englishmen revere the memory of Nell Gwynne, and speak of her with a smack of unconscious envy. They seem to consider her as one of the peculiarly fortunate of this world. They keep her portrait at Hampton Court, among some more treasures of the same sort; they study her picture as history with affectionate pride; they value any rag or relic which her touch has made holy; they are as excited and pleased over any new fact concerning her as a devotée would be over a garment which his favorite saint had used.

> Mark Twain at this time was writing his *Yankee in King Arthur's Court*—a terrible arraignment of royalty and nobility—and his mind was filled with instances and examples. His blood grew hot remembering them.

There are shams and shams; there are frauds and frauds, but the transparentest of all is the sceptered one. We see monarchs meet and go through solemn ceremonies, farces, with straight countenances; but it is not possible to imagine them meeting in private and not laughing in each other's faces.

The system has for its end the degradation of the many

to exalt the few, the misery of the many for the happiness of the few, the cold and hunger and overworking of the useful that the useless may live in luxury and idleness.

The system of our Indians is high and juster, for only merit makes a man chief, and his son cannot take the place if there is another man better fitted for it.

Observe how monarchies and nobilities are sprung upon a heedless and ignorant people. Chiefs rise by the one divine right—capacity, merit. One of these shows merit for war and government above all the rest, he conspires with a faction of the chiefs and is made king. The body of the people ignored, allowed no vote, their desires in the matter held to be of no consequence by these upstarts. The conspirators make the succession permanent in this king's family, and the crime is complete. It is the same sort of crime that surprise and seizure of a weak community's property by a robber gang, and the conversion of the community itself into slaves, is. All monarchies have been so built; there was never a throne which did not represent a crime; there is no throne today which does not represent a crime. A monarchy is perpetuated piracy. In its escutcheon should always be the skull and crossbones.

What a funny thing is monarchy and how curious its assumptions. It commits a crime and assumes that lapse of time removes the criminality; it does a dishonest thing and assumes that lapse of time removes the taint, as if it were a mere smell, and perishable; it does a shameful thing and assumes that lapse of time transfigures it and makes it a thing to be proud of. It assumes that a wrong maintained for a dozen or a thousand years, becomes a right. It assumes that the wronged parties will presently give up and take the same view—that at least their descendants will. Now, by an effort one can imagine a family of bears taking pride in the historic fact that an ancestor of theirs took violent possession of a bee tree some centuries ago, and that the family have had a right to it ever since. We can get that far without any trouble, but there the allegory fails; for the bees would attack the bears every day for a thousand years. You can make a man understand how time turns a wrong into a right, but you can't make a bee understand—in his present undeveloped stage. What the bee lacks is the thrill of awe. He will get that by and by, then he will be a very good Englishman.

Let us take the present male sovereigns of the earth—and strip them naked. Mix them with 500 naked mechanics, and then march the whole around a circus ring, charging suitable admission, of course,—and desire the audience to pick out the sovereigns.

They couldn't. You would have to paint them blue. You can't tell a king from a cooper except you differentiate their exteriority.

What is the chiefest privilege remaining to nobility? That you shall not laugh at it. No other class is exempt. If you would know how vast a privilege it is, observe that to accord it to any thing, or being, or idea, is to give it eternal life.

No god and no religion can survive ridicule. No church, no nobility, no royalty or other fraud, can face ridicule in a fair field and live.

There are in Connecticut, at this moment and in all countries, children and disagreeable relatives chained in cellars, all sores, welts, worms and vermin.—Cases come to light every little while—two recent cases in our state. This is to suggest that the thing in man which makes him cruel to a slave is in him permanently and will not be rooted out for a million years. To admit that slavery exists in any country is to admit that you may describe any form of brutal treatment which you can imagine and go there and find it has been imagined, and applied, before you.

Find absolute power unrestrained by a trained public opinion and you will know without going to inquire, that *le Droit du Seigneur* exists there. Observe, it existed in Scotland; there are traces of it in England, you find it lodged in the big medicine man of various savage tribes.

In some savage lands it was an *honor* to the girl and her family. In modern times it is an *honor* to a subject to be reigned over (that is to have his liberty debauched) by a family called royal—a family with no decenter right than a medicine man. The stupid loyalty of today is the same sentiment unaltered that made *le Droit* possible, and the degradation is the same in quality and quantity—the form of it is changed, that is all.

Loyalty is a word which has worked vast harm; for it has been made to trick men into being "loyal" to a thoustand iniquities, whereas the true loyalty should have been to themselves—in which case there would have ensued a rebellion, and the throwing off of that deceptive yoke.

Note for Yankee

The first thing I want to teach is *disloyalty*, till they get used to disusing that word *loyalty* as representing a virtue. This will beget independence—which is loyalty to one's best self and principles, and this is often disloyalty to the general idols and fetishes.

I use compulsion in establishing my several breeds of Protestant churches, because no missionarying has ever been accomplished except by force which was not contemptible by comparison of the paltry result with the gigantic outlay of cash and labor.

The building of the Mansion House: A dissenter could not be Sheriff of London, because he would have to take the Sacrament according to the Anglican Rite. The City passed a by-law, fining any man 400 pounds who refused to run (for Sheriff) when asked, and 600 pounds for refusing to serve, after being elected. A blind man and a bedridden one were thus robbed of a thousand pounds each. In this way 15,000 pounds were collected—enough to build the whole Mansion House, in that day—a hundred years ago.

In a constitutional—figurehead—monarchy, a royal family of chimpanzees would answer every purpose, be worshiped as abjectly by the nation, and be cheaper.

Instead of giving the people decent wages, Church and gentry and nobility made them work for them for nothing, pauperized them, then fed them with alms and persuaded themselves that alms-giving was the holiest work of God, and the giver sure to go to heaven, whereas one good wage-giver was worth a million of them to the State.

The device of "loyalty" to King or Party should be a sheep. He is the counterpart and exactest twin and representative of the King's slave and the Party's slave. Follows his leader—to hell or heaven, it's all one to him, he hasn't got independence enough to think it any of his business.

September 12, 1888. Read Browning last night in a private house to 130 people, the ladies in the majority. Have made speeches several times at banquets where half were ladies. Have read and lectured a good many times at matinées where of course ladies were largely in the majority.

In all such places failure may be counted upon. In fact hardly anything can prevent it but a carefully organized *claque*. Not a half-hearted claque, but a brave one—a claque which will not allow itself to be disturbed.

For several reasons. To begin with, ladies are cowards about expressing their feelings before folk; men *become* cowards in the presence of ladies. Here then is what you are to expect: Your first piece goes well—the men forget themselves when they applaud. Consequently you go at your second piece with good heart, and do it well. This time, the applause has an undecided flavor about it; the men have not reasoned that it was the ladies who failed to support them when they applauded before, they have merely noticed that the support was lacking. After that they are afraid, and a dead silence follows the third reading. You are as exactly equipped now for the fourth piece as if a bucket of cold water had been poured over you. If you are wise, you will now tear your audience all to pieces with a roaring anecdote, then say you are smitten with a killing headache, and dismiss them, for no man can read or talk against unresponsiveness.

The Elmira Reformatory contains 850 convicts, who are there for all manner of crimes. People go there and lecture, read, or make speeches, and come away surprised and delighted. They can't understand it. They have astonished themselves by the excellence of their own performance. They can't remember to have ever done so well before. Afterwards, they always say that for a splendid audience give them a houseful of convicts; it's the best audience in the world. They puzzle and puzzle over it and are not able to get away from the apparently established fact that an audience of convicts is the most intelligent and appreciative in the world. Which is all a mistake. The whole secret lies in the absence of ladies. Any 850 men would be just as inspiring, where no dampening female person was in sight, with her heartful of emotions and her determined repression, choking it down and keeping the signs of it from showing on the outside.

> In his later years Mark Twain might have revised his opinion of female audiences. Long before his death, the convention that restrained women from open demonstration of their enjoyment had disappeared. He frequently and with great delight talked or read to colleges like Barnard, and always came home enthusiastic over his reception.
>
> Also, had he lived until today he might have found less to rave about concerning kings. He could have transferred his animus to dictators.

For any man or woman not rich or of noble rank, there was an imaginary difference between England and hell, a hundred years ago.

The institution of Royalty in any form is an insult to the human race.

The man who believes there is a man in the world who is better than himself merely because he was born royal or noble, is a dog with the soul of a dog—and at bottom is a liar.

If the master of a kingdom is so important that God will not entrust his appointment to men but appoints him Himself, it then follows that the master *of* that master is a still more important officer and so this one must *especially* be divinely appointed. Therefore one is logically compelled to say—"Nell Gwynne, by the Grace of God monarch of Great Britain etc."

People seem to think they are citizens of the Republican

Party and that that is patriotism and sufficiently good patriotism. I prefer to be a citizen of the United States.

October 15, 1888. I found yesterday that a prominent citizen (who has two skunk friends on the Street Board) had at last succeeded in getting the light moved from the Gillette Street corner to the mouth of Forest Street, thus leaving our gates smothered in Egyptian darkness. The city government has done me many a mean trick, in sixteen years, and I stood the strain and kept the peace; but to frightfully inconvenience me to accommodate a person like the said citizen was a little too much. So I went down last night and contracted for electric light at my own cost, and police protection at my own cost, and took measures to transfer my citizenship to some other town. So after next June I shall have the satisfaction of paying a possibly very large tax every year to some town in which I do not live, and paying not a cent in Hartford any more forever, except on the house and grounds.

> As we hear no more of this violent self-banishment perhaps it never became official. He may have reflected that to vote in Hartford he must remain a citizen, and he did like to vote there with Twichell and the others.

Publishing Memorandum

Sherman (Life of) proves to be unprofitable. Demand a reconstruction of contract placing power in my hands where it belongs. Refused? Go into court. Second: Demand dissolution. Go into court. Can I be held for debts made beyond the capital? I will buy or sell out.

Since the spring of 1886, the thing has gone straight down hill, towards sure destruction. It must be brought to an end, February 1, at all hazards. This is final.

That is to say, his publishing enterprise so magnificently started by the Grant Life—had been steadily going down hill ever since. Furthermore, all his available cash—all he could earn and borrow—was going into the type machine. It was easy to see that "the business must be brought to an end by Feb. 1," but it would go on steadily declining for another six years after that—it would take the panic of '93 and '94 to give it its final quietus.

November 23, 1888. At noon, was coming up a back street; two poorly dressed girls, one about ten, the other twelve or thirteen years old, were just behind me; was attracted by the musical voice of the elder one and slowed down my gait to listen; by and by the younger said—"Yonder they are"—"Where?" "Way down the street—don't you see?" The elder threw back her head and gushed out a liquid "hoo-oo-oo-ooh!"—The most melodious note that ever issued from human lips, it seemed to me. Nothing has equaled it in my hearing, but the rich note of the woodthrush. I resolved to track that child home—and did. She entered a poor frame dwelling next to and north of a frame building that had a sign "Sigourney Tool Co." on its front. Then I followed the younger girl home, at least to a house in front of John Hooker's grounds. So I shall be able to find one or the other, by and by. I mean to educate that girl's voice. She will make a stir in the world sure.

One wonders if he ever remembered it again. He had many such impulses—some of them he followed to fulfillment. He had educated Gerhardt, discovered quite accidentally; he had provided money for the dramatic education of William Gillette, and there were other instances of the sort. But the drain upon him was very heavy now, and his responsibilities increasing; also, his mind was very full and he may have never remembered the beautiful voice.

To Mrs. S. L. Clemens—

Happy New Year!

The machine is finished and this is the first work done on it.

S. L. Clemens
Hartford, Dec. 31, 1888.

(sample enclosed)

He thought it was—that his troubles were nearing their end. They had hardly begun. The machine would be "finished" so many times, after that, and always at fearful cost in money and mental stress.

Three pages farther along follows this triumphant entry:

Eureka!

Saturday, January 5, 1889, 12:20 P.M. At this moment I have seen a line of movable type, *spaced and justified by machinery!* This is the first time in the history of the world that this amazing thing has ever been done. Present:

J. W. Paige, the inventor;
Charles Davis
Earll | mathematical assistants and
Graham | mechanical experts
Bates, foreman, and
S. L. Clemens.

This record is made immediately after the prodigious event.

S. L. Clemens

Laid into the notebook are two examples of the typesetter's work—satisfactory examples. But then, almost immediately, Paige began to tinker with it—perhaps there was need—perhaps it was only Paige's pernickety habit of not being able to let well enough alone. Two days later comes another note:

Monday, Jan. 7—4:45 P.M.

"The first proper name ever set by this new keyboard was *William Shakspeare.* I set it at the above hour; and I perceive, now that I see the name written, that I either misspelled it then or I have misspelled it now."

The space bar did its duty, aided by the electric connection and steam, and separated the two words, preparatory to reception of the space.

Surely the test of a novel's characters is that you feel a strong interest in them and their affairs—the good to be successful, the bad to suffer failure. Well, in John Ward you feel *no* divided interest, no discriminating interest—you want them all to land in hell together, and right away.

As the cow and the Christian think—I mean that process which the cow and the Christian regard as thinking, when the subject is religion and the evidences.

A few months ago I was told that the Johns Hopkins University had given me a degree. I naturally supposed this constituted me a Member of the Faculty, and so I started in to help what I could there. I told them I believed they were perfectly competent to run a college as far as the higher branches of education are concerned, but what they needed was a little help here and there from a practical commercial man. I said the public is sensitive to little things and they wouldn't have full confidence in a college that didn't know how to spell John.

However, one thing seemed certain enough, anyway—the degree constituted me a member of the governing body and doubtless the head of it; so I proceeded upon that.

March 9, 1889. No more experiments (on the machine). Definite work alone left to do. Four months sure; that is, July 10. No new devices or inventions.

It has a tragic sound today. Evidently he did not know Paige yet.

March 11. Made this proposition to Mrs. Richardson today: That in lieu of the present contract, she dramatize the Prince and Pauper for *me*; I to pay her $500 upon delivery of the manuscript to me, June 1 or July 1, be her work good or bad. If the play *succeeds*, I to pay her another $500 (this to be the first $500 received by me as profits) after that, I to pay her $5 every time the piece is played. She will answer Thursday.

In the matter of pensions England has never made any distinctions between public service and private shame, except to pay highest for the latter. Consider the Dukes of Grafton and Richmond and the progeny of Nelson. England pensions the rich whore with millions, the poor private with a shilling a month, she was always shabby and a humbug.

March 22, 1889. Mother said, to Livy, "What is the name of the sister of ——"

"Mrs. Corning?"

"Yes, Mrs. Erastus Corning."

I was present. Livy explained that *this* was genuine mental telegraphy for no mention had been made of the Cornings. Last week four or five days ago—occurred some talk about Mrs. Pruyn of Albany, the sister under consideration.

I proposed to take down the three sentences immediately, and doubted if even immediately would be soon enough to get them exactly, so unsure a thing is human testimony. It is agreed that this report is exact.

You know how absent-minded Twichell (Rev. J. H.) is and how desolate his face is when he is in that frame. At such times he passes the word with a friend on the street and is not aware of the meeting at all. Twice in a week our Clara (aged 15) had this latter experience with him within the past month. But the second instance was too much for her and she woke him up, in his tracks, with a reproach—she said—

"Uncle Joe, *why* do you always look as if you were just going down into the grave, when you meet a person on the street?"

And then went on to reveal to him the funereal spectacle which he presented on such occasion. Well, she has met Twichell three times since then, and would swim the Connecticut River to avoid meeting him the fourth. As soon as he sights her, no matter how publicly placed, nor how far off she is, he makes a bound into the air, hurls arms and legs into all sorts of frantic gestures of delight, and so comes prancing, skipping and pirouetting for her like a drunken Indian entering heaven. She feels as embarrassed as the Almighty.

Elmira, August 18, 1889

We have been here two months, in which time Brer W. (Whitmore, his business secretary) has written me some three mere notes about the machine. I wrote once and asked him to tell me anything there was to tell from time to time. No answer. Wrote him and asked him to keep Fred in practice while the machine is stopped. No answer.

The machine stopped August 2—not a line from him to say why, or how much is to be done on it. Suppose it were a sick child of mine? Would he give me any news about it?

> It was, in fact, a sick child—it was generally sick, and every cure—every partial cure, for there were no complete ones, was terribly costly.

My adventure at 2 A.M., clothed with nightshirt and checkered summer parasol when I chased the dog Bruce over the hills, and finally encountered the colored preacher who was afraid of ghosts and took me for one.

We Americans worship the almighty dollar! Well, it is a worthier god than Heredity Privilege.

Better a deity that represents the labor of your hands and your contribution to the world's wealth than a deity which represents not a contribution, but a robbery; for no king or noble has ever lived who was not a robber, and the successor of robbers, since no kingship or nobility was ever yet conferred by the one and only authority entitled to confer it—the mass of the nation.

October 13, 1889. Proposed my idea (of buying the remains of Columbus and bringing them over to the fair of '92) to the N. Y. World Committee on ideas—but shan't *name* the idea until I hear from them.

These wretched American women who buy titles (and noble tramps) with their money—mongrel breeders; should have a bench show of their children.

February 1, 1890. Sir Wm. Gull is just dead. He nursed the Prince of Wales back to life in '71, and apparently it was for this that Mr. Gull was granted Knighthood, that doormat at the threshold of nobility. When the Prince seemed dead Mr. Gull dealt blow after blow between the shoulders, breathed into his nostrils, and literally cheated Death.

Monarchy? Why is it out of date? It belongs to the state of culture that admires a ring in your nose, a head full of feathers and your belly painted blue.

That kind of so-called housekeeping where they have six Bibles and no corkscrew.

That government is not best which best secures mere life and property—there is a more valuable thing—manhood.

I always come to introduce Stanley every time he goes off to hunt up some mislaid person in Africa and gets forgotten.

William Penn achieved the deathless gratitude of the savages by merely dealing in a square way with them—well—kind of a square way, anyhow—more rectangular than the savage was used to at any rate. He bought the whole state of Pennsylvania from them and paid for it like a man—paid $40 worth of glass beads and a couple of second-hand blankets. Bought the whole state for that. Why you can't buy its *legislature* for twice the money now.

> Memoranda concerning the machine and its trouble—its shortcomings—become monotonous, but just one more, to show the torture of mind he must have endured.

December 20, 1890. About three weeks ago the machine was pronounced "finished" by Paige, for certainly the half-dozenth time in the past twelve months. Then it transpired—I mean it was discovered—that North had failed to inspect the *period*, and *it* sometimes refused to perform properly. But to correct that error would take just one day, and *only* one day—the "merest trifle in the world." I said this sort of mere trifle had interfered often before and had always cost ten times as much time and money as their loose calculations promised. Paige and Davis *knew* (they always *know*, never guess) that this correction would cost but one single day. Well, the best part of two weeks went by. I dropped in (last Monday noon) and they were still tinkering. Still tinkering, but just *one hour*, now, would see the machine at work, blemishless, and never stop again for a generation; the hoary old song that has been sung to weariness in my ears by these frauds and liars!

December 29. The "one hour" lasted till last Thursday; it was reported to me by Whitmore that it got to work again that day. The next day I sent down a new (proposed) contract prepared by Robinson.

The machine broke down again *that day*! Remains so still.

February 7, 1891 Saturday night, 10 o'clock. Wrote a note to Paige saying I now hold myself as released from any further effort or expense in behalf of the machine. I told him today that this was going to be my last negotiation, and then I was done; that I should not renew the insurance or pay out any more money!

But this was open mutiny, not only as to Paige, but himself. He had got to a point where he did not own the machine—the machine owned him. He might perhaps have thrown the whole thing overboard, present it to Paige in a word —which may have been, though it is by no means certain, just what the latter wanted.

(*Copy of letter to Gas Company*)

Hartford, Feb. 12/91

Dear Sirs:

Some day you will move me almost to the verge of irritation by your chuckle-headed Goddamned fashion of shutting your Goddamned gas off without giving any notice to your Goddamned parishioners. Several times you have come within an ace of smothering half of this household in their beds & blowing up the other half by this idiotic, not to say criminal, custom of yours. And it has happened again today. Haven't you a telephone?

Ys

S L Clemens

February 20. It is more than two weeks since I have seen Paige or the machine. Am deep in work—the "Date and Fact game," "Col. Sellers,"[1] etc.

Huck comes back sixty years old, from nobody knows where—and crazy. Thinks he is a boy again and scans always every face for Tom, Becky, etc.

Tom comes at last from sixty years' wandering in the world, and attends Huck and together they talk of old times; both are desolate, life has been a failure, all that was lovable, all that was beautiful is under the mold. They die together.

Mark Twain went back to Hannibal in 1902, while John Briggs, his old playmate, was still

[1] The Sellers story here mentioned was the *American Claimant*, published in 1892.

alive. They did meet and talk over old times, but both were in good mental health.

Paige, the microbe.

May 2. Finished the book [American Claimant] which I began to write Feb. 20—71 days.

May 29, 1891, 1:30 P.M. Tried to send a telegram through telephone and couldn't. They charge you for the use of this deaf-and-dumb thing.

Bill Styles, lobbying in behalf of a candidate for U. S. Senator—in the legislature—spoke of the low grade of legislative morals, "kind of discouragin', you see, it's so hard to find men of so high type of morals that they'll *stay bought.*"

From Mr. Hall, May 25, 1891

In re your letters from the other side: For all letters containing not less than 3500 words, McClure is to pay you $1000 per letter. If they contain more than 3500 words so much the better. If the letters contain less than 3500 words he is to pay you at the rate of $300 per thousand words.

I telegraphed Hall to accept these terms for me.

P.S.—Changed, June 3. Letters to contain 5000 to 6000 words, $1000 per letter.

> The cost of American living had become almost prohibitive, and his finances were being scraped from the bottom of the treasure chest. Business was so bad that not only was there no money coming in from it, but he must provide considerable sums to keep it going. A memorandum shows that of the several amounts coming to Mrs. Clemens, from her investments, nothing

would be left after turning over money required by the machine and the publishing business—a ghastly situation. They had decided upon European residence. The Hartford house, their home for seventeen years, full of beautiful memories, would be closed.

CHAPTER XXI

European Residence

MARK TWAIN and his family sailed on the *Gascogne* June 6, 1891. Mrs. Clemens was last to leave the house, the home she would never enter again.

At Sea

June 6, 10:30 A.M. (first breakfast) went to it—then put down for second breakfast 12:30. Before these hours, 6 to 9—you can have coffee, tea and an egg, or chop, to stay your stomach.

One deck steward to 200,000 passengers. Began at nine to hunt for him and pray to him—got the order to him at 10:15, at 10:30 he has not appeared, and I have retreated from the sight of the starving family.

A woman springs a sudden reproach upon you which provokes a hot retort—and then she will presently ask you to apologize.

Twenty young wheelmen paying a specific sum apiece, in charge of a personal conductor who wheels them all over Europe and relieves them of all care and expense.

With such seas as this they could practice on these long decks all day if they chose.

One man says they do practice, two hours after midnight and spin along silently like ghosts.

The strenuous insistent muffled burr or buzz of the

propeller flange, like the humming bird's buzz—lulling and not unpleasant.

June 8. Certainly the sunniest and most beautiful day the Atlantic ever saw. But little sea—though what there is would be seriously felt on a smaller vessel. This one has no motion.

The phosphorescent waves at night are very intense on the black surface.

Life preservers: Square blocks of cork—Nicholson pavement—over my head, supported on slats.

I have often yearned to know how you get them down and how you use them, and I think it a mark of the perfection of my native procrastination that I continually put it off. Are there ten in our 300 who have done differently?

Divans all around a great square salon, occupied by silent folk in the squeamish stage. A piano in there—hated by the above.

Contrasts between the menu here and that of the old Cunarder, with the candles out at eleven, without notice.

June 11, 1891. The loneliness of a ship at 4 A.M. Saw just one person, for an instant, flit thru the gray of yesterday's dawn. Very rough—winds singing—first wet deck. Electrics seem to burn dim. Smoking sty stunk unendurably.

Susy: (of the French) "Their gesticulations are so out of proportion to what they are saying."

Hell or Heidelberg, whichever you come to, first.

This is the first hint of the story he was to write a few years later called *The Man who Corrupted Hadleyburg*; at least, the first hint of the sentence "Hell or Hadleyburg."

At Heidelberg

Went up to Königstuhl, and recognized old Gretchen—the two girls seem to recognize me (gave me hopes) but didn't; two red-headed children I attributed to the younger (fat) one. I was a skittish young thing of 42 in those days.

We have our old room now, No. 40.

> He refers to their German sojourn in 1878, when for a time they had lived at the Schloss Hotel, and he had worked in a small cottage farther up the hill.

Europe has lived a life of hypocrisy for ages; it is so ingrained in flesh and blood that sincere speech is impossible to these people, when speaking of hereditary power. "God Save the King" is uttered millions of times a day in Europe, and issues nearly always from just the mouth, neither higher nor lower.

The first gospel of all monarchies should be Rebellion; the second should be Rebellion; and the third and all gospels and the only gospel in any monarchy should be Rebellion against Church and State.

Want milk but they don't have it—would be too conspicuous not to drink wine. The wine increases my rheumatism, too.

Arrived at Ouchy, Thursday Sept. 17 ('91) noon.

September 19, Saturday—depart from Grand Hotel, Beau Rivage, at 2 P.M., for Castle Chatillon on Lac Bourget, for boat trip down Rhone.[1]

[1] See "Down The Rhone" in Vol. *Europe and Elsewhere*, Mark Twain's Works. Also, *Mark Twain—a Biography*, Chapter CLXXVI.

Three idiots took a boat just as I was walking to the Beau Rivage and soon were being swept down toward the bridge, they pawing the water innocently with their ignorant oars. The owner of the boats watched awhile then sent a boat after them and saved them, so the world is better off by three fools.

The river for miles is a raging plane of white caps; the Mistral is just howling.

Higginson visiting Emily Dickinson at her father's house in Amherst, 1870:

"It was at her father's house, one of those large square brick mansions so familiar in our older New England towns, surrounded by trees and blossoming shrubs without, and within exquisitely neat, cool, spacious and fragrant with flowers."

There—if there is any region on the continent of Europe where such houses exist, I have never found it.

As long as time shall last, history will spit in England's face for her treachery to Napoleon's trust in her. Some have looked around for the cue, and found it in England's fright. Excuses must have been scarce when that one was chosen.

Following the Rhone trip the family settled in Berlin, where the next entry is made.

The highest of all professions—the stilling of human pain—the saving of human life.

When you lie low, how welcome is the face of the doctor, in that time of uncertainty when you can't tell for sure just where you are going to.

And without a doubt Berlin is the place to come to to finish your medical education, for certainly it is a luminous center of intelligence—a place where the last possibilities of attainment in all the sciences are to be had for the seeking. Berlin is a wonderful city for that sort of opportunity. They teach everything here. I don't believe there is anything in the whole earth that you can't learn in Berlin except the German language. It is a desperate language. *They* think it is the language of concentration. They hitch a cattle train of words together, and vestibule it, and because there isn't a break in it from one end to the other, they think that is concentration, and they call it so. An officer gave me this word the other day, got it out of a naval handbook—"Untersecretariatsapplicant."

I wrote a chapter on this language 13 years ago, and tried my level best to improve it and simplify it for these people—and this is the result—it merely concentrates the alphabet with a shovel. It hurts me to know that that chapter is not in any of their textbooks and they don't use it in the Universities. If I could get an Imperial decree it would help the reform along.

But the fact is they ought to adopt our language. It is so simple and easy, whereas (here follows a long involved German sentence). But never mind about that, you are here to learn—you are here to perfect yourself in your great calling. And that is the thing to do. A half-educated physician is not valuable. He thinks he can cure everything.

This note was evidently part of an address to medical students.

We hate the critic and think him brutally and maliciously unjust, but he could retort with overwhelming truth: "You will feel just as I do about your book if you will take it up and read it ten years hence."

Move from Körnerstrasse to Hotel Royal, Unter den

Linden 31 December '91—six chambers and one dining-room and one parlor.

Left the family there and on the 4th day of Jan. '92, Livy and I went down to Ilsenborg in the Hartz Mountains—ostensibly four, but really seven hours from Berlin.

Stayed eight days in the house of Pastor Oberman. He and his wife lovely people. The stoves in our parlor and bedroom not satisfactory. I caught a heavy cough.

The entire society of the village consisted of the old Fürstin vom Reuss, her daughter the Princess, and the pastor and his wife—four people. We made it six.

The doctor and his wife were not in society; he was a baker's son and climbed to his doctorship by native gifts and hard work.

The second evening the Fürst vom Stolberg-Wernigerode and his son came over on the annual visit to his sister, the old Fürstin. He is a very handsome man, and the proudest unroyal prince in Germany, and the richest. He brought several carriage-loads of young princesses with him. Our party of six (which included the doctor and his wife) were the only people there below the rank of prince. Livy and I shook hands with the Fürst, and passed on, and I missed seeing the awful thing that followed: The doctor's wife put out her hand and the Fürst let on that he didn't see it. Poor thing, instead of taking warning, she raised her hand *higher*, imagining he hadn't seen it. He *ignored* it. It was tragic. She had a cry that night.

We came away at midnight, after a good supper and a pleasant and sociable time. I made the usual number of blunders in matters of etiquette.

The night before we came away the old Fürstin and the Princess came over to supper and spent the evening. They are lovely people and good English scholars. The Fürstin is a poet, too. I spun yarns and she translated them to the company.

> How leniently he deals with these people of rank. Imagine what he would have said had that incident occurred in England. He would not have referred to that prince as "proud." He would have combed the dictionary to find adjectives to convey his scorn.

Came up to Berlin Jan. 12, to lecture on the 13th, intending to go back to Ilsenborg and stay two months.

Went to our cousins' (Frau and General von Versen) ball after the lecture; we all came home at 2 A.M. and I have been in bed ever since—three weeks—with congestion of the lungs and influenza.

When I had been in bed eleven days Frau von Versen came, Jan. 24, and brought a note, inviting me on the part of the Emperor to come to the Palace at 11:30 A.M. and witness the consecration of some flags. I wrote my thanks and regret. Frau von V. came in again that day or the next and said that the Emperor had commanded her to prepare dinner for him and me in her house—the date of the dinner to be the day that I should be well enough.

A day or two ago Jean was overheard to say—after some talk about this approaching event—"I wish I could be in Papa's clothes"—pause and reflection—"but it wouldn't be any use, I reckon the Emperor wouldn't reconnize me."

Tasteless slovenliness and ugliness of German papers—even worse than French. French books are marvels of taste and fine workmanship—proving that they have printers there; whereas, if one saw only the papers he would think they hadn't even apprentices. How clear and clean and beautiful a London or New York paper looks beside the German and French papers.

I am reconciled to our display heads now. They tell me

at a glance the contents of a column. But here I must spell the column through, and it takes an hour.

When the King and Queen of Würtemberg were here they double-banked the "Holy Land" with soldiers, who shouted: "He's coming!"

I would like to be Emperor awhile.

> Apparently he has almost recovered from the fierce attack of king-phobia that had caused him to rage, through the period of writing the *Yankee in King Arthur's Court.*

Feb. 14. Prof. Helmholtz called.

The Court Gazette of a German paper can be covered with a playing-card. In an English paper the movements of titled people take up about three times that room. In the papers of the Republic of France from six to sixteen times as much. There, if a duke's dog should catch a cold in the head they would stop the press to announce it and cry about it. In Germany they respect titles, in England they revere them, in France they adore them, that is, the French newspapers do.

Been taken for Mommsen twice. We have the same hair, but upon examination it was found that our brains were different.

Thirty days sick abed—full of interest—read the debates and get excited over them, though I don't understand. By reading keep in a state of excited ignorance. Like a blind man in a house afire—flounder around—immensely, but unintelligently, interested, don't know how I got in and can't find the way out but I am having a booming time all to myself.

Don't know what a "Schelgesetzentwurf" is, but I keep as excited over it and as worried about it as if it was my own child. I simply live in the Sch—it is my daily bread. I wouldn't have the question *settled* for anything in the world. Especially now that I have lost the "Offentliche Militärgerich" circus. I read all the debates on that question with a never-failing interest, but all at once they sprung a vote on me a couple of days ago and did something, by vote of 100 to 143, but I couldn't find out what it was.

Here they recognize two sects, Catholic and Lutheran (which appear to differ from each other nearly as much as a red-headed man differs from an auburn-haired man). These receive State support; and their schools receive State support. Other sects are taxed to support these sects and schools, and have to run their own churches and schools at their own cost. It is infamous.

Just as infamous as it is with us—where no church property is taxed and so the infidel and the atheist and the man without religion are taxed to make up the deficit in the public income thus caused.

I went to church the first Sunday, and on Tuesday came a tax of twelve marks for church support. I have not been since. I can't afford religious instruction at that price. Only the rich can be saved here.

Feb. 20, 1892. Dined at General (lately Lt.-Gen.) von Versen's.[1] Sat at the right hand of the Emperor. His brother, Prince Heinrich, sat opposite. Prince Radolin (Chamberlin) further along; fourteen at table; mainly great military and naval people. Two of my friends besides the von Versens were there. Rottenborg and Rudolph Lindau, both of the Foreign Office. After dinner, six or eight officers came in, and all hands adjourned to the big room out of the smoking-room, and held a "smoking par-

[1] General von Versen had married a second or third cousin of Mark Twain.

liament," after the style of the ancient Potsdam one, till midnight, when the Emperor shook hands and left.[1]

Feb. 26. Day before yesterday the Emperor made a speech (as Markgraf of Brandenburg) to the little Brandenburg Parliament, assembled here, at a banquet in the Palace. Complained sharply of the grumblers who are dissatisfied with the government and suggested that if they don't like the way things are they had better shake the German sand out of their slippers and leave.

The speech has made a great stir. That of the odious (proposed) Schulgesetz, and the lack of bread and work resulted in a mob gathering in front of the Palace yesterday, of people out of work. They uttered revolutionary cries. Baker's bread was distributed to them but they threw it away.

At Jean's school this morning the children were forbidden to speak of the matter but said they would tell her *out* of school.

Crowds of the proletariat drifting up and down the "Holy Land" today but the Emperor rode out as usual, and after him I saw the whole force of royal carriages following—apparently all the royal women and all the children have turned out to show that they are not afraid.

> He was still far from well, and was commanded by his doctor either to remain in his room or go to a warmer climate. He chose the latter and with Mrs. Clemens went to Mentone, in the south of France, then to Italy.

Pisa, March 25 & 26. Echo in Baptistery is the noblest and sweetest and richest and most resonant and long-sustained musical strain in the world. It is nearest like a chord of flutes, perhaps, or one of those orchestral combinations in Wagner with silver horns in it—but nothing

[1] For a fuller account of what happened at this dinner see *Mark Twain—a Biography*, Chapter CLXXIX.

can do more than merely approach it remotely, no combination of voices or instruments can reproduce or adequately imitate it—for there is no building but this one where the strain would not have a noticeable flatness about it as compared with this noble roundness and fullness.

Saturday, April 30, 1892. Came from Rome to Florence yesterday. This is the Hotel Grande Bretagne and Arno—called the best in Florence. It is a vast confusion of halls and sleeping-holes, a huge congerie of rats' nests, furnished with rubbish, probably bought at pauper auctions. The cook *is* the best in Florence, no doubt. He is first class; the rest of the hotel is fortieth class.

In Rome two weeks ago young Corbett told me of his adventure in Campagna with his friend Martin, when two terrific dogs came for them, and their peasant guide put up a prayer to the Virgin and she vouchsafed a miracle which saved them.

To Twichell, in America

Dear Joe:

. . . The dogs of the Campagna (they watch sheep without human assistance) are big and warlike, and are terrible creatures to meet in those lonely expanses. Two young Englishmen—one of them a friend of mine—were away out there yesterday, with a peasant guide of the region who is a simple-hearted and very devout Roman Catholic. At one point the guide stopped, and said they were now approaching a spot where two especially ferocious dogs were accustomed to herd sheep: that it would be well to go cautiously and be prepared to retreat if they saw the dogs. So then they started on, but presently came suddenly upon the dogs. The immense brutes came straight for them, with death in their eyes. The guide said in a voice of horror, "Turn your backs, but for

God's sake don't stir—I will pray—I will pray the Virgin to do a miracle and save us; she will hear me, oh, my God she surely will." And straightway he began to pray. The Englishmen stood quaking with fright, and wholly without faith in the man's prayer. But all at once the furious snarling of the dogs ceased—at three steps distant—and there was dead silence. After a moment my friend, who could no longer endure the awful suspense, turned—and there was the miracle, sure enough: the gentleman dog had mounted the lady dog and both had forgotten their solemn duty in the ecstasy of a higher interest!

The strangers were saved, and they retired from that place with thankful hearts. The guide was in a frenzy of pious gratitude and exultation, and praised and glorified the Virgin without stint; and finally wound up with "But you—you are Protestants; she would not have done it for you; she did it for me—only me—praised be she for evermore! and I will hang a picture of it in the church and it shall be another proof that her loving care is still with her children who humbly believe and adore."

By the time the dogs got unattached the men were five miles from there.

Sunday, May 22, 1892. Tried to make the Johnsons, Browns, Sarah Orne Jewett, Mrs. James T. Field, and Mrs. Washington, understand (with Clara's help) the old puzzle of Whitmore taking me around the loop in his buggy. Of course they all laughed and laughed, at my stupidity at first, but it was a puzzle before they got done with it.

> It was a problem that from time to time puzzled him all his life. The driveway in Hartford led past the house to a loop. Driving in one day with F. G. Whitmore, Clemens said: "Whitmore, go around to the left when we reach the

loop, then when we come back to the house I shall be on the side next the step." "No," said Whitmore, "it won't make any difference which way we go around the loop, the result will be the same—you will be on the outside. "Try it," said Clemens, and Whitmore did so, with the result as he had prophesied. Clemens, however, was still unconvinced and made him try it again, going around the loop first one way and then the other, insisting that there must be a difference in the result. He confessed his mistake at last, but all his life it troubled him, and in almost every one of his notebooks there is a diagram of the loop and an attempt to show that his first conclusion was correct.

June 29 (on a trip back to America). Lake Shore and Michigan Southern and N. Y. Central. Today a man timed the train and said we were making 65 miles an hour. The porter said we sometimes make 70, and that over a distance of 400 miles we average 62. Over *there* the fastest train goes from Frankfort to Nauheim in forty minutes—25 miles. It takes the express nine hours to go from Berlin to Frankfort. Slow.

He was back in the typesetter tangle again and the entanglement of his business affairs. His life could have been so simple, so unharrassed, but for these things.

Union League Club, noon. I breakfasted here yesterday about ten. Sat around till 2 P.M. should say. Loafed down to Glenhem Hotel and in my room enjoyed the prodigious downpour of rain awhile; then went to bed—three or four P.M., and was soon absorbed in The Little Minister with shutters closed and gas lit. Hours and hours afterwards—

no idea how many, for no clocks were in hearing, but my instinct and the diminished street voices assured me it was about 2 A.M.—I suddenly thought "My watch has run down of course" and I hopped out of bed, got the thing from my vest on a wall hook and put it to my ear. Yes, it was silent. Opened it, took a careless glance—apparently 11:30 P.M. Been stopped more than two hours, I said:—listened—no tick hearable; wound it up, closed it; after a moment unclosed it and listened to make sure it had started up again; it hadn't; shook it, listened, shook it again, then it started up and I put it back in the vest pocket and returned to bed. I finished my book as quickly as possible—say in half an hour—then rushed myself to sleep, to capture what was left of the night (morning). When I woke I felt well rested up. Rose and looked at my watch—6 A.M. True time is about 8:30, I said, and ordered breakfast and the paper brought to my room. Ate the breakfast, read the World through, wrote a letter or two, began *A Window in Thrums*; by and by dressed and went up Fifth Avenue—noticed the clock in front of Fifth Avenue Hotel—took out my watch to set it. By George, it and the clock were precisely together!—10:14. What was it that called me out of bed the very instant that my watch had run down and stopped the night before?

This is the very counterpart of Mr. Child's adventure with his watch, in Florence.

The family were at the Villa Viviani, near Florence, and he presently returned to them.

Settignano, March 4, 1893: 9:30 P.M. Mr. Cleveland has been President now two or three hours, no doubt.

Driving from Prato this afternoon, a child darted across the road under the noses of the horses, was knocked down, and disappeared. Vitorio pulled the horses to a dead standstill, suddenly, and men ran out to gather up the remains. The child was actually not hurt. The men pulled it out from under the carriage and stood it on its feet. A singular escape. The family were well frightened. I was not along.

March 22. Sailed in the Kaiser William II, at 11 A.M.

His business worries kept him ferrying back and forth between Europe and America.

Tuesday, March 28. The usual brilliant sunshine, the usual soft summer weather. Sea polished and nearly flat—almost a dead calm. We have never had a sea that disturbed the dishes on the table to speak of.

Wednesday, March 29. Nice ball on deck, with colored electric lights. I opened it with Capt. Störmer—waltzed with overcoat. Danced a Virginia reel, with Longfellow for a partner.

Good Friday, March 31. Exceedingly rough—a deal of rain. A very sturdy ship, but of course this sort of sea makes her roll heavily—as it would any ship.

April 1. A wild wind and a wild sea yesterday afternoon. Several falls but nobody hurt. Went to bed at eight and slept till 8. Still a heavy sea this morning.

April 3 Monday. Arrived 6 P.M.

Tuesday, Mr. Hall, evening. Howells came for couple hours.

Thursday, 6th. Dined with Andrew Carnegie, Prof. Goldwin Smith, John Cameron, Mr. Glen. Creation of League for absorbing Canada into our union. The paper read and discussed. Carnegie also wants to add Great Britain and Ireland.

April 7. Dined with Rudyard Kipling and wife. Charles Warren Stoddard there.

> The notes which follow sound dream material, and they were:

Monday noon, April 10. At the Paige compositor—Connecticut Co., 18th and Broadway till 2:30 P.M. Fifty machines well along in building. One will be finished July 1. Present capacity of factory one machine a day. Factory to be built when location decided upon, five machines a day.

Considering proposition of fifteen million company one hour from Chicago. They offered to give the Conn. Co. two million dollars of their bonds, all the land they need, and five million cash, if they will build a factory on their land. This proposition is in writing.

The company intend to market 10,000 machines (rented) with all possible dispatch. All the printers are hurrying the company.

The above machines are for this country alone.

The company tells me that my royalty will be collectible on all foreign machines manufactured by them. By the end of this year the company will be making one machine a day, next year two—the year after, five.

The fifty now in the works will be completed one after the other soon.

> What a child he was: the company and the factory were no more than the airy fabric of Paige's vision. There was no real manufacturing plant, no machines under way, except in Paige's imagination. Paige must have been a hypnotist to impose so repeatedly on Mark Twain. But he imposed on others as well. At the end of this note Clemens adds that the Conn. Co. is paying him (Paige) $5000 a month until the first ma-

chine is sold or rented. But perhaps that was just a part of the vision, too.

"Put all your eggs in one basket—and watch that basket." Andrew Carnegie.

Mark Twain now went to Chicago, taking young Hall along, as secretary. Paige was in Chicago by this time, possibly negotiating the matter of the "land" which had been offered. Sixteen days following the "dream" just related, Mark Twain wrote:

April 23, 1893. Great Northern Hotel, Chicago.

Paige called three days ago. He called again tonight. I asked him if his conscience troubled him any about the way he had treated me. He said he could almost forgive me for that word. He said it broke his heart when I left him and the machine to fight along the best way they could, etc. etc. I tried to bring him to book, and finally he said that he was considering a contract offered by his Land Co. and had carried it back today modified in this way. Instead of accepting one-half their capital stock of fifteen millions, he had amended the contract asking for one-half a million dollars cash and no stock. They will accept or reject this proposition tomorrow. They may accept and offer him less. Whatever they offer he will take in cash and send me one-half. When his European patent affairs are settled, he is going to put me in for a handsome royalty on every European machine. We parted immensely good friends. . . . In the last contract he even got me to assign my 9/20 interest in the foreign patents, after I had all that they had cost up to that time. He is a very extraordinary man—the smoothest talker I ever saw. I tried to impress upon him that I would compromise and square matters for two or three hundred additional royalties on the machine—and for less than that indeed, as I did not care for the money involved, the 500 royalties producing much more than I shall ever need, but then I wanted some trifling evidence that I could exhibit to myself, in proof that I had not been dealt with in an absolutely shameless conscienceless way.

In reply I got an abundance of gilt-edge promises but nothing more.

Charles E. Davis was here two or three nights ago. He said he still holds the paper which Paige dictated to him one day, to quiet him, in which he says that no matter what happened he and I would always share and share alike in the results of the machine, or words to that effect. Paige shed even more tears than usual. What a talker he is. He could persuade a fish to come out and take a walk with him. When he is present I always believe him—I cannot help it. When he is gone away all the belief evaporates. He is a most daring and majestic liar. He said he had put one million three hundred thousand dollars into that machine since he began it. Then as much as $800,000 must have gone into and out of his large pocket within the last two years. He is absolutely frank in his confessions of misconduct. He said he never intended to sign the Fairchild contract—he was only playing Fairchild.

He meant to scoop some money out of him, and he did; that is not his exact expression. I cannot recall the words but they were still more conscienceless and atrocious than this. He said he got several thousand dollars out of Fairchild. He said he played Mallory for all he was worth. That he never intended to have any dealings with Mallory from the beginning, but that he got $16,000 out of him and made himself strong and able to go ahead without any help from Mallory or Fairchild.

Up to this point the note was dictated to Hall. Clemens himself now adds:

Said he paid those men back, afterwards. Seemed to

take considerable credit to himself for it. However, in Ward's office he took credit to himself for granting $2,000,000 to North, the inventor of the Justifier, when (as he said) he hadn't need to grant him a cent unless he chose; whereas, as *I* understand it, North took legal steps against him before he yielded.

Clemens never seems to have been openly violent with Paige. Once he wrote:

Paige and I always meet on effusively affectionate terms, and yet he knows, perfectly well, that if I had him in a steel trap I would shut out all human succor and watch that trap, until he died.

May 13. Saturday. Room 268 (?) Kaiser Wilhelm II. Cast off at 10:15 A.M.; discharged pilot at 12:30. Only half a trip of passengers.

Wednesday, May 24. Sailing along the Balearic Islands, this forenoon. Due at Genoa tomorrow night. A perfectly smooth voyage, but unspeakably tedious. I am older by ten years than I was when I left New York. The fact is, the voyage is *too* smooth.

It was not the smooth voyage that had aged him; it was the gnawing uncertainty of his business future. The publishing firm, now conducted by a Mr. Hall, had undertaken to issue a large set of books entitled Library of American Literature, edited by Edmund Clarence Stedman and to be sold by subscription. Agents were already taking orders for it, but money for its manufacture was required faster than could be provided for by the initial payments received from subscribers. Large sums of money were needed and the notes at the bank were growing.

When a cackling hen is far away and is saying K-k-k-k-k-k KWACKO! you hear nothing but the first syllable of her last word—just a single strenuous note, pitched on a high key, all the rest is lost in the intervening distance. At a distance this fiend-owl's note sounds like that. Close by it is soft and dovelike and it is not so very unlike a flute note. It is quadruple time—one utterance to the bar, followed by three quarter-note rests, thus

h-o-o-o ________ h-o-o-o ________ h-o-o-o-o ________ h-o-o-o-o ________ ________ ________

The monotony of it is maddening. You beat time to it, and count the hoots and the rests—you cannot help it. You count till your reason reels. Low and soft as the note is, it is marvelously penetrating; it bores into the skull like an auger. It can distress you when it is 150 yards away; at a third of that distance it is unendurable. When you have counted fifty hoots and 150 rests you have reached the limit of human endurance. You must turn and drive the creature away or your mind will go to ruin.

To Hall July 26. Will come over mid-October with idea for new magazine, if L.A.L. [Library of Amer. Lit.] is then out of the way.

> Then presently we find him again on the way to America. That demon, the machine, had called. He was never able to resist that summons.

August 29, 1893. Sailed from Breman, with Clara, in the Spree, Capt. Meissel. Lunched with Mr. Platte, President of the North German Lloyd.

Spree table admirable—Kaiser Wilhelm II table detestable.

Took room at Players, Sept. 29th (1.50).

In the first place God made idiots. This was for practice. Then he made proofreaders.

Proofreaders could stir Mark Twain to very high flights of wrath. Once to his business partner, Webster (his nephew by marriage) he wrote:

Charley, your proofreader is an idiot; not only an idiot, but blind, and not only blind, but partly dead.

Some of the spacing—*most* of it, in fact—is absolutely disgraceful, but this goddamned ass never sees it. By God he can't see *anything*; he is blind and dead and rotten, and ought to be thrown into the sewer.

Jan. 15, 1894. This is a great date in my history—a date which I said on the 5th would see Paige strike his colors. A telegram from Stone says he has done it. Yesterday we were paupers with but three months' rations of cash left and $160,000 in debt, my wife and I, but this telegram makes us wealthy.

In all the 40 notebooks there is not a more tragic entry than that.

There are people who can do all fine and heroic things but one—keep from telling their happiness to the unhappy.

Love seems the swiftest, but it is the slowest of all growths. No man or woman really knows what perfect love is until they have been married a quarter of a century.

Today, Jan. 19, sent cable at noon to Livy—"Nearing success."

2 P.M. Jan. 31—Mr. Rogers' office. The great Paige Compositor scheme consummated. At 2 P.M. I cabled

Libby, Paris, "A ship visible on the horizon, coming down under a cloud of canvas."

Friday, Feb. 2, 1894. Sent this cablegram to Livy in Paris last night, to be put on her breakfast plate this morning (our 24th anniversary), "Wedding news: Our ship is safe in port. I sail the moment Rogers can spare me."

Livy's answer this morning is—"We rejoice with you and congratulate you on your well-earned success."

> He had fallen in with the great oil financier, the elder H. H. Rogers, who had taken a hand in his affairs. His dream seemed to be coming true.

A thing long expected takes the shape of the unexpected when at last it comes.

We can secure other people's approval if we do right and try hard. But our own is worth a hundred of it and no way has been found out of securing that.

Ships that Pass in the Night. Get two—send one to Paris.

Drill—that is the valuable thing. Drill—drill—*drill*—that is the precious thing. For, from drill comes the automatic, and few things in this world are well done until they can *do themselves.* If teachers would but drill—drill—drill in the language! But God never made a language-teacher out of a sane person yet. When he can't get an idiot He won't play.

Oh Death where is thy sting! It has none. But life has.

It is more trouble to make a maxim than it is to do right.

Write Ambassador Wayne MacVeigh—how to stop bomb-throwing.

Of all God's creatures there is only one that cannot be made the slave of the lash. That one is the cat. If man could be crossed with the cat it would improve man, but it would deteriorate the cat.

> A good many of his maxims were used in Pudd'nhead Wilson, then in course of publication.

An occasional compliment is necessary, to keep up one's self-respect. The plan of the newspaper is good and wise: When you cannot get a compliment in any other way pay yourself one.

As shy as a newspaper when referring to its own merits.

Familiarity breeds contempt—and children.

Like the mendicant who passes the hat for gratuitous literary contribution and yet would be ashamed to be caught passing it for coppers.

A man should not be without morals; it is better to have bad morals than none at all.

God pours out love upon all with a lavish hand—but he reserves vengeance for his very own.

There are those who scoff at the schoolboy, calling him frivolous and shallow. Yet it was a schoolboy who said: "Faith is believing what you know ain't so."

When in doubt, tell the truth.

> Some of his maxims required a good deal of reconstruction, but this last one—perhaps the greatest he ever uttered, appears to have undergone no change.

In spite of fair outlook at the beginning of the year, the one definite thing that happened that spring was the failure of Charles L. Webster & Company, Mark Twain's publishing-house. The business which had begun so prosperously ten years earlier had dwindled to bankruptcy. Yet it was not all sorrow: Mark Twain was free. Loaded with debt (for he refused to settle at less than the face value of his obligations), but free from haunting uncertainties. His friend, H. H. Rogers of the Standard Oil Company, took his affairs in hand, and Mark Twain hurried back once more to Europe, to finish his story of *Joan of Arc,* begun at Florence, two years before. He still had faith in the machine, and his spirits were high. From Rouen, where he went to visit Joan landmarks, he wrote Rogers—with glee, we may be sure—his most recent adventure.

Dear Mr. Rogers:

Yours of the 24th Sept. has arrived filled with pleasantness and peace. I would God I were in my room in the new house in Fairhaven, so'st I could have one good solid night's sleep. I might have had one last night if I hadn't lost my temper, for I was loaded up high with fatigue; but at two this morning I had a W.C. call and jumped up in the dark and ran in my night-shirt and without a candle—for I believed I knew my way. This hotel d'Angleterre must be a congeries of old dwellings—if it isn't, it is built up in a series of water-tight compartments, like the American liners, that go clear to the top. You can't get out of your own compartment. There is only your one hall; it has four rooms on each side of it and a staircase in the midst; would you think a person could get lost in such a place? I assure you it is possible; for a person of talent.

We are on the second floor from the ground. There's a W.C. on the floor *above* us and one on the floor *below* us. Halls pitch dark. I groped my way and found the upper W.C. Starting to return, I went up stairs instead of down, and went to what I supposed was my room, but I could not make out the number in the dark and was afraid to enter it. Then I remembered that I—no, my mind lost confidence and began to wander. I was no longer sure as to what floor I was on, and the minute I realized that, the rest of my mind went. One cannot stand still in a dark hall at two in the morning, lost, and be content. One must move and go on moving, even at the risk of getting worse lost. I groped up and down a couple of those flights, over and over again, cursing to myself. And every time I thought I heard somebody coming, I shrank together like one of those toy balloons when it collapses. You see, I was between two fires; I could not grope to the top floor and start fresh and count down to my own, for it was all occupied by young ladies and a dangerous place to get caught in, clothed as I was clothed, and not in my right mind. I could not grope down to the ground floor and count *up*, for there was a ball down there. A ball, and young ladies likely to be starting up to bed about this time. And so they were. I saw the glow of their distant candle, I felt the chill of their distant cackle. I did not know whether I was on a W.C. floor or not, but I had to take a risk. I groped to the door that ought to be it—right where you turn down the stairs; and it was it. I entered it grateful, and stood in its dark shelter with a beating heart and thought how happy I should be to live there always, in that humble cot, and go out no more among life's troubles and dangers. Several of the young ladies applied for admission, but I was not receiving. Thursdays being my day. I meant to freeze out the ball if it took a week. And I did. When the drone and burr of its music had ceased for twenty minutes and the house was solidly dead and dark, I groped down to the ground floor, then turned and counted my way up home, all right.

Then straightway my temper went up to 180 in the shade and I began to put it into form. Presently an admiring voice said—"When you are through with your prayers, I would like to ask where you have been, all night."

Truth is stranger than fiction—to some people, but I am measurably familiar with it.

If you tell the truth you don't have to remember anything.

Now that our second-hand opinions, inherited from our fathers, are fading, perhaps it may be forgivable to write a really honest review of the Vicar of Wakefield and try to find out what our fathers found to admire and what not to scoff at.

Now what *was* the accident that brought Shakespeare into notice after two centuries of neglect and oblivion—was it a chance remark of a monarch? An idea there; make kings read all the new (native) books; and once every year proclaim the names—just the names—of the few that particularly pleased them.

Truth is the most precious thing we have. Economize it.

It takes me a long time to lose my temper, but once lost I could not find it with a dog.

He was perfectly frank about it and said he wanted to go to hell: said he had got used to reading the (Paris) N. Y. Herald and couldn't do without it.

It would seem that France was not born to create civilizations; yet she has one glory which not all the eons left in the slow wasting magazine of time can dim or obliterate. Let her content herself with the reflection that it was across her firmament that those two prodigies swept, astonishing the world, Napoleon and Joan of Arc,—that wonderful man and that sublime girl who dwarf all the rest of the human race.

Sailed from Southampton for America. "New York," Feb. 23, 1895.

> Another wild rush to America; publishing matters, and to attend the machine's funeral, the latter having finally come to an end in December, failing completely to stand the test.[1] His only interest now was his Joan book, and a lecture tour which he proposed to make around the world, to pay his debts.

Bob Ingersoll's tale of the Presbyterian saint who went from heaven to hell on a cheap excursion ticket—and couldn't sell his return ticket.

Noise proves nothing, often a hen that has merely laid an egg cackles as if she had laid an asteroid.

Paris. Clara left parasol in a cab. Susy left a couple of bundles in cab. Mrs. C. left porte-monnaie on a counter. I left some things in a cab—but said nothing about it. There are 26,244 cabs, each makes as many as thirty courses a day, moving about 45 persons. Two persons out of three leave something in the cab; thirty articles a day per cab; 10,000 a year per cab. 262,440,000 articles a year for the 26,244 cabs, if there are that many cabs and if my estimate is right.

[1] See *Mark Twain, a Biography*, Chapter CLXXXIX.

Man has been called the laughing animal, to distinguish him from the others, but the monkey laughs and he has been called the animal that weeps—but several of the others do that. Man is merely and exclusively the Immodest Animal, for he is the only one who covers his nakedness, the only one with a soiled mind, the only one under the dominion of a false shame.

Sunday morning: Six or eight people who came over with me in the Paris—three or four of them went up to London with our multimillionaire, to be shown his glory. It was a month ago; but to this day these men can think of nothing else, talk of nothing else. They are as happy and stunned and blessed as if they had been to heaven and dined with God.

Clara says it tires her to have to keep on deciding that she isn't sick, so persistently and so watchfully.

New York, May 18, 1895. Noon. Arrived at 9. Cable from London says that Tichborne Claimant has published an affidavit confessing that he is Arthur Orton, son of a Wapping Butcher. I was in London twenty or twenty-two years ago, during his trial for perjury, and spent an evening in his society with a number of his devoted adherents. He had a marvelous memory. He played his part well. He was sent up for fourteen years; served his term, then came over here and was a bartender in the Bowery.

Jean's comment on the Emperor of Germany's dinner invitation: "Papa, the way things are going, pretty soon there won't be anybody left for you to get acquainted with but God."

Master Mechanic on the L road who said: "You are enough like Mark Twain to be his brother."

Elmira, May 24, 1895. Terms offered to Pond: He to have one-fourth of the profits outside Frisco and one-fifth inside Frisco. He to lecture me there six consecutive nights and three matinées, all in the same week.

His reply by telegraph, May 25, "Terms accepted. See letter."

That is, for the lecture tour around the world. Mrs. Clemens and Clara would accompany him; Susy and Jean (aged 23 and 15) were to remain with their Aunt Sue (Mrs. Theodore Crane) at Quarry Farm, Elmira, New York.

Accompanied by Major and Mrs. J. B. Pond, who would go with them as far as Vancouver, the lecture party left Elmira the night of July 14th (1895). Their last glimpse was of Susy, under the light at the end of the platform, waving good-bye. They never forgot that picture.

CHAPTER XXII

The Way to the Coast

JULY 17, '95. Sailed from Cleveland in the Northland. Fine and swift; her length must be as much as 350 feet. Spacious decks for promenading. Just as luxurious and comfortable as a great ocean liner or a Fall River boat. I have seen no boat in Europe that wasn't a garbage barge by comparison. Think of those European tubs! Sunny, balmy, perfectly delicious voyage—I know nothing anywhere to compare with it. Been away four years and have dropped back into the dark ages in some—many—respects.

Evening. It is an ideal summer trip. The long approach to Port Huron through narrow ways, with flat grass and wooded land on both sides, and on the left a continuous row of summer cottages with small-boat accommodations for visiting across the little canals from family to family, the groups of summer-dressed young people all along, waving flags and handkerchiefs, and firing cannon—our boat replying with four toots of the whistle and now and then a cannon and meeting steamers in the narrow way, and once the stately sister-ship of the line crowded with summer-dressed people waving—the rich browns and greens of the rush-grown far-reaching flat lands, with little glimpses of water away on the further edges, the sinking sun throwing a crinkled broad carpet of gold on the water—well, it is the perfection of voyaging. Boat is a split between Fall River and ocean liner. With this difference—carried no freight—passengers only.

He does not mention it, but most of that eager greeting was for himself—it having been announced that he was on that boat, setting out on a voyage around the world, to free himself from debt.

July 18. Island of Mackinac. Masonry walls with towers of Middle Ages pattern, an inheritance from French early days, no doubt.

At St. Paul, July 24. Lectured both here and at Minneapolis.

Winnipeg, Manitoba. Read in Winnipeg second night.

July 28, Sunday morning. An hour's talk with a bright girl—part Indian, with French name—correspondent of Toronto Globe. Has been a factory girl. Was president of a combine of 500 working girls who appealed to the electric car company for a Sunday car service; the year before that the pulpits had pulled in 5000 majority against it; the 500 girls reduced that to 750 majority two years ago. The pulpit got the next struggle put off three years. It occurs a year hence; then the thing will be carried the other way.

Toronto is 12 miles long, one way, within the city limits; the poor live at one end and work at the other—and not a car on Sunday. These families are as exiled as if the Atlantic flowed between them, but as long as God and the clergy are gratified what of it.

Standards. There are no standards—of taste in wine, cigars, poetry, prose, etc. Each man's own taste is the standard and a majority vote cannot decide for him or in any slightest degree affect the supremacy of his own standard.

Sunday on the Continent is a blessing. In England and America it is a curse and certainly ought to be abolished—no—stripped of its power to oppress. Here on this sunny Sunday morning I heard the happy laughter of the only bird that does laugh by nature—the martin—for the first time in more than a generation. He was my favorite as a boy. Beautiful color—and is a kind of swallow. Man his friend; provides him with a house and never harms him. In France they would hunt him.

Must write up the pretty story where the 16 Yale boys got to treating the two Yale veterans and at 11:30 P.M. found they had used up 14 quarts of champagne and were aghast. What *should* they do to raise the money.

Steward: "That's all right; the two old gentlemen paid for it while you passed by escorting them to their room with a song of honor."

July 31. Drove with the Gibsons to the 49-foot fall (Rainbow?) and the wonderful fountain which Lewis and Clark, 1805, found to be blue and retained its blue color for half a mile down the Missouri.

On the way a young cowboy, showing off, was tumbled over the horse's head. The horse fell on him but fortunately did not kill him.

Butte, Mont., Aug. 1. Beautiful audience. Compact, intellectual and dressed in perfect taste. It surprised me to find this London-Parisian-New York audience out in the mines. [He gives a list of the numbers read]:

Dead Man.
Christening.
Frog.
Old Ram.
Smallpox.
Watermelon.
Crusade.
Golden Arm.

One hour and 30 minutes. Just right. Left out the Duel.

Splendid big negro soldiers; obedient, don't desert, don't get drunk; proud of their vocation, finest and pleasantest soldiers—and Pond says great in battle. Some of these have been in the service ten and fifteen years, and my escort 24 years. They all have the look and bearing of gentlemen. The earliest ones were not educated and could not perform clerical duties; but the later ones can; been in public school. As a rule the army can't sing the "Star-spangled," but Burt ordered these to be taught, and they can sing it.

The band, all colored but leader, made beautiful music.

Ceremony of fetching the colors. All uncovered when the colors passed by—I did, after first blunder. Another—was asked to throw away my cigar when the colors approached.

Chaplin (colored) is a commissioned officer, approved by the Senate. Is saluted like other officers.

Goodwill. They take a pride in it. *I* think the negro has found his vocation at last.

Clark's Fork of the Columbia—green water and lovely. Never saw a green stream in America before. Following this perfectly lovely stream all of the afternoon.

Portland, Ore., Aug. 9. Splendid house, full to the roof. Great compliment to have a lofty gallery packed with people at 25¢ as intelligent and responsive as the others. Floor and dress circle full too, many standing, and the sign up early: "Standing Room Only."

> Everywhere he was welcomed, and had crowded houses, Olympia, Tacoma, Seattle—the returns rolled in.

Aug. 15. Young boy came to interview me this morning.

Asked me in strict detail precisely the questions which I have answered so many million times already:

"First visit?
Pity about the smoke.
Where do you go from here?
Have you had good houses?
Have you enjoyed the trip?
Your family with you?
Where do you go from Australia?
How long will the trip take you?
Are you going to write a book about the voyage?
What will be the character of it?" (tempted to say hydrophobia, seamanship and agriculture.)

A stretch of 18 miles in which there is not a single place named Victoria. En route to Vancouver, Aug. 15. This shows that we are not under the British flag.

Letter sent to Rudyard Kipling:

Vancouver, B. C., Aug. 16, 1895.

Dear Kipling: It is reported that you are about to revisit India. This has moved me to journey to that far country in order that I may unload from my conscience a debt long due you. Years ago you came from India to Elmira to visit me, as you said at the time. It has always been my purpose to return that visit and that great compliment, some day. I shall arrive next January, and you must be ready. I shall come riding my Ayah, with his tusks adorned with silver bells and ribbons, and escorted by a troop of native Howdahs, richly clad and mounted upon a herd of wild bungalows, and you must be on hand with a few bottles of ghee, for I shall be thirsty.

Victoria, B. C., Hotel Driard, Aug. 22. Lectured last night—house full. The Governor-General and Lady Aberdeen and their little son in Highland costume, present. Several bars of "God Save the Queen" played when they entered, the audience standing. They came at 8:45, 15 minutes late. I wish they would always be present, for it isn't permissible to begin till they come; and by that time the late comers are all in.

Was conducted to their box, when I was done, by the Aide de Camp. It was in every way pleasant.

A kitten walked across the stage behind me last night. The audience laughed in the wrong place. I did not know why till after the reading.

Friday, Aug. 23. Sailed for Australia in the Warramoo.

Strange how these great brown gulls (species of albatross) can scrape the tip of one wing along the surface of the water over all depressions and elevations and never touch it. Have watched them for hours.

The recurrent dream. Mine is appearing before lecture audience in my shirt-tail, a most disagreeable dream.

Honolulu Roadsted, Aug. 31. Reached here last night at ten. Not allowed to land. Required to cast anchor and unload our 700 tons of freight in lighters. *Cholera.* Malignant form. Eight deaths this morning, five deaths reported for yesterday.

500 seats booked for my lecture. Can't get ashore to deliver it.

Young Mrs. Corbett says her mother (then Miss Diamond) came here with me in the Ajax, 29 years ago.

Oahu—Just as silky and velvety and lovely as ever. If I might I would go ashore and never leave. The mountains right and left clothed in rich splendors of melting color, fused together. Some of the near cliffs veiled in slanting mists—beautiful luminous blue water; inshore brilliant green water.

Two sharks playing around, laying for a Christian.

By order, the blue uniforms changed for snow-white duck this morning. I bought a suit of it—coat and pants—for $3.

Aug. 31. Five new cases today, five deaths.

This town has 25,000 people now, one-third white.

The Bennington came out and anchored a little to the windward flying the yellow flag at her foremast. There had been a death on board (cholera) and some of our passengers were worried. A protest was sent and the Commander said his ship had been thoroughly fumigated and all his people were healthy, but if any fell sick would go to sea at once.

Sharks playing around our stern all day. Could not catch any.

The most marvelous of sunsets.

We have the snake liar and the fish liar always with us. Now I find we are getting toward the atmosphere breathed by the boomerang liar. The first officer has seen a man escape behind the trees but his pursuer sent his boomerang high over and beyond the tree; then it turned, descended and killed the man. The Australian passenger has seen it done to *two* behind two trees, with one throw. Maturin Ballon *heard* of a case where the boomerang killed a bird and brought it back to the thrower.

Passengers who had taken rooms in this ship were not allowed to come on board at Honolulu. One lady prisoner wrote our Captain an imploring letter.

Sept. 1. Lying at anchor till midnight.

And so they must sail away. For thirty years he had dreamed of going back to the Islands, only to meet this disappointment. One is reminded of Moses and the Promised Land.

Sept. 6. Crossed the equator at 4 P.M. yesterday. Clara kodaked it.

Sept. 8. Today is Sunday and tomorrow Tuesday. It is said that Monday has dropped out because the sailors don't like to lose their Sunday holiday—as if they couldn't have it just as well on an ostensible Sunday as on a real one.

At night. 50 miles from Sidney, very dark. Schools of porpoises come streaking it to the ship from out the black distances like luminous sea serpents. A porpoise 8 ft. long would look like a glorified serpent 30 to 50 ft. long, every curve of the tapering long body perfect and the whole snake dazzlingly illuminated by the phosphorescent splendors in the waters. The color was that of the glow worm and wonderfully intense. The night was so dark that the actual surface of the sea was not distinguishable, and so it was a weird sight to see this spiral ghost come suddenly flashing along out of the solid gloom and stream past like a meteor.

In Australia

Oct. 3. Sent £437.13.6 to T. A. Dibbs, Commercial Banking Co. of Sydney. I asked him to send it to Mr. Rogers.

> He had set out to pay off the debts resulting from the failure of the Charles L. Webster Pub. Co. and had been steadily remitting to Mr. Rogers for this purpose. This was probably his first remittance from Australia.

Oct. 4. Melbourne. Dr. Fitzgerald froze and then lanced this damned carbuncle; then gave me an opium hypodermic. It is the loftiest of all human vocations—medicine and surgery. Relief from physical pain, physical distress. Next comes the pulpit, which solaces mental distress; soothes the sorrows of the soul. These two are the great professions, the noble professions. The gap between them and the next is wide—an abyss.

The most diligent industry in Victoria and New South Wales is apparently horse-racing. There does seem to be a perfectly amazing amount of it. The interest in it seems to be universal and intense. The Melbourne Cup comes off presently, and it is the event of the year.

(Australian) Convicts rose to great worth and prominence and wealth. They left descendants who should not be ashamed of them and probably *are not*. A redeemed career is certainly a thing for the man himself to be proud of, and this just pride in it should extend to his posterity. Many of the convicts were mere boys, and were transported for long terms of years for stealing a rabbit or a hatful of turnips, to stave off starvation. In fairness they should not be called criminals.

The Sabbath is kept in Australia. They actually haven't any Sunday edition of the dailies. It is said the pulpit fears it could not run in competition (in interest) with them.

No Sunday cable car service in forenoon.

When people get to be as good as this no amount of horse-racing can damn them.

I have spent my entire stay in Melbourne in bed with a carbuncle.

> This visitation of carbuncles had begun in Elmira. In one place he wrote: "The dictionary says a carbuncle is a kind of jewel. I never cared much for jewelry."

Since the beginning of the world there have been 225,-000,000,000 savages born and damned and 28,000 saved by missionary effort.

NOTEBOOK

Remember the Bishop from China who said—"4/5 of the human race know not God. God can't do all the work; we must help."

CHAPTER XXIII

Australia and New Zealand

Oct. A darling climate. Drove to Agricultural College, eight miles, open wagon, brilliant sunshine, ninety-two in shade, but perfectly comfortable (dry heat). Just like middle of June. Saw pupils shearing sheep. The fleece when spread out is as big as a bedquilt. Tarstick for wounds to heal them and keep off flies.

The sheep are shorn dirty—buyer prefers it—and the shorn sheep looks as white as snow.

The 40 students work at all farming, every other day. On alternate days study and hear lectures. They are taught the beginnings of sciences (like chemistry, etc.) that bear upon farming, and all practical farming.

Can't see that the British Govt. has any more authority here than she has over the constellations. She seems merely to furnish governors, and the colonies pay the salaries. She has a veto, but she doesn't seem to venture to use it. She can't even force a governor that the colonies object to. She furnishes seven worships and the colonies pay interest on their cost.

The railroad is the only thoroughly European thing here. That is, they build fine stations and then have all the idiotic European railway system in perfection—slow trains, no drinking-water, no sanitary arrangements, every conceivable inconvenience; an utterly insane system—the jackass system.

Many convicts were terrible people no doubt, but ought to have been hanged, not transported. Transportation, in the conditions, was a cruel punishment, and unfair—hanging was the man's right.

Convicts were assigned to Tom, Dick and Harry, to work. Story of one who for a fault was made to walk 14 miles and get an official flogging, then walk back with his torn back—others warned that if they washed his wounds or succored him in any way they would get the like.

New Zealand

Nov. 6. A lovely summer morning, brilliant blue sky. After a few miles from Innercargill passed through level green vast pastures filled with sheep—beautiful clean green expanses.

In these sheep pastures all the cattle are jet black—a hardy breed brought from Scotland to withstand the rather severe winter.

Idiots argue that Nature is kind and fair to us, if we are loyal and obey her laws, and we are responsible for our pains and diseases because we violate the laws—and that all this is judged. Good God! Cholera comes out of Asia and cuts me down when I have taken every pains to have myself and house in good sanitary conditions. Oh, in that case, my *neighbors* violated Nature's law—and Nature makes *me* responsible, takes it out of me—and that is called just! Very well, the caterpillar doesn't know what the laws are—how then are these people going to excuse nature for afflicting that helpless and ignorant creature? It would save those people a world of uncomfortable shuffling if they would recognize one plain fact—a fact which a man willing to see cannot be blind to, namely, that there is nothing kindly, nothing beneficent, nothing friendly in Nature toward any creature, except by capricious fits and starts; and that Nature's attitude toward all life is profoundly vicious, treacherous and malignant. This caterpillar two inches long and the thickness of a cedar pencil—when getting ready to turn into a great nice moth—partially buries his body in a little trench—and Nature has *got him,* the spores of a peculiar fungus are blown about by the wind, they lodge in a wrinkle of his neck and begin to sprout and grow; the roots force their way into the worm and along through the body, and the worm slowly dies and turns to wood, preserving all its details, like a petrifaction.

We easily perceive that the peoples furtherest from civilization are the ones where equality between man and woman are furthest apart—and we consider this one of the signs of savagery. But we are so stupid that we can't see that we thus plainly admit that no civilization can be perfect until exact equality between man and woman is included.

That forgotten and discredited invention of the devil, the gong, still flourishes in Australia and the ringer of it is still merciless and bangs it like a demon gone mad.

The peremptory, big, frowsy blond waitress in the station—and dressy. Made me homesick, she was so like our home-made article.

It is the strangest thing that the world is not full of books that scoff at the pitiful world, and the useless universe and violent, contemptible human race—books that laugh at the whole paltry scheme and deride it. Curious, for millions of men die every year with these feelings in their hearts. Why don't *I* write such a book? Because I have a family. There is no other reason. Was this those other people's reason?

The Larrikins of Sydney and Melbourne used to hail me "Hello, Mark; good night, Mark" and of course I

Man has been called the
laughing animal to distinguish him from the others —
but the monkey laughs; & he has
been called the animal that
weeps — but several of the
others do that. Man is merely
& exclusively the Immodest
Animal, for he is the only one
that covers his nakedness, the
only one with a soiled mind; the
only one ~~degraded~~ under the ~~[illegible]~~
~~degrading~~ dominion of a false shame.

Sunday morning. Six
or eight people who came
over with me in the Paris
the other day. Three or four
of them went up to London
with our multi-millionaire
to be shown his glories.
It was a month ago; but
to this day these men
can think of nothing
else, talk of nothing else.

EXAMPLES OF MARK TWAIN'S NOTEBOOK ENTRIES

Clara says it tires her to
have to keep on "deciding
that she isn't sick" so persistently & so watchfully.

=

New York, May 18/95—noon.

Arrived at 9. Cable from London
says the Tichborne Claimant
has published an affidavit
confessing that he is Arthur
Orton, son of a Wapping
butcher. I was in London
twenty or twenty-two years
ago during his trial for
perjury, & spent an evening
in his society with a number
of his devoted adherents.
He had a marvelous memory.
He played his part well. He was
sent up for 14 years; served his
term, then came over here & was
a bar-tender in the Bowery

SPECIMEN PAGE OF MARK TWAIN'S NOTES

responded. Here in Timoru I have a chance to attend a corner meeting of the Salvation Army and hear their brass music and singing but am deprived; the ungodly on the outskirts hail me friendly, and my stay would not do, unless I were willing to interrupt the Army's work.

The fact that man invented imprisonment for debt, proves that man is an idiot and also that he is utterly vile and malignant. How can a prisoner pay a debt? Was the idea of it to pay the creditor in revenge?

Nov. 27. Livy's birthday. I claimed that her birthday has either passed or is to come; that it is the 27th as the 27th exists in America, not here where we have flung out a day and closed up the vacancy.

Today we reached Gisborn in a big Bay (Poverty Bay) but did not go ashore to lecture. A big sea running. A tub of a steam launch came out turning summersets, and took off 25 and put on about 15 people, men, women and children, in a most primitive basket. Any unskillfulness would have cost lives, but there was none.

Prohibition

What marriage is to morality, a properly conducted licensed liquor traffic is to sobriety.

In fact, the more things are forbidden, the more popular they become.

He embodied these thoughts in an interview he gave to a reporter of thc *Licensing Guardian,* N. S. W.

Mark Twain on Prohibition

(From the *Licensing Guardian*, N.S.W.)

"What do I think of Prohibition?" Nothing, for the simple reason that there is no such thing. When men want drink, they'll have it in spite of all the laws ever passed; when they don't want it, no drink will be sold. Without wanting to know the experience of America, you people in Australia have an object lesson in temperance legislation. There is supposed to be no drink sold on Sundays in Sydney and Melbourne. Yet I, a stranger, can see that plenty of it is sold, that the most inveterate boozer can get all he wants while he is able to pay for it. Now, if Prohibition cannot be enforced on one day of the week, it cannot be enforced all the year round and year after year. If men cannot do without a drink from Saturday night till Monday morning it is certain that they cannot wait longer. The way in which your Sunday-closing law is evaded will give you an idea of the so-called Prohibition districts in America. The front door is closed, but the back is opened; instead of open honest drinking, you have sly boozing; instead of having the traffic under the supervision of the law, and conducted in the interests of order and morality, there is no supervision at all and the trade is conducted under the most demoralizing conditions. The manner in which these absurd liquor laws are broken breeds contempt for law in general. Then, while intensifying, instead of eradicating the evil, these laws give rise to smuggling, and informing and perjury. So now you see why in the States and Canada they are often repealed on the very first opportunity. The only approach to Prohibition I have seen is in those English towns where hotels shut during certain hours. There I've seen thirty customers refused and told to wait until the house legally opened. Such a thing would never have happened in Prohibition Maine, where a man gets served at any hour.

"Ah," sighed our distinguished visitor. "Why don't the temperance agitators remember Edmund Burke's words? Lawful indulgence is the only check on illicit gratification. Abolishing matrimony would not stamp out fornication. Well, what marriage is to morality a properly conducted licensed liquor traffic is to sobriety. In either case a certain human propensity is regulated so as to be a blessing; while left to itself, or subjected to repressive efforts, it would be a curse."

Here Mr. Mark Twain—where is the middle initial of the Yankee name—looked at his watch and said: "Time is pressing; come let us solve the liquor problem in our own way. What are you going to have? Isn't it curious how drink always follows the flag? For instance, I take a cocktail wherever I go. That doesn't suit the British constitution. In those German forests where the British constitution was reared, beer, according to Tacitus, was popular. Here's luck to *The Guardian* and confusion to teetotalism."

Palmerston North. Lectured there, Dec. 2. Club Hotel. Memorable Hotel. Stunning Queen of Sheba style of barmaid, always answered the bell and then got up on her dignity and said—lighting fires, brushing clothes, boots, etc., was the chambermaid's business. Would she please tell the chambermaid? No answer. Exit. Why do you answer the bell?

Sign up saying landlord will not hold himself responsible for baggage. No keys to the door. Drunken loafers making noise downstairs. Said he had keys, but didn't know they was going to be wanted and it would take a long time to sort them out; hadn't any labels or numbers on them. Elderly and not very handsome woman said she'd given up her room if she'd known people was so particular. *She* wasn't afraid to sleep without a key. Got a key at last—midnight.

Early in the morning baby began—pleasantly—didn't mind baby—then the piano, tin kettle, played by either the cat or a partially untrained artist—certainly the most extraordinary music—straight average of three right notes to four wrong ones, but played with eager zeal and gladness—old, old tunes of 40 years ago, such as I heard at Timoru—and considering it was the cat—for it *must* have been the cat—it was really a marvelous performance. It convinces me that a cat is more intelligent than people believe, and can be taught any crime.

Rooms astonishingly small—partitions astonishingly thin—parlor the size and shape of a grand piano. Very funny hotel. Landlord shows lady through with his hat on. Fat, red, ignorant, made of pretty coarse clay, possibly mud.

At Waitukuran, Dec. 2. Stopped 20 minutes for luncheon. I sat at head of table, then Livy, Clara and Smythe. Mirror in front of *them.* But Livy hadn't her glasses on and couldn't see anything in it. I saw two pictures on the distant wall and made up my mind that one of them was the Death of —— Broke into the conversation—"Do you remember when the news came to Paris?"

"Of the killing of the prince?"

"The very words I was going to say. But *what* prince?"

"Napoleon."

There was no conclusion. The picture was *not* his murder—so it was not the picture itself that I conveyed to her but my *notion* of what the picture was.

Dec. 5. Left for Hawera 8 A.M. Yesterday lunatic burst into my parlor and warned me that the Jesuits were going to cook (poison) me, in my food, or kill me on the street at night. Said a mysterious sign was visible upon my posters and meant my death. Said the Century was a Jesuit magazine; that the editors were a man and his two sisters, that they were Jesuit tools and were steeped in carnage and murder. Had written them and so charged them, and they were dumb and could not deny the charge. Saved Haweis's life by warning him that there were three men on his platform who would kill him if he took his eyes off them for a moment during his lecture. He has saved so many lives in 20 years in that way that they put him in the asylum.

Lectured.

In the "Garden Region" they never had a drought; the grass is green and fat the year round. The grass is the only beauty we saw today. The country looks like one vast clearing—covered, stretch after stretch, with prone and charred great trees and vast roots—little frame cottages old and paintless, sprinkled about the distances, also a sprinkling of neat, new-painted ones. Settlement was retarded by Maori hostilities, but peace has reigned for years, now, and the government lands have been thrown open for occupation.

Plenty dogs attend my lectures. They have had a fight only once, at Omoru. At Napier, sign up, "Dogs positively forbidden in the dress circle." Tacit permission to fill up the rest of the house.

Inscription on Monument

"Who fell in defense of law and order against fanaticism and barbarism." i.e.—Patriotism. This is the most comical monument in the whole earth. Try to imagine the humorless deeps of stupidity of the idiot who composed that inscription—and the dullness of the people who don't see the satire.

Small earthquake this morning. Not enough to shake down the church bell.

In Rome along at first you are full of regrets that Michael Angelo died; but by and by you only regret that you didn't *see* him do it.

It is often the case that a man who can't tell a lie thinks that he is the best judge of one.

We are all inconsistent. We are offended and resent it when people do not respect us; and yet no man, deep down in the privacy of his heart, has any considerable respect for *himself*.

Dec. 13, Friday, 1895. Sailed from Wellington, New Zealand, today at 3:15 P.M. in the Mararoa. (Returning to Australia.)

Now let us have a storm, and a heavy one. This is the damnest menagerie of mannerless children I have ever gone to sea with.

In the past year have read Vicar of Wakefield and some of Jane Austen. Thoroughly artificial.

Back to Australia

Tuesday, Dec. 17. Reached Sydney 9 A.M. Day before yesterday it was full Sydney summer—95 in the shade, and as hot as 115 at Horsham. Then came a "burster"—kind of hurricane—out of the south—the twin of the Texas "Norther"—and knocked the mercury down 36 degrees in four hours. The dust blew. It will be cool weather now for a spell.

Rain. Praying subject up again. Rev. Dr. Strong has been trying to explain why prayers for rain are not a proper sort to make. The usual result: a nest of ignorant hornets waked up—violent, vituperative, insulting people. One of them quotes passages from the New Testament to show that what thing soever a righteous Christian prays for, *he will get it*—otherwise God would be violating his contract. Then almost in the next sentence this logician says—"God reserves the privilege of exercising His own judgment as to which things prayed for He will grant."

Went to see "For the Term of His Natural Life." Even when the chain gangs were humorous they were still a most pathetic sight. The play goes far to enable one to realize that old convict life—invented in hell and carried out by Christian devils.

Thursday, Dec. 19. En route for Scone. War scare between England and America.

The war scare. A few days ago among the cables was: "The Board of Trade has cabled the N. Y. Chamber of Commerce: 'Pleasure boats will not be allowed to obstruct the movements of the British warships.' Reply of Chamber of Commerce: 'We hope your warships will be better than your yachts.'"

Nobody saw the first joke till the latter was cabled two days later, then there was a shout.

Monday, Dec. 23, 1895. Sailed from Sydney for Ceylon (via Melbourne, Adelaide, etc.) in the P. & O. steamer Oceana, at 1 P.M.

Twenty male and female cranks—rivals of the Salvationists—in no uniform but waterproofs (it was raining) sang hymns on the dock, and a man (this seems to be the main feature of both organizations) begged contributions, walking back and forth and holding his hat up toward the passengers. As he moved away they sang the Doxology.

Lascar crew in this ship, first I have seen. White costume, like petticoat and pants—barefoot—red shawl for belt—straw cap, brimless, on head, with red scarf around it. They are rich dark brown, with short straight black hair; whiskers fine and silky and jet black.

Shipped about £200 to Mr. Rogers through Mr. Gibb's bank, at Sydney.

From time to time in the Australian notes he undertakes poetry descriptive of the picturesque Australian animal life. Example:

Land of the Ornithorhynchus,
  Land of the kangaroo,
Old ties of heredity link us,

Here he pauses for breath and to dig up a rhyme, apparently without success, for presently he proceeds:

Land of the fruitful rabbit,
  Land of the boomerang,

Another pause, equally hopeless, then

Come forth from thy oozy couch,
  Oh Ornithorhynchus dear,
And greet with a cordial claw,
  The stranger that longs to hear
From thy own lips the tale
  Of thy origin all unknown.
Thy bone where flesh should be
  And flesh where should be bone.
And fin of fish where should be paw.
  And beaver trowel tail,
And lungs of beast and teeth of beast,
  Where gills ought *to* prevail.

Come, kangaroo, the good and true,
  Foreshortened as to legs,
And body tapered like a churn,
  And sack marsupial fegs;
And tell us why you linger here
  Thou relic of a vanished time,
When all your friends as fossils sleep,
  Immortalized in rhyme.

New Years, 1896. Sailed at noon for Ceylon.

Jan. 4. Lying in roadstead at Albany all day. At seven strong breeze, got up the anchor. Small pilot in elaborately gold-laced uniform, stood by our giant uniformed Captain on the bridge and began a fine piece of seamanship. Our stern pointed straight at the head of the narrow buoyed channel; we set a jib to help and turned around in our tracks in spite of the strong wind.

In the Indian Ocean

Plenty cats on board. Carlyle Smythe [his agent] says it is British law that they must be carried. Instances case of a ship not allowed to sail till she sent for a couple of cats and the bill came: two cats 20 shillings.

The jackass (bird) laughed for us. Vulture, red, bald, queer, sloped head, featherless, red places here and there on body, intense great black eyes, set in red featureless rim, dissipated look. A businesslike style, a selfish, conscienceless, murderous, aspect. The very look of a professional assassin, and yet a bird which does no murder.

One must say it very softly, but the truth is that the native Australian is as vain of his unpretty country as if it were the final masterpiece of God, achieved by Him from designs by that Australian. He is as sensitive about her as men are of sacred things—can't bear to have critical things said about her.

Jan. 6. At midnight went to sleep with eight bells in my ear; slept; woke and heard two bells; slept, woke and heard four bells; slept, woke, heard seven bells; slept, woke and heard one bell; slept, woke, heard two bells, and the bugle call to breakfast. Took my coffee in bed—kind of a fool of a night.

He mislays his notebooks from time to time, now, and his notes get rather mixed, in consequence. We shall try, however, to straighten them.

Jan. 6, '96. In the Indian Ocean

Some ungoverned children on board. The irritating thing about ungoverned children is that they often make as orderly and valuable men and women as do the other kind.

What an eventless existence life at sea on a long summer voyage is. No life visible; now and then a school of porpoises; and at intervals a solitary albatross; once a week a ship, far away. Peace, everlasting peace, and tranquillity. But it is infinitely comfortable and satisfying. Before we see land again it is possible that we and the English and Australians on board will have been war enemies for sometime without knowing it. However, a ship is a world of its own—one does not trouble himself about other worlds and their affairs.

There are canaries in this ship, also cats—but the cats get no proper chance.

Jan. 8 Wednesday. At noon yesterday we crossed the 100 meridian of East Longitude. The sun was directly overhead.

The more I see of modern marine architecture and engineering the more I am dissatisfied with Noah's Ark. It was admirably unfitted for the service required of it. Nobody but a farmer could have designed such a thing, for such a purpose.

This is the best library I have seen in a ship yet. I must read that devilish Vicar of Wakefield again. Also Jane Austen.

On this voyage I have read a number of novels. Prince Otto—full of brilliancies of course—plenty of exquisite phrasing—an easy flowing tale, but—well, my sympathies were not with any of the people in it, I did not care whether any of them prospered or not. There is a fault somewhere; it could have been in me.

Jan. 8. Lat. 20—30 S: Lon. 100—26E. Every mile northward adds to the heat now. Today is roasting hot. Linen will be put on tomorrow, no doubt. Punkas started today; strips of cloth they hang above the tables and are kept in motion by Indian boys who pull the ropes. Very good fan.

The sea is a splendid Mediterranean blue today with a delicate but pronounced copper tint on the shady side of the waves. This is ideal sailing—long, slow, gentle rocking of the ship, soothing and lulling as a cradle motion, the atmosphere filled with peace and far-from-the-worldness —just enough breeze to keep your fat from melting and running down and greasing your clothes.

The porpoise is the clown of the sea—evidently does his wild antics for pure fun; there is no sordid profit in it.

How curiously unanecdotical the Colonials and ship-going English are. I believe I haven't told an anecdote or heard one since I left America. But Americans, when grouped, drop into anecdotes as soon as they get a little acquainted. Come to think, I *have* started an anecdote once or twice, but didn't finish it. One is pretty sure to be interrupted, and with a remark which is foreign to the subject and is a quite thorough extinguisher. Which is well enough, for the interrupter goes right ahead, and you couldn't get in again if you wanted to.

Zangwill's "Master" is done in good English—what a rare thing good English is! and the grammar is good, too —and what a very, very rare thing that is! The characters are real, they are flesh and blood, they are definite; one knows what they will do in nearly any given set of circumstances. And when there is an incident, an episode, it comes about in a natural way, and happens just as it would happen in actual life.

Swore off from profanity early this morning. I was on deck in the peaceful dawn, the calm and holy dawn. Went down dressed, bathed, put on white linen, shaved—a long, hot, troublesome job, and no profanity. Then started to breakfast. Remembered my tonic—first time in three months without being told—poured it in a measuring-glass, held bottle in one hand, it in the other, the cork in my teeth—reached up and got a tumbler—measuring-glass sprang out of my fingers—got it, poured out another dose, first setting the tumbler on washstand—just got it poured, ship lurched, heard a crash behind me—it was the tumbler, broken into millions of fragments, but the bottom hunk whole—picked it up to throw out of the open port, threw out the measuring-glass instead—then I released my voice. Mrs. C. behind me in the door: "Don't reform any more, it isn't any improvement."

To the smoking-room—an interminable trip through a dark tunnel to the second saloon—a lady showed me the way—up two flights along canvas-roofed deck, a dart across the bridge, a spring through a ray of rain for the smoking-room door—made it without catching a drop—slipped on a grating and fell sprawling on the swimming deck—the reform interrupted again.

CHAPTER XXIV

Ceylon and India

SATURDAY, Jan. 18. Arrived at Colombo about five days ago—I with a very bad cough. Exhausted by four P.M., went to bed in Bristol Hotel.

The most amazing varieties of nakedness and color and all harmonious and fascinating. Ingredients—shining black body, nine-tenths naked, one or more bright colored rags and you have the perfection of dress—grace, combined with convenience, comfort, beauty.

Presently into this intoxicating whirl and drift and confusion of lovely colors and beautiful forms an offensive discord is included—twelve prim little pious Christian black girls, marching two and two from a missionary school, and dressed precisely as they would be dressed on a summer Sunday in an English or American village.

It would be difficult to match this thing for the two qualities of surprise and shock. A promising way to do it would be to discharge a flock of these nearly nude Singalese into the midst of the grave and proper church drift of an American or English town on a Sunday morning.

"Papa salaam, papa,"—a poor little girl touching my foot—pretty little beggar girl. Beggar boy said, "How do, Father."

The only entirely nude person was a black boy of three or four, and even his nudity was not absolute, for he had a piece of string around his middle.

News at Colombo from Dec. 23 to Jan. 14, Dr. Jameson had been defeated and captured and Krüger had magnanimously turned him over to his own queen for punishment. Cecil Rhodes, Premier, had resigned (his deportation had been demanded by Krüger) and had said in a speech at Kimberley that his career was not ended, it was just beginning.

Bombay, Jan. 20. Been shut up all the time with this infernal cough. It does not improve. I wish it was in hell.

The hotel noises begin about five in the morning. Hindu servants yelling orders to each other from story to story. It is equal to a riot and insurrection for noise. And there are other noises—roofs falling in, windows smashing, persons being murdered, crows squawking, canaries screeching, fiendish bursts of laughter, explosions of dynamite. By seven o'clock one has suffered all the different kinds of shock there are and can never more be disturbed by them either isolated or in combination, then the noises all stop for hours.

Servant, Brampy, beautiful black hair, combed back like a woman and knotted at the back of head—tortoise-shell comb, sign he is a Singalese—small mustache—jacket—under it a white gown from neck to heels—I did not like to undress unless his back was turned.

Bombay[1]

When we arrived in this hotel the manager, a German, came up to see our room, with three native servants to see to arranging things. A vast glazed door opening upon a balcony needed opening or cleaning or closing or something. A native went at it and seemed to be doing it well enough, but not to the manager's mind. He didn't state that fact, or explain where the defect was, but briskly gave him a cuff and *then* an arrogant word of explanation or command. The native took the shameful treatment with

[1] See *Following the Equator*.

meekness, saying nothing and not showing in his face or manner any resentment. I had not seen the like of this for fifty years. It carried me instantly back to my boyhood and flashed upon me the forgotten fact that this was the *usual* way of explaining one's desires to a slave. I was able to remember that the method seemed to me right and natural in those days. I being born to it and unaware that elsewhere there were other methods; but I was also able to remember that those unresented cuffings made me sorry for the victim and ashamed for the punisher. My father was a refined and kindly gentleman, very grave, rather austere, of rigid probity, a sternly just and upright man, albeit he attended no church and never spoke of religious matters and had no part or lot in the pious joys of his Presbyterian family, nor ever seemed to suffer from this deprivation. He laid his hand upon me in punishment only twice in his life and then not heavily: once for telling a lie, which surprised me and showed me how unsuspicious he was, for I knew I had told him a million before that. He punished me only those two times and never any other member of the family at all, yet he commonly cuffed our harmless slave boy Lewis for any little blunder or awkwardness and even gave him a lashing now and then which terrified the poor thing nearly out of his wits. My father had passed his life among his slaves, from his cradle up, and his cuffings proceeded from the customs of the times, not from his nature. When I was ten I saw a man fling a lump of iron ore at his slaveman in anger—for merely doing something awkwardly, as if that were a crime. It bounded from his skull and the man fell and never spoke again. He was dead in an hour. I knew the man had a right to kill his slave if he wanted to, and yet it seemed a pitiful thing, and somehow wrong, though *why* wrong I was not deep enough to explain if I had been asked to do it. Nobody in the village approved of that murder, but of course no one said much about it.

Jan. 22. Invited with the family to lunch with Lord Sandhurst, Governor of Bombay, of Government House, Malaber Point, tomorrow. I knew him in London years ago. Had to decline—not able to go out before the lecture day after tomorrow, lest my cough jump on me again.

Sunday, Jan. 26, 1896. Bombay. It was Mr. Gandhi (delegate to Chicago World's Fair Congress of Religions) who explained everything to us yesterday at the Jain Temple.

Our good Mahatma of later years.

From there went to the house of a wealthy Parsee, to assist at a gathering in honor of Knighthood being conferred upon H.H. The Prince of Palitana.

Huzzas outside announced arrival of Prince. Large stately man, ropes of pearls and green rubies (?) around his neck—the very ideal of an Indian Prince. The young prince with him had been to the Chicago Fair.

Preparing his book, "Following the Equator" Mark Twain spoke of these "green rubies." Mrs. Clemens going through the manuscript, noted:

Perhaps you don't care, but whoever told you that the Prince's green stones were rubies told an untruth. They were superb emeralds. Those strings of pearls and emeralds were famous all over Bombay.

To which note Mark Twain added:

All right, I'll make them emeralds, but it loses force. Green rubies is a fresh thing. And besides it was one of the Prince's own staff liars that told me.

Sunday we lunched at Governor's House with their Excellencies the Governor and Lady Sandhurst; and at 4 P.M. visited the Towers of Silence with three Parsee gentlemen. Five towers. One 300 years old—the first built —and small.

An adult funeral passed along, the bearers roped together with white, the mourners following, then the dog. Later a child.

Row of vultures fringed the top of the lower wall. When the iron gate was opened and the corpse carried in, Clara and Smythe had a glimpse through the distant iron door of the vultures flying down in.

On top of a tall cocoa shaft (topless) stood a vulture—looked like an intentional ornament.

I was not feeling well and thought something must be the matter with my liver. I consulted a physician—a highly celebrated man with a quaint English all his own.

"It is not that your liver were in disorder, but some of your other guts."

Then he continued—"In this country I would that one shall take care not of one gut alone but of all his guts, including the heart. Let him do this and he shall not be conscious ever that he ails—which is to say he shall never think to show that he has any guts at all."

Two interesting hours with Prince Kumar Shri of Pulitana, and his young son and little daughter,—along with Merriweather. The others saw the Rani, his wife—she never goes out of the house, of course. She is a fluent speaker of English.

Jan. 31, Baroda: Lectured in the great hall of the palace where the Durbars are held. The Gaikwar Resident, and 200 guests, 4:30 P.M. (Great King.)

Saw the elephants etc., but failed—quite unnecessarily —to get to the Jewel House five minutes distant. It is claimed here that no monarch in the world can match this mass of magnificence.

The Maharani was behind the screen, up high--at the lecture—with two ladies of her household.

This is the romance: About 15 years ago Great Britain deposed the Gaikwar (family name, not a title) for cause, and imprisoned him at Madras—then looked around for a substitute. Good deal of a hunt—heirs were scarce; but found the nearest heirs in three little brothers, obscure peasants making mud pies in the village and having a good time accordingly. G.B. did not appoint the eldest—a little too old to be molded, maybe; nor the youngest—too long in minority; took the middle one. The eldest is now Commander in Chief of the Gaikwar's forces, and the youngest is in England studying for the bar. He will be a judge here some day, no doubt.

The G. is a fine and cultivated gentleman—been to Europe five times. I liked this palace, but not the new one.

Three long gray apes capered across the road.

Train of laden camels—the only creature in the world never seen in a wild state and whose original habitat is not known.

Good library in the palace—my books there, you see.

"Your American threats of war we merely smile at." Speech of an English lady (who is a little ignorant of history) to Mrs. Clemens. I should have quoted the Revolution (2,000,000 against 10,000,000) now 70 against 45.

The gold cannon is solid—a Gaikwar made it to get ahead of his predecessor who had made the silver one. They are six-pounders, or four-pounders, or somewhere along there. They have thin steel cores and are used for salutes at mighty intervals, and not heavily loaded.

Slept all the way back to Bombay—10 P.M. till 7 A.M. Our own bedding and towels.

Some unthinking people criticise Adam—find fault with him because he was weak, and yielded. Oh, that is not fair, that is not right. He hadn't had any experience. We have had ages and ages of experience and tuition—we who criticise him and yet see what we are—just see what *we* are when there is any forbidden fruit around. I have been around a good deal, but I have never been in any place where that apple would be safe—except Allahabad. Why, it is the *prohibition* that *makes* anything precious. There is a charm about the forbidden that makes it unspeakably desirable. It was not that Adam ate the apple for the apple's sake, but because it was forbidden. It would have been better for us—oh infinitely better for us—if the *serpent* had been forbidden.

Consider the patience of these poor people. At seven this morning I went around the long veranda of this hotel to see Smythe, and by a door I saw a Hindu manservant squatting, waiting to be on call. He had polished his master's yellow shoes and now had nothing to put in the time with. He was barefooted, the morning cold, the tiles frozen. There he sits now, just as before, waiting—9 A.M.

Not more than a tenth of the Ganges's bed has water in it. Great crowd of natives and huts and flags on that sandspit. It is the fag end and finish of the great January meet, when two million natives swarm to Allahabad to bathe in the sacred waters.

A sick man was carried by in a palanquin—the dirty Ganges bath has healing powers.

All the way yesterday was through parched land, sown

thick with mud villages in all stages of crumbling decay. It is a sorrowful land—a land of unimaginable poverty and hardship.

Thought this would all become commonplace in a week; three weeks of it have only enhanced its fascinations. I think I should always like to wait an hour for my train in India.

If we had got to the Mele this morning we might have seen a man who hasn't sat down for years; another who has held his hands above his head for years and never trims his nails or hair, both very long; another who sits with his bare foot resting upon a lot of sharp spikes—and all for the glory of God. Human beings seem to be a poor invention. If they are the noblest work of God where is the ignoblest?

Four cramped little palanquins at the railroad station, said to contain Hindu ladies—dirty cotton, or duck, boxes, shut up tight all around so nobody can see in—the person must sit up in there, she can't lie down. There they stood in the sun, waiting, the bearers standing by.

Feb. 8. Today and yesterday lay abed and starved a cold. This evening went to Belvidere and dined with the Lieut. Governor of Bengal—Sir Alexander MacKenzie and a dozen—private dinner party.

Calcutta, Feb. 12. Packed theater.

Calcutta, Feb. 13. Packed house—jammed.

Bought a silver mug for my niche as one of the founders of the Players, New York.

No bells in the room. The servant lies by your door nights, on the stone floor.

Barney is slow and not sure. Mousa is quick, and not sure. Barney was to put a glass of water on my stage table. He seemed to understand perfectly after I had explained, behind the scenes, four times and pointed to the stage. What he finally did was to put a vast empty glass on the stage and a full one behind the scenes.

Big concerns have a little one-horse conveyance for each clerk. Nobody walks in the hot months.

Feb. 14, 4:30 P.M. Left Calcutta for Darjeeling in the official car of Mr. Barclay, Chief of Traffic. Till dark through rich vegetation. Rush, coco and bamboo.

Feb. 15. Sound sleep all night. Up early refreshed. Put on double suit of flannels—bright and frosty. What a gushing spray of delicate greenery a bunch of bamboo is!!

Everybody is plowing—and numerous—these villages. They are but 300 yards apart. There are dozens of them in sight all the time. In effect this is one mighty city made up of villages—a city of hundreds of miles long and broad and contains a population of from 200 to 300 millions. The biggest city I was ever in.

India the Marvelous!

What a garden Bengal is! Heard in the smoking-room on ship that most self-complaisant of all poems—"Greenland's Icy Mountains"—"They call us to deliver their land from error's chains." The call was never made.

When that hymn was written there were 1,200,000,000 of deeply religious heathen in the globe and 12,000,000 Christians—i.e. genuine, ardent Christians. It was this tail that was proposing to wag that dog. It has not wagged it. In forty million years it will not wag it. It has never made the faintest impression, missionarying, upon those vast bodies of heathen—never can in the very nature of things. In all history, go back as far as you will no nation has ever changed its religion by persuasion, but only by compulsion—by a king's command. Kings can't do that now and so the missionary business is played out. Traitors to religion are of the same stuff as other traitors, the poorest material in the camp.

And this is India! Tropical, beautiful, and just alive with villages.

One everlasting stretch of naked men and boys plowing the field, but not a woman or a girl—not one! Come, let us introduce Austrian, Bavarian and French civilization, and Christianity, right away.

"Where every prospect pleases and only man is vile." That described India and it also describes the average Christian.

Feb. 21. Left for Lucknow about 1 P.M. Hot as the nation. The flat plains the color of pale dust, and the dust flying. Tiffin at two at Janpur City. No doubt all these old native grayheads remember the mutiny.

Sunday, 23d. Drove with Major and Mrs. Aylmer (16th Lancers) and Capt. and Mrs. Dallas, in the regimental drag over the whole of Colin Campbell's march, and also out to the Imam Bara.

Was dined by the United Service in the ancient and elegant Chutter Munzil Palace (umbrella palace)—very large—it is the Club's Sumptuous Home. In my speech quoted what Walcott said lately in the Senate about England.

Major Aylmer's native orderly, in uniform, brought the invitation, riding on a picturesquely dressed camel—a stately sight.

Agra, Feb. 28. Mousa was drunk again last night; second time in two weeks. At midnight was sleeping like a log on the marble steps of the great portico with his head on the bare flags.

Lectured; drove from there—two carriages full—to the Taj Mahal, arriving at 11:30—clear sky and splendid full moon. At that moment, to our surprise, an eclipse began and in an hour was total—an attention not before offered to a stranger since the Taj was built. Attempts were made to furnish an eclipse for the Prince of Wales in 1876, and in recent years to 20 other princes of that house, but without success. However, Col. Lock, Political Agent, has much more influence than any of his predecessors have had.

At noon gave Mousa a note to carry to Smythe and bring an answer and told him he could consider himself discharged at 7 this evening. He laid his fingers against his forehead as usual, made the usual inclination, gently said—"Wair good" (very good) just as he always does when receiving an order, and that was all. Turned and went about his errand. In his noiseless barefeet—it was pathetic. Was it Indian fatalism which accepts without murmur whatever the two million gods send, or had he had this experience so often that it no longer affects him?

Mousa had apparently a bad attack of fever in Lucknow before he got drunk. Livy was full of compassion and gave him a teaspoonful of liquid hell-fire—quinine. Six hours later he turned up and she offered him another dose. He said gravely, "Scoose me—no sick no more." She and Clara beseeched, but he only said, "Scoose me," putting his fingers to his forehead and making his humble bow. If he has had any fever since he has concealed it.

March 19. Susy's birthday—24 years old. [Note—

added later: "and we did not know that it was to be her last."]

By all accounts England is the home of pious cant; and cant of a most harmful sort. Gen. Sir William —— told me that more than half the hospital contents all over India is syphilis; bad, very bad cases; these fine hearty young fellows come out here to defend England and England makes no provision for their natural passion—infamously betrays them to their destruction, knowing her treachery, but afraid to go in the face of cant. Then those 70,000 young men go home and marry fresh young English girls and transmit a heritage of disease to their children and grandchildren.

Clean women subject to rigid inspection ought to be kept for these soldiers. Any other course is treachery to the soldiers.

This B. I. Company had a dead python landed once. A year later this ship brought one to Calcutta zoo. Our Captain was instructed to see for himself that this one was alive before he accepted it. The man, a half-caste, said, yes he was alive; and opened the door of the box and gave the snake a punch with an old umbrella and asked him to show up. The snake snatched the umbrella and made a rush, and showed up on deck—forty feet long and as big as a barrel. Everybody went aloft, but the half-caste said: "There's no harm in him, he just had a feed that will last him two years; come a couple of you and take him by the tail and help me steer him into the box." Which they did without trouble.

For six hours now it has been impossible to realize that this is India and the Hoogli (river). No, every few miles we see a great white columned European house standing in front of the vast levels, with a forest away back—La. planter? And the thatched groups of native houses have turned themselves into the negro quarters, familiar to me near forty years ago—and so for six hours this has been the sugar coast of the Mississippi.

March 27. We have slept on deck these two nights. Very hot, and mosquitoes troublesome elsewhere.

CHAPTER XXV

Leaving India

To Mauritius via Madras and Colombo

March 28, '96 at sea.

Our Captain is a handsome Hercules; young, resolute, manly, and has a huge great splendid head, a satisfaction to look at. He has this odd peculiarity: he cannot tell the truth in a plausible way. He is the very opposite of the austere Scot who sits midway on the table: he cannot tell a lie in an *un*plausible way. When the Captain finishes a statement, the passengers glance at each other privately, as who would say—"Do you believe that?" When the Scot finishes one, the look says—"How strange and interesting." The whole secret is in the matter and method of the two men. The Captain is a little shy and diffident, and he states the simplest fact as if he were a little afraid of it, while the Scot delivers himself of the most atrocious lie with such an air of stern veracity that one is forced to believe it although he knows it isn't so. For instance: the Captain told how he carried home 62 children under seven, one voyage, nearly all of them bad, ungoverned creatures, because they had been allowed all their little lives to abuse and insult the native servants; and how a boy of seven was shoving a boy of three overboard one day when the Captain caught the victim by the leg and saved him—then slapped the persecutor, and straightway got a couple of stinging slaps himself from the persecutor's mother. The private comment among the ladies at the table was "Do you really believe she slapped him?"

Presently the Scot told how he caught a shark down on

the frozen shores of the Antarctic Continent, and the natives took the shark away from him and cut it open, and began to take out cigars and hair-brushes and hymn books and cork screws and revolvers and other things belonging to a missionary who had been missed from the Friendly Islands three years before; and when he demanded a share of the find the natives laughed in his face and would give him no part of it except a sodden wad of crumpled paper. But this paper turned out to be a lottery ticket, and with it the Scot afterward collected a prize of 500,000 francs in Paris. Everybody agreed that this was "remarkable and interesting," but nobody tried to throw any doubt upon it.

The Captain told how a maniac chased him round and round the mainmast one day with an ax, until he was nearly exhausted, and at last the racket brought the mate up from below who threw a steamer chair in the way, the maniac stumbled over it and fell, then the mate jumped on his back and got the ax away from him, and the Captain's life was saved. There was nothing unreasonable or unlikely about this, yet the Captain told it in such an unplausible way that it was plain nobody believed him.

Presently the Scot told about a pet flying-fish he once owned, that lived in a little fountain in his conservatory and supported itself by catching birds and frogs in the neighboring field. He was believed. He is always believed, yet he never tells anything but lies; whereas the Captain is never believed, although he never tells a lie, so far as I can judge.

My own luck has been curious all my literary life; I never could tell a lie anybody would doubt, or a truth anyone would believe.

> On the voyage from Australia Mark Twain had read some fascinating books on ant life, by Sir John Lubbock.

In Jeypoor I tried several of Sir John Lubbock's experiments, and got results similar to his. Then I tried some experiments of my own. These latter proved that the ant is peculiarly intelligent in the higher concerns of life. I constructed four miniature houses of worship—a Mohammedan mosque, a Hindu temple, a Jewish synagogue, and a Christian cathedral, and placed them in a row. I then marked 15 ants with red paint and turned them loose. They made several trips to and fro, glancing in at the several places of worship, but not entering. I turned loose 15 more, painted blue. They acted just as the red ones had done. I now gilded 15 and turned them loose. No change in result: the 45 traveled back and forth in an eager hurry, persistently and continuously, visiting each fane but never entering. This satisfied me that these ants were without religious prejudices—just what I wished; for under no other condition would my next and greater experiment be valuable.

I now placed a small square of white paper within the door of each fane; upon the mosque paper I put a pinch of putty, upon the temple paper a dab of tar, upon the synagogue paper a trifle of turpentine, and upon the cathedral paper a small cube of sugar. First I liberated the red ants. They examined and rejected the putty, the tar and the turpentine, and then took to the sugar with zeal and apparently sincere conviction. I next liberated the blue ants, they did exactly as the red ones had done. The gilded ants followed. The preceding results were precisely repeated. This seemed to prove beyond question that ants destitute of religious prejudices will always prefer Christianity to any of the other great creeds.

However, to make sure I removed the ants and put putty in the cathedral and sugar in the mosque. I now liberated the ants in a body and they rushed tumultuously to the cathedral. I was very much touched and gratified and went in the back room to write down the event; but when I came back the ants had all apostatized and gone over to the Mohammedan communion. I said that I had been too hasty in my conclusions, and naturally felt rebuked and humbled. With diminished confidence I went on with the test to the finish. I placed the sugar first in one house of worship, then another, till I had tried them all. With this result: that whatever church I put the sugar in, that was the one that the ants straightway joined. This was true, beyond shadow of a doubt, that in religious matters the ant is the opposite of man: for man cares for but one thing, to find the Only True Church; whereas the ant hunts for the one with the sugar in it.

I suppose that a missionary passes some of the bitterest hours that men are called upon to suffer in this life; hours heavy with self-reproach, humiliation, remorse; hours wherein the one side of his nature rises in revolt against the other side; where his heart fights against his head; where his duty comes into collision with his humanity. For he is but a man, like the rest, with the instincts and feelings common to his race. He must often feel a deep compassion for the parents whose heart he is breaking when he beguiles their children from the religion which those parents love and honor and leads them into paths which they regard as perilous, and puts upon them the shame of treachery and apostasy. It must be that sometimes the missionary is a parent himself and has suffered what he is now inflicting. And he will remember how careful he was to shield his children from religious influences foreign to his creed; how particular he was to see that the teachers were of the right theological tint before he trusted them in any school; how promptly he dismissed a servant, sometime or other, when he found out that that servant was a propagandist for another creed.

He will argue that the cases differ: that the servant was robbing his child of salvation, but that he is bringing salvation to this man's children. Then he will remember that *he* was the judge in the case of his child, and so he must allow this man to be judge in the case of *his* children. He cannot claim a right which he denies to another man.

However, when the missionary's field is the terrible New Guinea his self-reproaches are probably mild and infrequent. For his work there has had such benignant results that they must furnish balm for his troubled spirit. A few extracts from "New Guinea"—a missionary record, will support this proposition:

"When we first landed here the natives lived only to fight, and the victory was celebrated by a cannibal feast. Great was the chief who claimed many skulls; and the youth who wore a jawbone as an amulet was to be admired.

"Mr. Chalmers pointed out the spot where a Pari lad was killed and partly devoured by crocodiles. The widowed mother, the sisters and others relatives, ate raw the part saved, to evince their love to the deceased! . . ."

Now the tale changes; the missionary came in 1878. They labored for years. With this result:

"From this date there has been no fighting or killing all along the coast."

One of the circus men told me that in the Dutch settlements in Sumatra the soldiers' barracks are visited twice a week by women sent by the government, after inspection. A British General said that such a thing would raise a tempest in England, and cannot be ventured, although it is as much England's duty to provide safe women for the soldiers as it is to provide wholesome food for them. Half the soldiers in hospital are diseased. They go home and marry healthy girls and disease them.

The North American squaw straps her baby to a board and carries it over her back by a strap around her forehead; the Hindu and many savages carry baby astride the hip; these Malay nurses aboard pass a scarf over right shoulder and under left arm and baby sits in it as in a swing and folds his arms and head on nurse's shoulder and sleeps in great comfort. The best way yet of carrying a baby, after it is born.

The only way one can get even a dim idea of the tangled mystery of caste is to imagine it among one's friends, and hear gossips say:

"Archie Jackson has degraded the cotton thread; he has drunk from Alec Peterson's ice-pitcher, and been excommunicated and ostracized by the Daggetts and Barnards and Whitakers and all that caste. Dick Taylor has been caught listening to the reading of the Bible and has been branded on his terminus and exiled to Kalamazoo."

The upper castes regard us as the dirty peoples. Dirty is the right word; it accurately described what the Hindu thinks of us. Of course we must be disgusting objects to him; of course we often turn his stomach. He washes his garments *every day*; we come into his presence in coat, vest and breeches that have never been in the wash since they left the tailor's hands; they are stale with ancient sweat, tobacco smoke and so on. No doubt he says "Ugh!" and retches; but his feelings are not allowed to show outside, for he is a courteous being.

You say the Hindus are unspeakably indecent in their language—the grown people and the children alike. If they so earnestly desire to be cleanly, why do they do that?

Because according to their standard such things are not objectionable. Also, according to their standard lying is not a sin. They all lie and think it no evil. Another thing, you have noticed from the car windows that they publicly and without embarrassment indulge in various habits which to us are forbidden. By their standard this is no offense. In Japan formerly both sexes bathed naked in public. The newly arrived white people were disgusted. The innocent Japanese said—"What dirty minds these white people have." By their social creed all the details of the body were worthy of respect since the gods made them and no detail of it is contemptible or indecent. Each race determines for itself what indecencies are. Nature knows no indecencies; man invents them.

At Sea

How seldom one glances at the sea on this voyage. We sit on the promenade deck under the awnings from 7 A.M. till 11 P.M. and sometimes upon going to bed I realize that I have not consciously seen the sea the whole day.

The creatures that fly are by far the Lord's most important creation. He has provided for them a domain (home) forty miles deep which envelops the whole globe. The creatures that live in salt water are next in importance. He has provided for them a domain some miles deep which covers three-fifths of the globe's surface. Next in importance is Man, for to man he has given the skin which thinly covers two-fifths of the globe's surface. On one-fifth of it he can raise snow, icicles, sand, rocks, and nothing else; and on the other fifth he can raise enough food to keep his race alive, but it takes hard grubbing to do it, and then the weather that he must fight—the drought, the flood, the hail, the hurricane.

Macauley speaks of the public executioner's "odious" office. If it is an odious office, then of necessity the law that creates the office is an odious law, the law that creates death penalties is an odious law, the jury that applies the law penalty is an odious institution and the judge who pronounces the death sentence exercises an odious function; and the entire lot are legitimate objects of contempt and obliquy. Sanely examined, the offices of commanding generals and public executioners are in one detail identical; the one kills the public enemy by command of the law and for the country's good; the other does exactly the same thing for the same reason. If the one office is honorable it is irrational to deny that the other is likewise so. If you can contrive to prove that the one office is odious, contemptible, disreputable, you will find that you have proved the same of the other and that there is no honest way of getting out of this difficulty.

This is a good time to read up on scientific matters and improve the mind. For about us is the peace of the great deep. It invites dreams to study, to reflection. Seventeen days ago this ship sailed out of Calcutta and ever since barring a day or two in Ceylon there has been nothing in sight but a tranquil blue sea and a cloudless blue sky. All down the Bay of Bengal it was so; it was so on the equator, it is still so here in the vast solitudes of the Indian Ocean; 17 days of heaven, and in 11 more it will end. There will be one passenger who will be sorry. One reads all day long in this delicious air of course. Today I have again been storing up knowledge from Sir John Lubbock about the ant. The thing which has struck me most and most astonishingly is the ant's extraordinary powers of identification—memory of its friend's person.

The sermon yesterday morning had in it one of those old timers—one of those sillinesses—which the pulpit used to get eloquent over very frequently:—Christ gave His life for our race. Could a man be found who could do such a thing? Millions of men and millions of women have done more; they have freely given their lives to save even individuals who were in danger—and risked eternal damnation when they did it; for they rushed to the rescue without first squaring up their sin account with God.

Every volunteer in the army offers his life to save his country or his country's honor, and does it on the chance that his death may land him in hell, not on the great white throne, which was Christ's sure destination. For men to throw their lives away for other people's sake is one of the commonest events in our everyday history. It is ludicrous to see the Church make something fine out of the only instance of it where nothing was risked that was of consequence, for nothing was involved but a few hours of pain; and every girl takes a risk superior to that when she marries and subjects herself to the probable pains of childbirth, indefinitely repeated.

There seems to be nothing connected with the atonement scheme that is rational. If Christ was God, He is in the attitude of One whose anger against Adam has grown so uncontrollable in the course of ages that nothing but a sacrifice of life can appease it, and so without noticing how illogical the act is going to be, God condemns Himself to death—commits suicide on the cross, and in this ingenious way wipes off that old score. It is said that the ways of God are not like ours. Let us not contest this point.

If Christ was God, then the crucifixion is without dignity. It is merely ridiculous, for to endure several hours' pain is nothing heroic in God, in any case.

> A paragraph or two of this entry has been omitted, being a repetition of what he has said elsewhere.

There being 210 varieties of Christians in the world, each with a name of its own (remark in a notice of the dispute between Marcus Clarke and an ecclesiastic of the Church of England—a Bishop) and each believing itself to be the nearest right of all of them, the savage hates to give up a certainty for an uncertainty. He has no doubts concerning his own religion, and naturally hesitates to go groping among 210 kinds of doubt, lest he lose his way and lose *himself*. This is one of the reasons why missionary effort produces such barren results.

The notebooks contain nothing about Mauritius. It is likely that he wrote his notes in very extended form, on sheets of paper, which later he used without much change in his book—"Following the Equator." They sail from there April 28 for South Africa.

CHAPTER XXVI

In South Africa

May 4, 1896. On the drive to the Trappist Monastery, splendid spot of fire glowing at intervals a foot above the grass. It was a flower,—a flower the size of a child's fist, uplifted on a very slender stem. It suggested "torch." It was difficult to see how it could suggest anything else—unless perhaps "lamp." Inquiring, was told it is called the "lantern" flower. It is wrong. Lanterns are not perched on top of poles, but torches are, and street lamps.

Banana fields and pineapple. A grass-thatched hut peeping from a wilderness of broad banana leaves is just right. Any other kind of house does not harmonize. All through the two-hour drive, over the hills there were pleasant surprises. I could frame glimpses, with my hands, of rocks and grassy slopes and distant groups of trees that were exactly American—New England, New York, Iowa—remove the hands and let groups of tropic things—spiky plants, plants like bunches of vegetable swords, plumy tall palms, the cactus tree, the flat-roof tree, and so on—the illusion was gone. Again the road would be like a prairie road—sandy, deep rutted, the grassy expanses like their like in the prairie; couples and groups of negro men and women strolling along, dressed exactly like our darkies and with exactly the same faces—and I could imagine myself in Texas; then suddenly a gang of unmodified Zulus would appear, festooned with glass beads and with necklaces made of the vertebræ of snakes, the men's hair wrought into a myriad of little wormy forms, gummed with tar, the women's greased with red clay, the robust naked legs of both sexes shining with oil—and the illusion was gone again. In the plains of India I got a vast level stretch to look exactly like an alkali flat and was back in Nevada again, but just then an elephant moved into the field of vision and destroyed the illusion.

Pietermaritzburg, Capital of Natal, May 15

Big room in the Imperial, brilliantly sunny. It is a sincere and genuine old-time English inn, with all which that implies of order, neatness, gentility, serenity and homelike comfort. A landlady with a welcome and welcoming face and the look and the pleasant ways that one remembers in one's mother. Good food, well cooked. A tame kitten with a friendly spirit and willing to be sociable—sign of a right spirit in the house. The chambermaid a young Indian woman with soft black eyes and the expression of a Madonna; beautiful with the beauty of goodness. A lumbering great Zulu porter, fire-builder and general utility man, with a perfect disposition and less perfect English. A coal fire in the grate, a chilly blustering night outside. Last night, I mean. Lamps, books, pipes. Life is worth living.

At seven this morning the Zulu brought Smythe's coffee. Smythe said, "Bring me a biscuit please"—and waited, till his coffee was cold—cold and beginning to freeze. Then the Zulu came and said, "Misses say she can't spare a basket."

Pretoria, May 23. Audience composed chiefly of Africanders and direct descendants of the old Boers; hard to start but promptly and abundantly responsive after that.

Visited the prison with the Chapins, Mrs. Hammond and Smythe. The man in chief command there was a du Plessis. Thoroughly Dutch, but his name dates him back to the Huguenot immigration of two centuries ago, following the revocation of the Edict of Nantes. Found I had met Hammond many years ago when he was a Yale Senior—visitor at Gen. Franklin's. An English prisoner heard me lecture in London 23 years ago. Guard barred me off from crossing a line—called the "death-line." Made a talk—or a speech—sitting. Explained to the prisoners why they were better off in jail than they would be anywhere else; that they would eventually have gotten into jail anyhow, for one thing or another, no doubt; that if they got out they would get in again; that it would be better all around if they remained quietly where they were and made the best of it; that after a few months they would prefer the jail and its luxurious indolence to the sordid struggle for bread outside; and that I would do everything I could, short of bribery, to get the government to double their jail terms.

> These prisoners were the Jameson raiders, who in an endeavor to carry out one of Cecil Rhodes plans had been captured by Boers.[1] President Kruger ("Oom Paul"), who had but a meager sense of humor, heard of Mark Twain's comments—in the jail, and to a reporter—and ordered that the prisoners be more rigidly confined. Clemens when he heard of this paid a visit to President Kruger (see entry May 26) and "explained his joke," with the result that the treatment of the prisoners improved and they were presently discharged. (See entries May 30 and June 4.)

What sort of insanity is it—that moves banqueteers to appoint as chairman the one man among them who is destitute of qualifications for the place? It is no exaggeration to say that in nine cases out of ten this is the case.

[1] For a clear elucidation of the Transvaal (South African Republic) difficulties and the Jameson raid, see *Following the Equator*.

The man begins by saying he is no speaker—a fact which should persuade him to say no more but sit promptly down and appoint some one who is a speaker to do his work for him. Then he goes stumbling along through his imperfectly memorized speech of welcome and compliments to the guest of the evening and nearly always losing courage when he comes to one of his happy jokes, delivering it in such a shamefaced wish-I-hadn't-started-in-on-it way as to make it impossible for the table to respond to it in any but an artificial manner, a sort of spectral laughter that blows a chill upon the speaker and the whole place.

It is a cruel custom and immeasurably stupid. If the chairman would add *any* remark about *anything* in the world, after he has finished his compliments, it would save the guest; for anything *except* a compliment is text enough, it is all a guest needs at a convivial gathering.

May 26. A most superb moon came up at sunset, huge, round, and intensely and splendidly white, in the spaces not occupied by the "Man." But the new feature, the striking feature, was this: that there didn't seem to be any man there, or any definite figure or form, but only a tumble and confusion of pale, vague, rich, spectral smoke-wreaths occupying the Man's accustomed place and covering a deal more space than he ever does when he is present.

Visited President Kruger. He was in ordinary everyday clothes, and sat in an armchair, smoking Boer tobacco (the common black kind), his head and body bent forward. He had a bad cold and a very husky voice. He said he felt friendly toward America, and that it was his disposition to be lenient with the American captives.

Talking of patriotism what humbug it is; it is a word which always commemorates a robbery. There isn't a foot of land in the world which doesn't represent the ousting and re-ousting of a long line of successive "owners," who each in turn, as "patriots," with proud swelling hearts defended it against the next gang of "robbers" who came to steal it and *did*—and became swelling-hearted patriots in *their* turn. And this Transvaal, now, is full of patriots, who by the help of God, who is always interested in these things, stole the land from the feeble blacks, and then re-stole it from the English robber and has put up the monument—which the next robber will pull down and keep as a curiosity.

May 28. Drove in the afternoon with Poultney Bigelow; and after lecture he and I went to the sumptuous bachelor house of a German friend of his and had supper and comfortable fire (cold night) and hot whiskey and cigars; and good talk about Helmholz and Mumson and Vierchow.

I think the Veldt in its sober winter garb is as beautiful as Paradise. There were unlined stretches day before yesterday where it went rolling and swelling and rising and subsiding and sweeping grandly on and still on, like an ocean, toward the remote horizon, its pale brown deepening by delicately graduated shades to rich orange and finally to purple and crimson where it washed against the wooded hills and naked red crags at the base of the sky.

These darkies—just like ours—are not quite so big and brawny as the Natal Zulus. And the language seems to have no Zulu clicks in it; seems to have no angles or corners in it, no roughnesses, no vile S's or other hissing sounds—very, very mellow and rounded and flowing. The women have the sweet soft musical voice of ours, too. I followed a couple of them a mile to listen to the music of their speech and the happy ripple of their laugh.

What a curious thing a detective story is. And was there ever one that the author needn't be ashamed of, except the "Murders in the Rue Morgue"?

Smythe says of Browning: A man asked him the meaning of a passage in Sordello. Browning puzzled over it awhile then said—"Once there were two who knew"—glancing skyward, then touching his own breast—"Now there is only One."—glancing again skyward.

Miss Rhodes, middle-aged sister of Cecil and the Colonel (one of the four) told Smythe in the hotel in Pretoria that the prisoners were furious because I praised their lodgings and comforts; Smythe said the Colonel said—either *he* was a damn fool or *I* was. He seems to be in doubt. I'm not. We are all fools at times; this is his time. The prisoners ought to have had a policy and stuck to it. But no—Butters and others were for conciliating the Boers (which was wise). Col. Rhodes and others were for *driving* them—which wasn't.

In the train, bound for East London, *Brown,* whom I last saw in prison in Pretoria, says the brutalities of the jail guards were awful. They've had an African chief in there, and some of his people, since last August—never brought to trial yet—no shelter from rain or sun. Put a big black in the stocks for throwing his soup on the ground; stretched his legs too far apart and set him with his back downhill. He couldn't stand it and put back his hands on the ground to support himself. Guard ordered him to stop it—and kicked him in the back. The powerful black wrenched the stocks asunder and went for the guard; a Reform prisoner pulled him off and thrashed the guard himself.

Queenstown, Cape Colony, June 4. Arrived 7 this morning 16½ hours from Bloemfontein.

"All that a man hath will he give for his life." To *save* it he will. But ask a man of 50, "If you were dead now what would you give to have your life restored?" He wouldn't give a brass farthing.

The American characteristic is Uncourteousness. We are the Impolite Nation. In this detail we stand miles and miles above, or below, or beyond, any other nation savage or civilized.

We are called the Inventive Nation—but other nations invent. And we are called the Bragging Nation—but other nations brag. And we are called the Energetic Nation—but there are other energetic nations. It is only in uncourteousness, incivility, impoliteness, that we stand alone—until hell shall be heard from.

The black savage whom the Boer has driven out was brimming over with good nature and comradeship and friendliness, and he was the cheeriest soul, and had the easiest life in the world; and it was always on tap and ready. He went naked; he was dirty; he housed himself like a cow; he was indolent; he worshipped a fetich; he was a savage, and all his customs were savage; but he had a sunny spirit, and at bottom a good disposition.

He was replaced by the Boer, a white savage, who is dirty; houses himself like a cow; is indolent; worships a fetich; is grim, serious, solemn, and is always diligently fitting himself for heaven, probably suspecting that they couldn't stand him in the other place.

At billiards Carlyle Smythe beats me to death—by fluking. Now I have ruled fluking out, neither beats the other more than five points in a hundred. We *count* a fluke, but retire. We make the same number of flukes in each game, but the trouble before was that he generally piled three flukes on top of the first, but I *never* could.

> It was his habit to make new rules driving billiards: Sometimes a rule for some special shot.

At Laurence Hutton's table two or three years ago, Henry Irving spoke across to me and asked if I had heard the story about such and such a man, etc. It cost me something to say no, but I said it. Then he started to tell the story—hesitated—said—you are sure you haven't heard it? I braced up again and said—no, perfectly sure. He went on, a sentence or two further, and once more interrupted himself to inquire if I was absolutely certain I hadn't heard it. Then I said: "I can lie once, I can lie twice, for courtesy's sake; but I draw the line there; I can't lie the third time, at any price: I *have* heard the story, for I invented it myself." And that was the truth.

In Australia a man dropped in to talk with me at a club and I saw in a moment that he was a person with a local story-telling reputation and that he was going to show off before the company. He began to remark upon the slowness of the New Zealand railway service and I saw that he was working up the atmosphere for an anecdote and presently he launched the anecdote. Anecdote about how he advised the conductor to put the cowcatcher on the other end of the train "because we are not going to overtake any cows, but there is no protection against their climbing aboard at the other end and biting the passengers." I could have embarrassed him a little by reminding that there are no cowcatchers on Australian trains; and I could have embarrassed him still more, perhaps, by showing him that I had printed that little tale when he was a boy. In fact I invented it for use in a lecture, a hoary long time ago.

Sunday, June 14. Very heavy sea on tonight. Our ship lies in sight half a mile away, but we may not be able to get across the bar tomorrow.

The human imagination is much more capable than it

gets credit for. This is why Niagara is always a disappointment when one sees it for the first time. One's imagination has long ago built a Niagara to which this one is a poor dribbling thing. The ocean "with its waves running mountain high" is always a disappointment at first sight; the imagination has constructed real mountains, whereas these when swelling at their very biggest and highest are not imposing. The Taj is a disappointment though people are ashamed to confess it. God will be a disappointment to most of us, at first. I wish I could see the Niagaras and Tajs which the human imagination has constructed, why then, bless you, I should see Atlantics pouring down out of the sky over cloud ranges, and I should see Tajs of a form so gracious and a spiritual expression so divine and altogether so sublime and so lovely and worshipful that—well—St. Peter's, Vesuvius, Heaven, Hell, everything that is much described is bound to be a disappointment at first experience.

Tuesday, June 16. Lying at anchor before East London, Norham Castle, a large and very fine ship. Smythe and I came aboard yesterday afternoon, although we are due to sail this afternoon; but the tug might not be able to cross the bar if a great sea should be running, and there is a considerable sea today; it dashes itself against the big stone breakwater near the mouth of the river and bursts up in a vast white volume with laced edges, apparently 100 feet high.

Thursday, June 18. Cablegram saying the Drummond Castle has gone down off Plymouth, 400 lives lost. This at Port Elizabeth.

What ought to be done to the man who invented the celebrating of anniversaries? Mere killing would be too light. Anniversaries are very well up to a certain point, while one's babies are in the process of growing up: they are joy-flags that make gay the road and prove progress; and one looks down the fluttering rank with pride. Then presently one notices that the flagstaffs are in process of a mysterious change of some sort—change of shape. Yes, they are turning into milestones. They are marking something lost now, not gained. From that time on it were best to suppress taking notice of anniversaries.

If I were going to construct a God I would furnish Him with some ways and qualities and characteristics which the Present (Bible) One lacks.

He would not stoop to *ask* for any man's compliments, praises, flatteries; and He would be far above *exacting* them. I would have Him as self-respecting as the better sort of man in these regards.

He would not be a merchant, a trader. He would not buy these things. He would not sell, or offer to sell, temporary benefits or the joys of eternity for the product called worship. I would have Him as dignified as the better sort of men in this regard.

He would value no love but the love born of kindnesses conferred; not that born of benevolences contracted for. Repentance in a man's heart for a wrong done would cancel and annul that sin, and no verbal prayers for forgiveness be required or desired or expected of that man.

In His Bible there would be no Unforgivable Sin. He would recognize in Himself the Author and Inventor of Sin and Author and Inventor of the Vehicle and Appliances for its commission; and would place the whole responsibility where it would of right belong: upon Himself, the only Sinner.

He would not be a jealous God—a trait so small that even men despise it in each other.

He would not boast.

He would keep private His admirations of Himself; He

would regard self-praise as unbecoming the dignity of His position.

He would not have the spirit of vengeance in His heart; then it could not issue from His lips.

There would not be any hell—except the one we live in from the cradle to the grave.

There would not be any heaven—of the kind described in the world's Bibles.

He would spend some of His eternities in trying to forgive Himself for making man unhappy when He could have made him happy with the same effort and He would spend the rest of them in studying astronomy.

Cradock, Monday, June 29. Stopped off here for a day, yesterday evening, ten hours from Grahamstown, Victoria Hotel, in a side of the vast bare dust-blown square. Clouds of dust blowing along the powerful wind, like snow in New England on a raw March morning. Very nice and neat and comfortable hotel. Negro women can't understand English. Negro boy was ordered to bring fire and wood and build his fire. And sure enough he did bring fire on a shovel, a thing I had not seen before since I was a boy.

Kimberley, July 1. Went to the great crater, original Kimberley diamond mine, with Mr. Robeson, assistant engineer to Gardiner Williams; also to the great hoisting works of the DeBeers Consolidated Co. also to the diamond office and saw the day's take, £10,000 worth; also to the compound with him and Mr. Dallas and saw the natives dance.

Thursday July 2. Went with Mr. and Mrs. Robeson to the No. 2 washout and saw the concentrators—each one treats 300 carloads a day and the result is three carloads of slush and stuff which goes to the pulsator and the three are there reduced to a quarter of a load and this is examined by hand and the diamonds removed.

The whole DeBeers concern treats 8000 carloads a day—1600 lbs of stuff to each load—and the result is 3 lbs avoirdupois of diamonds—a big double handful, worth £10,000 or £12,000.

Damn the subjunctive. It brings all our writers to shame.

CHAPTER XXVII

England

> Susy Clemens died in Hartford, August 18, (1896), soon after the arrival in England (from South Africa) of the Mark Twain party. On the first word of Susy's illness Mrs. Clemens and Clara had sailed for America, Mr. Clemens remaining in England, where they had taken a house, at Guilford. When the following notes were made, the sorrowing mother and daughter had returned. Mark Twain's "Susy" notes follow this chapter.

Monday Sept. 21. Day after tomorrow the queen will have achieved the longest reign in the history of the English throne. She will come within twelve years of the longest reign in the history of any throne (?) Louis XIV seventy-two years.

Sept. 22. House-hunting again. England is the land of neat and pretty and shapely and polite housemaids. An ugly or ill-dressed or unpolished one is rare, very rare.

> They were presently located in Chelsea, on Tedworth Square, No. 23.

All the dogs here wear muzzles. Of course, they prefer it. Doubtless some ducal dog wore one, one day, merely because he had the toothache, or for fun, and then the others adopted it.

Making the fire. In England they lean the poker up against the grate so that the end of it stands over the coal—it makes the fire burn. You can make the fire warm up at either end or in the middle by placing the poker accordingly.

After we had noticed this standing poker every morning for a week when we entered the breakfast parlor, our curiosity finally prompted us to inquire.

What a funny muddle the Powers (sceptered burglars) are in today, with the Sultan massacring Armenians like pigs and the "Concert of the Powers" to act. (Because Russia holds all the cards.)

Don't try to pronounce an English name till some native shows you how. K'koobry, etc. The common Welch name, Bzjxxllwcp, is pronounced Jackson.

Chelsea, Oct. '96. In London it takes five weeks to find a house (furnished) that will suit both your convenience and your means. Five more to find a cook—not many are advertised, even in the Morning Post, where it is said they mainly go to be thought high class; and it takes the former occupant nine weeks to persuade the postmaster to respect his new address. We already had maids or maybe it would have taken eleven weeks to get them. Got a good man the first day to do odd jobs—carry up coal, black boots, scour knives, etc. He is the authorized messenger of the block and has to show a good character before the police authorities will appoint him.

More hugging and kissing by boys and girls and young men and maids in the streets at night and parks by day! And no chaffing them by anybody. I met a couple tonight, aged 17 and 14, a dozen times, around the garden. They ought to have done the blushing, but I presently found they could not be depended on, and had to do it myself.

The moral sense enables one to perceive morality—and avoid it. The immoral sense enables one to perceive immorality and enjoy it.

Oct. 24 '96. Wrote the first chapter of the book today. [*Round the World*. Later called *Following the Equator*.]

Max (Orell) that industrious dealer in literary old clo'. Thankful he has kept the respect &c. Let him venture to Sydney and see. But there is no harm in him. He merely fell into "literature" as a blind mule falls into a well. He continues in "lit" because he finds it cool and pleasant to soak himself in other people's water.

London is a collection of villages. When you live in one of them with its quiet back streets (Chelsea) and its one street of stores and shops (Kingsroad) little bits of stores and shops like those of any other village, it is not possible for you to realize that you are in the heart of the greatest city in the world.

Be careless in your dress if you must, but keep a tidy soul.

Our address discovered after three weeks of peaceful seclusion. Given to some reporter by Chelsea librarian? But how did *he* know me?

The long-legged, gray bird in the Grand Hotel Garden in Port Elizabeth that danced and showed off. Asked Clara to tell about him. And the one that played with the keeper at Jaypore.

Does the human being reason? No; he thinks, muses, reflects, but doesn't reason. Thinks *about* a thing; rehearses its statistics and its parts and applies to them what other people on his side of the question have said about them, but he does not compare the parts himself, and is not capable of doing it.

That is, in the two things which are the peculiar domain of the heart, not the mind,—politics and religion. He doesn't want to know the other side. He wants arguments and statistics for his own side, and nothing more.

Nov. 4 '96. Clara went with Mrs. Hopekirk Wilson yesterday and saw a young English girl of 20 (pupil of Leschetizky's) play before an audience for the first time. The girl's name is Goodson. Clara says she is not pretty, but has a most interesting face. She does not look English, but foreign—Russian, Clara thought. When she was ready to go on the stage Mrs. Wilson found that her hands were cold, from fright. She sent for hot water, but the girl said "No! No! No! I can't touch it! I have inked my master's initials on my nails as a talisman, and it would wash off!"

By that time it was necessary that she go on at once; and she did. She has a preternaturally grave face, and Clara said airs from the churchyard seemed to sift over the house as she stood solemnly glooming upon it from her place by the piano. Came the hoarse whisper from the prompter's hole "*Bow,* for God's sake *bow*!" She did it—a little wee machine bow—the applause of welcome crashing along all the time—for the audience (matinée, and almost all ladies) doubtless knew what Leschetizky had said about the girl—that she would be the greatest of all women pianists. She sat down and played—and retired under a splendid enthusiasm of applause and then encore, and went back and stood glooming out over this tossing sea of rejoicing noise. Hoarse whisper from the prompter's hole—"*Smile*, for God's sake *smile*!" which she did; a machine-made smile and it could have sat for the portrait of the Cheshire Cat in "Alice in the Looking Glass," or "Wonderland."

She made a great hit, was encored every time she appeared.

When we got to Australia we found that the story of my burial from Government House was the invention of a crazy man.

With the House Agent

The Water Co. has sent *me* no bill, but here is a notice requiring me to pay up at once and the man who delivered it to the servant brought oral notice that if I didn't pay the water would be cut off. Can you make *me* pay another man's debt?

Well, you see, they decline to know anybody in the matter but the *house*. It saves (them) trouble. They don't have to hunt up Mr. G. who may be in Egypt. They know you will pay G.'s bill and take it out of next rent rather than have your water cut off.

Have they such power?

Dear Sir, they have Imperial powers. I was going to say Sovereign Powers but that would be feeble—they have powers that the Sovereign cannot pretend to.

How comes that?

Well, their charters are as old as the time of the Stuarts—a time when the king had a finger in every pie—when he sold for a "king's share" his support to every promising adventure, like the capture and sale of foreign slaves, or the capture of English slaves with a water privilege of eternal duration and autocratic powers, or the giving away of States and Territories in America and elsewhere, to "merchant adventurers" and so on. The rest of those big monopolies have gone the way of all things perishable, but a water company is not perishable. A king's share in one of these old water companies, that was worth twenty pounds originally, is thrown on the market about once in a generation and it makes a mighty stir and exposes a revelation. A king's share in the new river came on the market four or five years ago and that twenty pounds worth sold for a fortune.

The dividends are incredible, and one wouldn't mind it so much if this surplus went to support the government, but it hurts when you know it goes to private pockets—the butcher and the baker—and that it is *they* that can lord it over you with their insolent notices and make you hunt up their debtors for them or pay their debts. Did you see the proposition the other day that London buy out the companies for £40,000,000? One million of that represents plant, no doubt,—represents pipes and reservoir and water, the other 39 represent "water." They charge for water not by any rule, but to value the building. A factory with one hydrant paid on its rental of £200 a year.

Two frowsy men with wheezy voices walking up and down the center of the street of dwellings wheezing out sentimental ditties, "Farewell my love, farewell my dear, farewell my syler (sailor) boy," and the pennies were thrown to them from the windows—by the sentimental housemaids? No doubt. *Any*body can collect pennies for *any*thing in London. It seems to be the paradise of the cheap adventure in music and piety. These two stalwarts had on seedy clothes and comforters wrapped around their necks. They looked as if they were on their way to Harrigan's to represent Thompson Street.

Grief can take care of itself, but to get the full value of joy you must have somebody to divide it with.

Nov. 26. We have now been in this house two months,

but *nothing* can persuade the fool post-office to send Mr. Garth's letters to his new address any oftener than four days in the week—the other three they come here.

Thanksgiving. We did not celebrate it. Seven years ago Susy gave her play for the first time; that was the last Thanksgiving jollification we ever had in our house. Mother [his wife's mother] died the day before Thanksgiving the following year. Ma died in 1890, the same year and month as Mother died.

The best way to cheer yourself is to try to cheer somebody else up.

Temperate temperance is best. Intemperate temperance injures the cause of temperance, while temperate temperance helps it in its fight against intemperate intemperance.

Fanatics will never learn that, though it be written in letters of gold across the sky.

Wrinkles should merely show where the smiles have been.

"We claim the right to deal with our servants as we think expedient"—an English Railroad Magnate.

At Johannesburg the manager of a great mine said—"We don't call our blacks slaves, but that is what they are, and that is what we mean they shall remain."

Dream-humor. In a dream last night a farmer was asked which of the two horses he had bet on. "One hundred pounds on each," he said.

Whereat there was a great storm of laughter from the young fellows present, because the man was bound to win one bet and lose one, and therefore might as well have made no bet at all,—no, that was not it—they laughed because *he* thought he was sure to win *both* bets—which they considered funny and absurd; and they also laughed because (as they said) he was bound to *lose* both bets—and that they regarded as very funny indeed.

It seemed quite sane in the dream. And that is where dream-things differ from waking-things: they can be thoroughly mad and incongruous, without the dreamer suspecting it.

London, Dec. 13 '96. Tonight at dinner Clara told of meeting a lady (Scotch I think) at Mrs. Hopekirk Wilson's today, who told her about a remarkable young relative of hers—a young girl, friend of Mrs. Wilson a few years ago in Leipzig. This said young girl was studying there—violin, and has turned out to be fine on that instrument. But suddenly she began to draw and paint, without instruction, and threw all her heart into it, and lost her passion for music. Somebody showed one of her pictures to the great Watt, R.A., and he said he must see her at once; she must be his pupil (he never would take pupils) and be his successor and continue his work.

George von Bunson is dying here in London. Mrs. Poultney Bigelow tells me that when he was at the height of his great popularity and influence in Berlin and politics, he made a liberal speech which infuriated Bismarck who was then chancellor, and Bismarck did him several vicious turns. Among others invited him to a State dinner at his house; went and spoke with each guest in turn; when he got to Bunson he looked him over from head to foot, then turned his back on him without a word. Bunson left (why the others didn't, also, is not stated). Later the Bunsons gave a ball and invited society—(they had six marriageable daughters). Society consists largely, if not mainly, of military officers. Bismarck intimated to his generals and colonels that he wanted all officers forbidden to accept invitations. Nobody much but ladies at the ball, by consequence; nobody to dance with. The Bunsons became ostracized. The daughters could not find husbands. That might be eight or ten years ago. Only one of them is just married.

Dec. 22 '96. It took piles of blankets to keep us warm last night. It was as cold as it would be at home at 30.—Yet it was really only 52. I brought the thermometer from the dressing-room where there was a fire. It was marking 59.

If you order a box of cigars here (as I did yesterday at this time, three blocks away) they may be two days getting it to you. I am expecting this result.

We are nothing but echoes. We have no thoughts of our own, no opinions of our own, we are but a compost heap made up of the decayed heredities, moral and physical.

London 11:30 Xmas morning. The square and adjacent streets are not merely quiet, they are *dead*. There is not a sound. At intervals a Sunday-looking person passes along. Once I saw a couple of postmen go along—once or twice I heard the rumble of wheels come out of the sepulchral distance—Queens Road, I should say.

Because of the smoothness and excellence of the paving, London is the least noisy city; but the silence of today! Oh, it is the silence of the tomb.

The family have been to breakfast. We three sat and talked as usual, but the name of the day was not mentioned. It was in our minds, but we said nothing.

They were remembering Susy, who as already told had died in August. A page or two farther along he would write of that tragedy.

The Church here rests under the usual charge—an obstructor and fighter of progress; until progress arrives, then she takes the credit.

Whatever the Church damns is saved; whatever it opposes prospers—like anti-slavery and evolution.

Some of the commonest English words are not in use with us—such as 'ousemaid, 'ospital, 'otel, 'istorian.

The several principles and mechanisms involved in the construction of an ant are as follows—that is a *good* ant, an ant that is made *right*: First, the antennæ—so called because they are part of the ant. Butterflies have antennæ, too, but that's a plagiarism. Next, the legs, six in number —one on each corner, and two in the middle. They are not all needed for general business—some are to get home on when the others have been chewed off; ants are always chewing each other's legs off, in arranging details connected with politics and theology.

CHAPTER XXVIII

Susy

In Paris I spoke of getting "dusted off" (lectured by Mrs. Clemens). Susy took up the phrase and was always seeing to it that Mamma did it before functions. "Mamma don't forget to dust him," and "Did you dust Papa off?"

She was *intense.* That was her marked characteristic.

Livy arrived after a year, at Elmira, by the very same train and at the same hour that she had left there a year before, with Susy on the platform, waving good-bye; and now Susy was lying in her coffin at the Langdon home.[1]

It is pleasant to know that while we were far away around the globe, Susy got a letter in Hartford which mightily pleased her from the great Madame Blanche Caccamesi saying (in substance) "I hear that the reason you did not stay and complete your vocal education is that your father was financially embarrassed and could not afford it. I would have completed it for you gratis for the sake of bringing out your noble voice and giving it to the world. I should have been repaid twice over."

She was very near-sighted. When she was little I was going upstairs with her, and I looked back when halfway up and through the dining-room door I saw the cat curled up like a worm on the intensely red cover of the round

[1] For the story of Susy's death the reader is referred to *My Father, Mark Twain*, by Clara Clemens, chapter XII, and to *Mark Twain —a Biography*, chapter CXCIII.

dining-table—a tortoise-shell cat—a striking picture. I called Susy's attention to it and was astonished to find that she was not able to see it.

In the other notebook[1] I have it wrong. Susy put out her hand and stroked Katy's face and said—"Mamma." That was the last time she spoke in this life. Poor troubled heart. It turned for help and comfort in its latest consciousness to the refuge that had never failed it. If anything *could* comfort Livy, it would be the thought that she was the last image that drifted across the poor child's perishing mind and her name the last utterance that fell from the dying lips.

She was a poet—a poet whose song died unsung.

Every now and then in her vivacious talk she threw out phrases of such admirable grace and force, such precision of form, that they thrilled through one's consciousness like the passage of the electric spark.

> He contemplated doing a small book about Susy, for private circulation. From time to time he wrote chapters of it, most of which were later included in his *Autobiography*. The book itself was never completed.

In this lament I wish to speak of my dead child as I would speak to my family, to my most private friends, without reserve, without conventions. For I am moved to pour out only praises and endearments, only homage and worship, over the dear and beautiful spirit that has vanished out of our life, and left it desolate. I wish to speak of her as she appeared to *us* of the family, not as she may, or may not, have appeared to others, even her comrades and intimates. To do this I must use franknesses of appreciation which would be out of place if I were speak-

[1] This notebook cannot be found.

ing to any but our nearest friends. It is to those friends—and those only—that this little paper will go. And I lay upon them the injunction—if I may do it without offense, that they allow none to see it but themselves.

Étrétat—Joan of Arc and Susy's suggestion. She liked "l'Arbre fée de Bourlemont,"[1] and said it was poetry, which greatly pleased me. She was fond of Joan's transitions from playful girl to official activities: "Messenger from the King!" And La Hire's speech when he backed up Joan's war methods.

She had no care about money, no notion of its value. She spent it, wasted it, lost it. Lost her opera glasses, her gloves, her parasol, her purse. It was always wise to examine a cab when she left it. In one day in Paris she left things in three different cabs. She was such a flutter-mill; always in the air; always singing, dancing, making her tongue fly.

She was full of little loving ways with her mother, whom she ennobled with pet names and enriched with ceaseless caresses. She would pet my hair, and fuss at it, sometimes—which always made me wish she would go on.

Sad at Viviani; at Venice; at Nauheim; the first winter in Paris (time of Ravachal) afraid of theaters and bombs; at La Bourboule (the riot in the Hotel threatened); at Berlin part of the time—but she was fond of Berlin; happy in Munich; unhappy in Maintz; in Marienbad; very happy in Hartford, the last months. Bayreuth, happy.

Yet through all her seasons of unhappiness there were outbursts of happiness—exaltations of it.

I cannot remember when she first began to carry around a vast Shakespeare. She was never without it. It was a

[1] A poem in his book on *Joan of Arc.*

trouble in traveling, but she had to have it. She was fond of Browning.

To us she was a prodigy. I mean, in speech she was that. We of the family believed, and still believe, that she had no equal among girls of her own age in this regard. Even the friends thought highly of her gift, though they could never see her at her best, which was in the unembarrassing limits of the family circle.

I did not hear her glorious voice at its supremest. That was in Hartford, a month or two before the end.

She was not industrious, except in the things in which she was gifted; she was indolent; she lived mainly in the clouds; hard, persistent work went against the grain with her. As a rule, I mean. She mastered the French and German and Latin grammars, and of course that does mean hard, persistent work. Still, as I say, she had a distaste for toilsome work—a trait which she got from me.

Copy of letter to Mr. Henry C. Robinson, of Hartford.

London, Sept. 28/96.

It is as you say, dear old friend, "the pathos of it"—yes, it was a piteous thing—as piteous a tragedy as any the year can furnish. When we started westward upon our long trip at half past ten at night, July 14, 1895, at Elmira, Susy stood on the platform in the blaze of the electric light waving her good-byes to us as the train glided away, her mother throwing back kisses and watching her through her tears. One year, one month, and one week later, Clara and her mother having exactly completed the circuit of the globe, and drew up at that platform at the same hour of the night, in the same train and *the same car*, and again Susy had come a journey and was near at hand to meet them.[1] She was waiting in the house she was born in, in her coffin.

[1] Susy had been brought from Hartford to Elmira, for burial.

All the circumstances of this death were pathetic—my brain is worn to rags rehearsing them. Yes, and cursing them—cursing the conception and invention of them. The mere death would have been cruelty enough, without overloading it and emphasizing it with that score of harsh and wanton details. The child was taken away when her mother was within three days of her, and would have given three decades for sight of her.

In my despair and unassuageable misery I upbraid myself for ever parting with her. But there is no use in that. Since it was to happen it would have happened.

With love S.L.C.

It tickled Susy—Jo Twichell's war-whooping, when he would meet Clara on the street in Hartford.

Susy had faults but the memory of them was submerged in that great darkness which descended upon us when her life was quenched, and I do not know what they were.

Susy and Clara—one on each side of me—selecting hickory nut kernels for me—"That's a good one." They beguiled me into many an indigestion and loss of sleep.

The last ms. of mine that ever I read to her was four-fifths of the last chapter of Joan—and the last words of that which I read were "How rich was the world, etc."

And to me these words have a personal meaning now.

When out of her head she said many things that showed she was proud of being my daughter. "It is because I am Mark Twain's daughter." The attentions shown us in Australia, India, etc.—"Katy" (to her maid), "that is *my* family."

In the burning heat of those final days in Hartford she would walk to the window or lie on the couch in her fever and delirium, and when the cars

> went by would say: "Up go the trolley cars for Mark Twain's daughter. Down go the trolley cars for Mark Twain's daughter." This was no more than a day or two before the end.

In various places Livy and Clara selected presents for Susy; in Bombay, in a Parsee gentleman's house, bales of goods were sent for, by him, and they selected a dress pattern for Susy of Indian crêpe, and were so particular to get the shade of pink exactly right—the "inside of a seashell," as they described it.

No member of the family with her when she died, except her young sister Jean (16) and Katy Leary, an old servant who had been with us sixteen years and is regarded as part of the family. The gardener and the coachman were also on the premises—old friends of Susy's; the one had served us 26 years, the other 10 or 12. The gardener brought a basket of roses for her every morning.

George Griffin, butler, colored, he was with us 18 years. He was always betting; Susy always tried to reform him. When he won a bet he always told us about it at breakfast—so that she could hear it.

Sometimes in those days of swift development in Paris her speech was rocket-like; I seem to see it go up and up and up, a soaring, streaming, climbing, stem of fire, and finally burst in the zenith and rain colored sparks all around. And I felt like saying "You marvelous child!" But never said it. To my sorrow I remember it, now. But I came of an undemonstrative race.

Many a time I said—"The two most pathetic, moving things in the English tongue to me are these: one is the refrain of a long-ago forgotten song, familiar to me in my earliest boyhood: "In the days when we went gypsying, a long time ago." The other "Departed this life"—and now this will be written upon *her* gravestone.

Livy saw her in her coffin. That was denied to me.

Madame Marchesi said she had a grand-opera voice—"Marvelous voice" was one of her expressions. Madame Blanche said her voice was competent for the part of Elsa and Elizabeth in Lohengrin and Tannhäuser; and later she added Isolde to this list—which was the equivalent of saying it was competent for any soprano part.

She went home to live on a hill—as commanded by these great teachers, valleys being forbidden—and gather vigor of body. Then to go back to Paris and prepare for the stage (opera).

Her voice was not only eloquent with feeling, but of almost (particularly after she got to Hartford) unexampled power and volume.

Bryn Mawr began it. It was there that her health was undermined.

Elmira, Aug. 24. Susy is dead and buried.

We stand stunned as before a space where an apparently strong house has stood five minutes ago—now swept away by a cyclone—not a vestige left.

She was perfectly happy in Venice with her mother and Jean—Clara and I in America. She lived in the gondola all the time.

She was sensitive to everything. The palmist (lady at a party) told her she would have an unhappy life and that with all her gifts she would fall just short of success. She would be a failure. It distressed her for days.

Susy became blind through the suffusion of blood on the brain and said to Charles Langdon "I am blind, Uncle Charlie, and you are blind."

She was so glad and proud to see "Pudd'nhead" on the stage. She took such interest in all my work—and I miss her so—and half the incentive is gone.

Those words touched her so: "And will you no come back again." I said the pathos was in the "no"—it wouldn't be as effective in English.

I seem like poor old Aaron Burr, standing in the midst

of the early morning, gazing out for the ship that had long ago gone down.

That poor child. She was human and was pleased with a compliment—and now that she is gone beyond the hearing of them, how richly they came flooding in! Here are these piles of letters from competent and discriminating friends in America, Germany, Italy, France, England, Scotland, filled with her praises—and the ears they would have so gratified are deaf, the pulses they would have quickened are still.

It is human to exaggerate the merits of the dead, and I find myself wondering if the praises in this multitude of letters have that defect. I do not know, in certain of the details, such as voice, literary gift, and some others—other witnesses are more competent perhaps than I; but in the matter of the *talking* gift I know myself that she was not merely remarkable, she was extraordinary.

When she was out of her head in those last days she found a dress of her mother's hanging in a closet and thought it was her mother's effigy or specter, and so thought she was dead, and kissed it and broke down and cried.

We wanted her to go around the world, but she dreaded the sea and elected not to go.

In the first week of August I proposed to myself a magazine article in which I intended to "prove" a certain thing by quotations—these to be the most familiar sentences in our language, sentences familiar to everybody. But I did not intend to put myself to the trouble of gathering these together myself. No, I would have the children do that and pay a small fee for each accepted one. I expected a harvest of them from Susy.

In this family she held the place of intellectual chief, as by natural right; none of us thought of disputing it with her. In depth of mind, in swiftness of comprehension, clearness of intellectual vision, in ability to reveal the meaning of an obscure page with a simple flash from her mind upon it and in the ability to transmute her thoughts into the crispest of English by instantaneous process, we knew her for our superior. And we did not resent it but were only proud of it.

Livy: "Others that are bereaved say 'Be comforted—time will heal the wound.' What do *they* know? They have not lost a Susy Clemens."

How is it that I, who cannot draw or paint, can sometimes shut my eyes and see faces (dark colored always, color of putty) most delicate and perfect miniatures and can note and admire the details. How is it? They are not familiar faces, they are new—how can I invent them? And what is it that makes perfect images in my dreams? I cannot *form* a face of any kind by deliberate effort of imagination.

CHAPTER XXIX

London Days

THERE is in life only one moment and in eternity only one. It is so brief that it is represented by the fleeting of a luminous mote through the thin ray of sunlight—and it is visible but a fraction of a second. The moments that preceded it have been lived, are forgotten and are without value; the moments that have not been lived have no existence and will have no value except in the moment that each shall be lived. While you sleep you are dead; and whether you stay dead an hour or a billion years the time to you is the same.

Write a novel in which part of the action takes place in heaven and hell, the next upon the earth. Let a woman in heaven watch the sweep of the ocean of fire at close quarters—a person passes by at very long intervals only; the ocean is so large. It is a solitude—so is heaven. She has sought for her daughter for a long time—she is watching hell, now, but not expecting her daughter to be there. Musing, she hears a shriek, and her daughter sweeps by. There is an instant of recognition by both—the mother springs in, perceiving there is no happiness in heaven for her any longer.

They try to help the situation of all the workingmen except the hardest worked one, the Prince of Wales. He does not get the benefit of the eight-hour law and ought to strike.

Not even sects are agreed upon morals and pieties. The Cardinal Archbishop cast-ironly forbids priests to go to theaters, whereas in Spanish countries priests are the main support of the hellish bullring.

The English clergy formerly rode to hounds, now they don't. In New England they used to take part of their salary in rum and get together on religious business and have a time with rum and pipes—now they discourage even the laity.

The believing Moslem knows that it is his duty to go to Mecca on pilgrimage, even when he is going to carry the plague to the unbelieving Europeans—and the European *allows him to do it.* The human being—with not a single exception in the whole earth—is a fool. And to his very marrow he is a hypocrite and a humbug.

I wish the Lord would disguise Himself in citizens clothing and make a personal examination of the sufferings of the poor in London. He would be moved, and would do something for them Himself

Satan, to newcomer (with discontent): "The trouble with you Chicago people is that you think you are the best people in hell—whereas you are merely the most numerous."

Saturday, Jan. 3, '97. The pedestal of the bronze, be-ruffled Charles I, is well clothed in wreaths of white flowers, with mottoes. This a lament by irreconcilable English 'legitimists,' to commemorate what they think was a calamity—the beheading of Charles, Jan. 21, 1649. They celebrate tomorrow (that apparently standing for Jan. 21 O.S.). Charles' back is toward Nelson, in the sky on his column top; he looks down Whitehall, past the Palace where he was executed and past the Horse Guards and Downing Street, political executive center of the vast British Empire, and his bronze glance strikes the great tower of Parliament, further down—the legislative center of the B.E.

In Hartford there is a family of American donkeys who shut themselves up Jan. 21 and snivel over Charles' death.

Feb. 18, '97. Brilliant morning (very rare). Some of the people looked glad to be alive. But not many. Walked an hour in the King's Road, as usual, between Markham Square and the Chelsea Polytechnic—back and forth. Shakespeare people all on hand as usual.

He was not a direct liar, but he would subtly convey untruth. He never dealt in any but large things, if you let him tell it. If by accident his trousers got stained in diverse tints, he would explain it by no actual lie, yet he would leave with you the impression that he got it sliding down a rainbow.

March 18, '97. I dreamed I caught a beautiful slender white fish 14 inches and thought what a fine meal it would make. I was very hungry. Then came the feeling of disappointment and sorrow; it was Sunday, and I could not take the fish home, for it would deeply grieve Livy to know that I had been fishing on the Sabbath. Then it occurred to me to catch a fish for *her,* and *that* would disarm her.

The dream is a perfect reflection of my character and hers, down to that last detail—there it suddenly breaks down. But in the dream it seemed quite natural that her religious loyalty should be bought for a fish.

The first thing a missionary teaches a savage is indecency. He makes him put clothes on. He is as innocent and clean-minded up to that time as were our first parents when they walked naked before the Lord and were not ashamed. He hid the knowledge of indecency from them; the missionary doesn't.

James I. In that day a suspected man was tortured into admitting a murder which he hadn't committed—then executed.

Victoria. Last week Lord Crowley (to try to save the name of Mrs. Charrington) confessed under oath on the witness stand (after kissing the Bible, no doubt) adultery with a prostitute in Brighton. The Judge said it must be corroborated by independent testimony or he could not accept the thing as being proved.

Also, the Scull girl voluntarily, without suggestion or invitation of any kind, confessed that she killed the child; the judge refused to hold her for trial because there wasn't sufficient independent testimony to make her confession good.

A foreigner in England wished to hire a maid, and knew that a maid and virgin are the same thing. The first applicant had merely heard that he wanted a house-servant but did not know in what capacity. She said she was a cook and asked what he wanted. He said—"I want a virgin. If you are not a virgin I do not want you. You do not look like a virgin." At this point the neighbors flocked to his rescue and he was removed to the hospital.

Dedication for Joan of Arc:

1870 1895

To my Wife
Olivia Langdon Clemens
this Book
is tendered on our wedding anniversary
in grateful recognition of her
25 years of
valued service as
my literary adviser
& editor

March 28. Twichell sends me a vast newspaper heading, the breadth of five columns "Close of a Great Career" in which it is said that I am living in penury in London and that my family has forsaken me. This would enrage and disgust me if it came from a dog or a cow, or an elephant or any other of the higher animals, but it comes from a man, and much allowance must be made for man.

London, April 13, '97. I finished my book today.

Boys whipping tops—never saw it in my life till in London, this time—yet was raised on books with woodcuts of boys doing it.

There is no such thing as Queen's English. The property has gone into the hands of a joint stock company and we own the bulk of the shares.

Everyone is a moon and has a dark side which he never shows to anybody.

None of us can ever have as many virtues as the fountain pen, or half its cussedness; but we can try.

I have traveled more than anyone else, and I have noticed that even the angels speak English with an accent.

May 18, '97. Finished the book *again.* Addition of 30,000 words.

Jan. 2, '97. Came Mr. White,[1] representing N. Y. Journal with two cablegrams from his paper.

[1] It has been stated that Mark Twain was then living at a London hotel. He was still at 23 Tedworth Square.

One (1) "If Mark Twain dying in poverty, in London, send 500 words."

(2) "Later. If Mark Twain has died in poverty send 1000 words."

I explained how the mistake occurred and gave him a cable in substance this:

"James Ross Clemens, a cousin, was seriously ill here two or three weeks ago, but is well now. The report of my illness grew out of his illness; the report of my death was an exaggeration. I have not been ill. Mark Twain."

Nobody would go to Bunyan's heaven now, since our improvements have made this life attractive, but it was a superior place in its day.

If Christ were here now, there is one thing he would *not* be—a Christian.

July 7, '97. London.

Yesterday Pond offered me $50,000 and all expenses for 125 nights on the platform in America. Mrs. Clemens is not quite willing, and I suppose I shall not accept.

London, July 10. Livy, Clara, and Julia Langdon[1] in a hansom. The horse fell, the whole front of the hansom wrecked, Clara thrown over and disappeared from Livy's view—fell on the struggling horse's rump, slipped down on to his hind legs in front of the wheels, scrambled out and had no severe hurt. Livy was flung on to the floor of the hansom and got two bruises on her face. Julie was not unseated and not hurt.

The horse scrambled to his feet, leaving Clara in front

[1] Niece of Mrs. Clemens.

of the wheel. She was on his hind legs and gripping one of his ankles with her hand when he scrambled up and spilled her off to the rear.

CHAPTER XXX

On the Continent

LEFT London at 8 A.M. Spent all the previous day packing, till midnight. Got Sue, Julie, Clara and Jean started down, at last. No lift boy, no clerk to take the money (Crescent Hotel). Nobody on deck but second hall porter. No cabs; said they should have been engaged the day before.

To Rochester in 45 minutes; to Queensborough within the hour. Left at 9:30 in the little steamer. Pretty indifferent food but not expensive. Arrived Flushing 5 P.M. Grand Hôtel des Bains—good and very cheap. Very quiet and cool; good bathing-beach. Orchestra of young women in white. Good music. Dutch women with good faces; plump; peasant dress.

On the Continent you can't get a rare beefsteak—everything is as overdone as a martyr.

We asked for the Zeeland Hotel, Flushing. The porter said in English—"It is not made" (built).

Railroad station made of tiles—brilliant, polished, strong colors; vividly readable map of tile—beautiful and good sense.

These villains cart you to the station nearly two hours before train time.

A very jolty road till we passed the German border, then smooth. It cost six of us $5 a day at Flushing.

You climb two flights of wide steps. Queer little church surmounted by a couple of very tall and exceedingly sharp pointed toothpick spires—sharp enough for birds to get impaled upon them. On one leaf of the ancient open door is carved an old-time knight in armor in deep relief—on the other a bishop. In the roomy vestibule are life-sized statues of six saints in niches, with their names labeled underneath them—St. Peter is one of them and has his golden key. One is labeled S. Clemens—just my name, just my initial. It was a proud thing to find an ancestor in such a place and in such company. Still, there have always been saints in our family. If I had my rights there would be one now. This one had on a helmet, probably used to be on the police force before he got promoted.

All around the church extends the churchyard; and it was noticeable that there were flowers on graves fifty years old. A quiet reposeful place, the shrubbery well tended.

Switzerland

Sunday, July 18, '97. Took up residence in Villa Bühlegg, Weggis.—with Sue, Julie Langdon and Ernst—seven persons. Terms frs 6 ($1.20) per day, per person, rent and food included, also candles and two lamps; and frs 14 extra per week to have the meals brought up and served in the house.

This trustful frau would not take pay for our five dinners yesterday, but said that it would go in the pension bill, in case we concluded to take the house; and so she let us go back to Lucerne ignorant of our names and address.

Swiss Thoroughness

The pharmacist took half an hour to mix one part litharge and two parts lard—got the proportions reversed twice and had to make the salve three times. Today, this one took as long, then took five minutes to coax the last vestige of the salve into the glass box. Told him I was in a hurry, and didn't *want* it all—it did not hasten him in the least. Then he got a label—set the receipt down in his book—then carefully copied on to the label (mislaying his glasses twice and hunting for them) then pasted the label on, did the box up in a piece of paper, which he measured before tearing it off; then went hunting for a match, then lit his candle and sealed the paper, in four places, and delivered it to me—a long job, but ended at last, with my patience. It was a good $40 worth of work, and all he charged for it was 7/10 of a franc—say 15c. That man will earn a fortune and yet die poor.

Patriotism

A man can be a Christian *or* a patriot, but he can't legally be a Christian *and* a patriot—except in the usual way: one of the two with the mouth, the other with the heart. The spirit of Christianity proclaims the brotherhood of the race and the meaning of that strong word has not been left to guesswork, but made tremendously definite—the Christian must forgive his brother man all crimes he can imagine and commit, and all insults he can conceive and utter—forgive these injuries how many times?—seventy times seven—another way of saying there shall be no limit to this forgiveness. That is the spirit and the law of Christianity. Well—patriotism has *its* law. And it also is a perfectly definite one, there are no vaguenesses about it. It commands that the brother over the border shall be sharply watched and brought to book every time he does us a hurt or offends us with an insult. Word it as softly as you please, the spirit of patriotism is the spirit of the dog and the wolf. The moment there is a misunderstanding about a boundary line or a hamper of fish or some other squalid matter, see patriotism rise, and hear him split the universe with his war-whoop. The spirit of patriotism being in its nature jealous and selfish, is just in man's line, it comes natural to him—he can live up to all its requirements to the letter; but the spirit of Christianity is not in its entirety possible to him.

The prayer concealed in what I have been saying is, not that patriotism should cease and not that the talk about universal brotherhood should cease, but that the incongruous firm be dissolved and each limb of it be required to transact business by itself, for the future.

Monday, July 19. Tea was forgotten in the arrangements. It has been added and costs $21 a month and we furnish the tea.

The hired piano came from Lucerne. It got wedged in the front door and stayed so two hours and blocked the way—the family on the inside, I on the outside, they anxious to get out, merely because they couldn't, I burning to get in, for the same reason. The piano with rent, handling and transportation, elevates the expense further.

Struck one economy anyhow—plenty good enough cigars at $5 a thousand, or $10 a barrel. In London the cheapest were $4 a hundred.

We are under the eaves of the Rigi and our part of the lake is fenced in in all directions by lofty mountain bulks —Pilatus the tallest. A most superb and impressive prospect.

Villa Bühlegg

It takes a person not born and reared among mountains a long time to find out that when he has looked across the lake at a towering bulk like Pilatus once, he has not yet seen it; that when he has looked across at it daily for 20 days he is not yet acquainted with it; that when he has done this for a hundred days it still has a thousand details, a thousand charms, fascinations, exquisitenesses, which have not yet been revealed to him; and he will by and by come to realize that such a mountain is a sublime mystery which is full-charged with beautiful secrets, which only a lifetime of daily observation can enable him to exhaust. Every slight drifting of the sun exposes to view for a moment a detail not discovered before—the next moment it is invisible again and may remain so for a year, possibly—until sun and atmosphere are exactly right for it once more. It may be a shepherd's hut, high perched among the breezy heights—it glows like a spark for an instant, and perhaps you might watch that spot for a year and never see it again. Every slight change of the ceaselessly changing atmosphere washes the mountain with new distributions of light and shade, new dreams of enchanting color.

In time the stranger to mountains finds the mastlike Pilatus is a new mountain every day, and may be gloated over with a new passion and a new delight every day and all the days, forever; that it is always beautiful; that its beauty is never twice the same, and never stales; that if he could sit in its benignant presence all his life his worship would be as deep and strong at the last as it was at the first; and the peace and healing it brought to his spirit in the beginning would abide with him to the end.

I can't tell our land from other people's when I prowl absent-mindedly around, so every now and then I step over the line and get warned off. A survival of the holy past. A thousand years ago when a man went poking through a wood, he had to blow his horn every few minutes as a protection. If he went silently he would be suspected of being a thief and shot.

They feed us lavishly. How do they manage it at the price? The languages used are German and French—mainly German.

The boats go stuttering by with a good deal of frequency—and packed with tourists. They charge only three francs fifty for the round trip to Fluëllen and back—a voyage of five hours.

Met a woman of 70 with a deep fruit-basket strapped on her back, and she stopped and remarked that the weather was very warm. I was of that opinion, too—the perspiration was flowing from me, washing boulders down the hill. This was about a third of the way up the mountain. She asked if I was on my way to the summit. I said no, it was too much of a climb. She said she had been up there to carry a load of peaches and pears, and was on her way down to get another load. I asked if she meant to carry that up, too. Yes, she said. Today? Oh yes, today. I tried to voice my admiration, but got tangled among the verbs and tenses and she bade me good-bye and resumed her brisk march down the slope without waiting to see where I was going to arrive with my speech. She was apparently not overheated, and was not perspiring. She was climbing 5000 feet, twice in the day, with a load of 100 lbs., descending the same distance twice, yet she seemed to think nothing of it. One ascent by itself would use me up.

July 31. Sunday. A smooth lake and a most quiet and peaceful day. Domestic picture. Grandmother, mother and two little daughters, sitting by the lake in front of their pretty villa. Grandma teaching one of the little girls her Bible lesson, the mother teaching the other one to fish.

In a dream I have at last encountered a humorism that actually remained one after waking. The crowned heads were adrift at sea on a raft. They all managed to stay amiable but Victoria—she was constantly cross. This was the origin of the V.C. With that sentence the dream ended.

Aug. 13. The Jubilee Singers sang at the Löwen last night—diviner, even than in their early days, 26 years ago. They came up to the house this morning and sang to us. They are as fine people as I am acquainted with in any country.

Monday Aug. 16. Last night there was a Fest and a torchlight procession of wheelmen from here (Weggis) to Vitznau and back. After midnight four villagers out in a boat—they had been drinking too much—got upset and three were drowned: a cook, a confectioner, and a locksmith all young men of the village. It has made a deep sensation. Today the people stand about in groups, talking low and looking sad. There is but one topic. Even our family finds itself personally affected by the tragedy; for we find that our fruitshop woman lost her son by it—a young fellow of 27. She and her daughter go on with their work today as usual (the poor have no emancipations from work) but they are very sad.

Villa Bühlegg, Weggis, Lake Lucerne, Aug. 18, '97. One year today since the great disaster fell. Livy went away to be alone. She took the steamer and spent the day solitary in an inn in an unknown town up the lake—a village. I spent the day alone under the trees on the mountain-side, writing some lines—a lament for Susy in the form of an allegory.

> Under the title "In Memoriam" it was published in Harper's Magazine, and is now included in the volume of his collected works "The $30,000 Bequest."

Unquestionably the person that can get lowest down in cringing before royalty and nobility, and can get most satisfaction out of crawling on his belly before them, is an

American. Not all Americans, but when an American does it he makes competition impossible.

Strip the human race, absolutely naked, and it would be a real democracy. But the introduction of even a rag of tiger skin, or a cowtail, could make a badge of distinction and be the beginning of a monarchy.

The Swiss seem to be at bottom good-hearted and they are courteous, though they exhibit no artificial polish; they are grave, not to say austere of countenance, independent, a trifle repellant in their manner; they have no vivacity, and if they know how to smile they keep that secret within themselves. They are furnished with machinery to smile with but they have no way of operating it. These remarks fit all the Swiss I have met, excepting about a dozen.

Notes for story—probably *The Mysterious Stranger.*

He had but one term for that large body which has such a fine opinion of itself—"the little stinking human race, with its little stinking kings and popes and bishops and prostitutes and peddlers."

He said: "The globe is a living creature, and the little stinking human race and the other animals are the vermin that infest it—the microbes. We dig into its skin to suck its blood (water) and we use its Niagaras and rivers for power. We sail its oceans in fleets which it is not conscious of and cannot see. We dig deep into the thin outer gold-leaf layer of its skin, 3000 feet, and it is not aware of it. Nothing hurts it but a bellyache, then it heaves with a trifling earthquake."

The absence of the Orienting faculty. In Innsbruck the portier of the Tivolier Hotel told me to go to the right two streets, then to the right again, a street or two, then to the left two streets—but he gave me a diagram, and that confused me. I said it showed that the third turn must also be to the right—and we made a test. Of course he turned out to be right.

I would as soon spend my life in Weggis as anywhere in the geography—Sept. '97.

CHAPTER XXXI

In Vienna

After two months in Weggis we find the Clemens family located at the Hotel Metropole, in Vienna.

VIENNA, Tuesday, Sept. 28, '97. Left Salzburg noon yesterday, arrived 7 P.M. in Vienna. Visited seven hotels last night before we could get a suitable lodging. Stopped at the Hotel Müller. Visited eight hotels today and then moved to the Metropole. We have never approached this record before.

Hotel Metropole, Vienna, Oct. 3, '97. At the next round table to ours sits a princess (daughter of the Dowager Empress Frederick, and granddaughter of Victoria); also the young daughter of the above and her intended, the young Prince Henry Reuss, called Henry III, whose mother and sister and uncle, the Prince von Wernigerode, in Ilsenburg, were in the Hartz Mountains six years ago. With them, a maid of honor, and a couple of Equerries. Good-looking people. They *all* smoke.

A man has sent me a Bible 250 years old (formerly the property of Queen Christina, of Sweden) to look at. It is as big as a trunk—and as uninteresting as an empty one. It has been in the room three days and we are getting tired of the responsibility. To people who value such antiquities it must be worth much money.

Sunday, Oct. 10. The princess did me the honor to send and invite me down to her parlor, this afternoon, and added the further honor of saying that if I was not yet strong enough to leave my quarters she would come up and see me. I went down at 4:30 and was received in a way which put me at my ease at once. She came to the door when I was announced and put out her hand and gave me a hearty grasp and shake, and said—"I am very, very glad to meet you and know you, Mr. Clemens—I have read your books and am familiar with them and they have given me great enjoyment." I said—"It is a great happiness to meet your Royal Highness, and what you have said makes me very proud." She gave me a chair and when she had seated herself I sat down and the talk at once flowed freely. She wanted to know how I came to get interested in Joan of Arc, and said she had read my book through three times and had then given it to a young girls' school which she had founded. Speaking of Joan's fate she said—"Poor child, but for the priests it would not have happened; but whenever *they* meddle, harm must come to somebody."

"Particularly when they and politics join teams and meddle *together,*" I said. She assented so zealously that I reminded her that *she* shouldn't have such opinions as that—they were proper to my sort of folk. But she said she *had* such opinions and feelings, and was used to putting them in words. There was some talk about the Greek situation, and I said she seemed to have a liking for politics. And so on, and so on. And she mentioned Gen. von Versen and regretted his death, and said she knew I had dined in his house to meet the German Emperor—said the Emperor had told her about it.

And then some talk about her daughter and the betrothal to the young Prince Reuss—said—"It took place in this room, a week ago today." I said that it must have been great fun and interesting. "Yes," she said, "to them —not so much so to me."

"I understand how that could be," I said, "it made you feel older than you wanted to feel." "That was it—yes; I suppose I shall get used to it, but as yet I am *not.* My daughter has always seemed to me a child, and now at 18, in presence of this event, she suddenly becomes a woman, and it isn't a pleasant surprise, considering how it ages me." And so on and so on—about the "Tramp Abroad," and the chapter on the German language; and then I rose, and she asked me to write in her autograph book, which I did; and she wanted me to send her my new book as soon as it was out—which I said I would be most glad to do; and she wrote her address—for me—her home address—for November; for now she is leaving here to visit her mother, the Empress Frederick; then will go to Roumania where her husband commands an army corps—then home to Breslau.

(Note added Dec. 16. Sent her the book. A cordial letter from her today.)

Nov. 6. Entertained by the Concordia last Sunday night. Made a speech in German.

Sitting to Hagenbarth these days for a bust.

Ten young American physicians called this evening. Very jolly time.

Nov. 24. Dined again with the Duc de Frias, one of the secretaries of the Spanish Legation. Speaks English like a native. Present, Clark of the English Legation, and the Prince of Thurn and Taxis. Fine men, all of them. The talk was of books altogether. A pleasant evening. The Prince speaks English nearly perfectly and is a fine man, worthy representative of that ancient house.

Dec. 1. Night before last, Madame Leschetizky came and took Clara and me to Ritter von Dutschka's to dine. Twenty persons at dinner; Count von Eulenberg (German Ambassador) and others came in after dinner. A remarkable gathering—no commonplace people present, no leatherheads. Princes and other titled people there, not *because* of their titles, but for their distinction in achievement. It was like a Salon of old time Paris. Madame Dutschka is large and stately and beautiful, cordial and full of all kinds of charms of manner, and ways and speech. She is Russian; appears to be about 30, but is really 52, and has a son 28. Count Kilmansegge, Governor of Upper Austria, and wife, and—but I cannot remember the name. The new baritone from Beyreut (von Rooy) sang—a wonderful voice. He is but 26 and has a future before him. Leschetizky played. A marvelous performance. He never plays except in that house, she says. He sacrificed himself for his first wife—believed she would be the greatest pianist of all time—and now they have been many years separated. If he had developed himself instead of her he would have been the world's wonder himself.

Note added July 19, '09. He is still alive and has his fourth (?) wife.

Buried treasure in a Missouri village—supposed by worn figures to be $980. Corrupts the village, causes quarrels and murder, and when found at last is $9.80.

> We have here probably the first hint of the great story he was to write a little later, *The Man That Corrupted Hadleyburg.*

Ecclesiastical and military courts—made up of cowards, hypocrites and time-servers—can be bred at the rate of a million a year and have material left over; but it takes five centuries to breed a Joan of Arc and a Zola.

Dec. 11. Cablegram from Keokuk, Ia. "Orion died today." He was past 73.

Dec. 30. No letter from Mollie yet; we do not know whether it was sudden or not.

> They went for the summer to a resort just outside of Vienna. Among the notes of that period are a good many axioms. It is noticeable that Mark Twain had become more bitter following Susy's death.

Kaltenleutgeben, July 4, '98. News that Sampson has destroyed the Spanish fleet in the Harbor of Santiago de Cuba; that our troops have closely invested the city and that it must surrender. Also that our transport fleet has at last arrived at Manila. Dr. E. S. Parker and Corneil Dunham are here to enjoy this news with us.

A person (Satan) who for untold centuries has maintained the imposing position of spiritual head of 4/5 of the human race, and political head of the whole of it, must be granted the possession of executive abilities of the highest order. In his large presence the other popes and politicians shrink to midgets for the microscope.

He hasn't a single salaried helper; the Opposition employ a million.

Some men worship rank, some worship heroes, some worship power, some worship God, and over these ideals they dispute—but they all worship money.

There is no law in the Bibles and the Statute Books limiting the appetites and the passions that has any but one function, to wit: to limit the law of God.

To ask a doctor's opinion of osteopathy is equivalent to going to Satan for information about Christianity.

You can't depend on your judgment when your imagination is out of focus.

The proper office of a friend is to side with you when you are in the wrong. Nearly anybody will side with you when you are in the right.

There is but one first thing to do when a man is wounded and suffering: *relieve* him. If we have a curiosity to know his nationality, that is a matter of no consequence, and can wait.

God's inhumanity to man makes countless thousands mourn.

Of the demonstrably wise there are but two; those who commit suicide, and those who keep their reasoning faculties atrophied with drink.

The radical of one century is the conservative of the next.

The radical invents the views. When he has worn them out the conservative adopts them.

There has been only one Christian. They caught Him and crucified Him early.

What God lacks is convictions—stability of character. He ought to be a Presbyterian or a Catholic or *something*—not try to be everything.

If all men were rich, all men would be poor.

Let us swear while we may, for in heaven it will not be allowed.

Familiarity breeds contempt. How accurate that is. The reason we hold truth in such respect is because we have so little opportunity to get familiar with it.

If I cannot swear in heaven I shall not stay there.

The unspoken word is capital. We can invest it or we can squander it.

If you wish to lower yourself in a person's favor, one good way is to tell his story over again, the way *you* heard it.

Spending one's capital is feeding a dog on his own tail.

Good breeding consists in concealing how much we think of ourselves and how little we think of the other person.

Truth is more of a stranger than fiction.

There are no grades of vanity, there are only grades of ability in concealing it.

When we remember that we are all mad, the mysteries disappear and life stands explained.

It is not best that we use our morals week days; it gets them out of repair for Sundays.

Truth is mighty and will prevail. There is nothing the matter with this, except that it ain't so.

All people have had ill luck, but Jairus's daughter and Lazarus had the worst.

The human race consists of the damned and the ought-to-be damned.

When you fish for love, bait with your heart, not your brain.

LIFE

We laugh and laugh,
Then cry and cry—
Then feebler laugh,
Then die.

The heart is the real Fountain of Youth. While that remains young the Waterbury of Time must stand still.

Christianity will doubtless still survive in the earth ten centuries hence—stuffed and in a museum.

Shut the door. Not that it lets in the cold, but that it lets out the cozyness.

It is an art apart. Saint Francis of Assisi said—"All saints can do miracles, but few of them can keep hotel."

It is easier for a cannibal to enter the Kingdom of Heaven through the eye of a rich man's needle than it is for any other foreigner to read the terrible German script.

Education consists mainly in what we have unlearned.

In this day of the telegraph man waits not for time or tide.

The altar cloth of one aeon is the doormat of the next.

"Good friends, good books and a sleepy conscience: this is the ideal life" (written in the Archduchess's album).

Concerning the difference between man and the jackass: some observers hold that there isn't any. But this wrongs the jackass.

It is easier to stay out than get out.

It is by the goodness of God that in our country we have those three unspeakably precious things: freedom of speech, freedom of conscience, and the prudence never to exercise either of them.

Truth is stranger than fiction, but it is because fiction is obliged to stick to possibilities; truth isn't.

Have a place for everything and keep the thing somewhere else. This is not advice, it is merely custom.

There are several good protections against temptations but the surest is cowardice.

Nature makes the locust with an appetite for crops; man would have made him with an appetite for sand—I mean a man with the least little bit of common sense.

There are many scapegoats for our blunders, but the most popular one is Providence.

When people do not respect us we are sharply offended; yet deep down in his heart no man much respects himself.

The universal brotherhood of man is our most precious possession—what there is of it.

Some of these observations he used in his books.

Through having mislaid his notebook, or for some other reason, this London note was omitted from the preceding book and here follows:

London, Jan. 7, '97. Last Sunday I struck upon a new "solution" of a haunting mystery. A great many years ago I published in the Atlantic "The Recent Carnival of Crime in Connecticut."[1]

That was an attempt to account for our seeming *duality*—the presence in us of another *person;* not a slave of ours, but free and independent, and with a character distinctly its own. I made my conscience that other person and it came before me in the form of a malignant dwarf and told me plain things about myself and shamed me and scoffed at me and derided me. This creature was so much its own master that it would leave the premises—leave its post—forsake its duties—and go off on a spree with other irresponsible consciences—and discuss their masters (no—their slaves).

Presently Stevenson published Dr. Jekyll and Mr. Hyde. That was nearer this thing. J. and H. were the dual persons in one body, quite distinct in nature and character and presumably each with a *conscience of its own.* Nearer, yes, but not near enough. Or, to put it differently, a truth and a falsity harnessed together; the falsity being the ability of the one person to step into the other person's place, *at will.*

I have underscored "conscience of its own." When I made my conscience my other person, and independent, with its own (original) character, it was a mistake. My conscience is a part of *me.* It is a mere machine, like my heart—but moral, not physical; and being moral is *teachable,* its action modifiable. It is merely a *thing*; the creature of *training*; it is whatever one's mother and Bible and comrades and laws and system of government

[1] Included today in his collected works.

and habitat and heredities have made it. It is not a separate person, it has no originality, no independence.

Inborn nature is Character, by itself in the brutes—the tiger, the dove, the fox, etc. Inborn nature *and* the modifying Conscience, working together make Character in man.

Jekyll and Hyde are correct in so far as each has its separate and distinct nature—*and*—conscience character.

But the Baltimore and other cases show that the two persons in a man have no command over each other (as falsely pretended in Jekyll and Hyde). The two persons in a man do not even *know* each other and are not aware of each other's existence, never heard of each other—have never even suspected each other's existence.

And so, I was wrong in the beginning; that other person is not one's conscience; and Stevenson was wrong, for the two persons in a man are wholly unknown to each other, and can never in this world communicate with each other in any way.

Now I come to my *new* notion.

The French have lately shown (apparently) that that other person is in command during the somnambulic sleep; that it has a memory of its own and can recall its acts when hypnotized and thrown again into that sleep, but that *you* have no memory of its acts. You are not present at all.

Very good. That *is* distinct duality. To this arrangement I wish to add this detail—that we have a spiritualized self which can detach itself and go wandering off upon affairs of its own—for recreation, perhaps. I am not acquainted with my double, my partner in duality, the other and wholly independent personage who resides in me—and whom I will call Watson, for I don't know his name, although he most certainly has one, and signs it in a hand which has no resemblance to mine when he takes possession of our partnership body and goes off on mysterious trips—but I *am* acquainted (dimly) with my spiritualized self and I know that it and I are one, because we have common memory; when I wake mornings, I remember that it (that is, *I*) have been doing, and whither it (that is *I*) have been wandering in the course of what I took to be unreality and called Dreams, for want of a truthfuler name.

Now, as I take it, my other self, my dream self, is merely my ordinary body and mind freed from clogging flesh and become a spiritualized body and mind and with the ordinary powers of both enlarged in all particulars a little, and in some particulars prodigiously.

For instance, to the ordinary vision, the vision of the X-ray is added—the invisible ray—and I am able to use it and see through opaque bodies. You have an instance of this in the biography of Agassiz. In a dream he saw through the stone that contained a fossil shell and woke up and drew a picture of that shell; and when he broke open the stone his picture was correct.

Waking I move slowly; but in my dreams my unhampered spiritualized body flies to the ends of the earth in a millionth of a second. Seems to—and I believe, *does*.

Waking I cannot form in my mind the minutely detailed and living features of a face and a form and a costume which I have never seen, but my dream self can do all this with the accuracy and vividness of a camera. Waking, I cannot create in my mind a picture of a room and furniture which I have not recently seen, or have never seen; but my dream self can do this to the minutest detail.

My dream self meets friends, strangers, the dead, the living—all sorts and kinds of dream people—and holds both rational and irrational conversations with them upon subjects which often have not been in my waking mind and which, in some cases could never have been in it. And these people say things to me which affect me in all ways; pleasurably, sadly, offensively, humiliatingly. They make me cry, they make me laugh, they make me rage, they make me fight, they make me run, they make me insult the weak, they make me cringe to the strong, and swallow the insults of the insulter. And I am always *myself*, not that other person who is in me—Watson.

I do actually make immense excursions in my spiritualized person. I go into awful dangers; I am in battles and trying to hide from the bullets; I fall over cliffs (and my *un*spiritualized body starts). I get lost in caves and in the corridors of monstrous hotels; I appear before company in my shirt; I come on the platform with no subject to talk about, and not a note; I go to unnamable places, I do unprincipled things; and every vision is vivid, every sensation—physical as well as moral—is *real.*

When my physical body dies my dream body will doubtless continue its excursion and activities without change, forever.

In my dream last night I was suddenly in the presence of a negro wench who was sitting in grassy open country, with her left arm resting on the arm of one of those long park-sofas that are made of broad slats with cracks between, and a curve-over back. She was very vivid to me—round black face, shiny black eyes, thick lips, very white regular teeth showing through her smile. She was about 22, and plump—not fleshy, not fat, merely rounded and plump; and good-natured and not at all bad-looking. She had but one garment on—a coarse tow-linen shirt that reached from her neck to her ankles without break. She sold me a pie; a mushy apple pie—hot. She was eating one herself with a tin teaspoon. She made a disgusting proposition to me. Although it was disgusting it did not surprise me—for I was young (I was never old in a dream yet) and it seemed quite natural that it should come from her. It was disgusting, but I did not say so; I merely made a chaffing remark, brushing aside the matter—

a little jeeringly—and this embarrassed her and she made an awkward pretence that I had misunderstood her. I made a sarcastic remark about this pretence, and asked for a spoon to eat my pie with. She had but the one, and she took it out of her mouth, in a quite matter-of-course way, and offered it to me. My stomach rose—there everything vanished.

It was not a dream—it all *happened*. I was actually there in person—in my spiritualized condition. My, how vivid it all was! Even to the texture of her shirt, its dull white color, and the pale brown tint of a stain on the shoulder of it. I had never seen that girl; I was not acquainted with her—but dead or alive she is a *reality*; she exists and she was *there*. Her pie was a spiritualized pie, no doubt, and also her shirt and the bench and the shed—but their *actualities* were at that moment in existence somewhere in the world.

The time that my dream self first appeared to me and explained itself (apparently I was for the moment dreaming) it was as insubstantial as a dim blue smoke, and I saw the furniture through it, but it was dressed in my customary clothes.

> He does not stick to his text—not altogether—as who can in any attempt to elucidate the shades of difference between under-conscious and semi-conscious dream personalities—our various and multiple selves? In the last paragraph we feel a touch of fiction, seldom entirely lacking with him, however much he tried to stick to the literal relation. Very likely he felt this himself, and so ended in this incomplete fashion.

Vienna, Jan. 19, '98. Tonight drove out to Leschetizky's house (wife and Clara along) to attend one of the fortnightly meetings of his piano class. About 25 of his great multitude of people present. The master sat at one piano, and each of his seven pupils in turn sat at the other. It was a wonderful performance. Young Voss, a handsome American, carried off the honors by a little. Now and then the master would let fly a rebuke, and play a passage as a pupil had played it, then play it as it *ought* to have been played. Beautiful as the pupil's work had been, the superior splendor of the master's touch was immediately recognizable. He gave one young lady a devastating dressing down—poured out wrath, criticism, sarcasm and humor upon her in a flood for ten—no, as much as twelve minutes. He is a most capable and felicitous talker—was born for an orator, I think. What life, energy, fire in a man past 70! And how he does play! He is easily the greatest pianist in the world. He is just as great and just as capable today as ever he was.

Last night, at dinner with us, he did all the talking for three hours, and everybody was glad to let him. He told us his experiences as a revolutionist fifty years ago, in '48; and his battle pictures were magnificently worded. Pötzl had never heard him before. He is a talker himself, and a good one, but he merely sat silent and gazed across the table at this inspired man, and drank in his words, and let his eyes fill and the blood come and go in his face and never said a word.

Among those who came to Mark Twain's apartment in Vienna was Ossip Gabrilowitsch, then a pupil of Leschetizky—less than a dozen years later to become the husband of Clara Clemens. In an article in the *New York Times,* last year (1930)—"Memoirs of Leschetizky"—Gabrilowitsch wrote:

"The Clemens drawing-room in Vienna was a rendezvous for distinguished men and women of all types and nationalities. Clara enjoyed great popularity in musical and social circles; and I was by no means the only young man in Vienna whose head was turned and whose heart sorely needed mending. 'Leschy,' with his usual keenness, quickly sized up the situation and made a witty remark to a group of young fellows gathered about him: 'Boys,' he said, 'it seems to me that you are all suffering from the same trouble—"Delirium Clemens."'

"Such little sallies of wit often flashed out in Leschetizky's remarks. He was a brilliant conversationalist, an engrossing story-teller and a mimic whose powers would have carried him far in the theatrical profession. He uttered many an epigram which his auditors cherished."

Wednesday, Feb. 2. Our wedding anniversary—28 years married. The first sorrow came in the first year—the death of Livy's father. Our Susy died Aug. 18, '96—the cloud is permanent now.

Feb. 4. Our betrothal day.

At the lecture the other night, Madame de Laschowska introduced us to Her Royal Highness Countess Bardi, a Princess of the Portuguese Royal House by marriage, sister to the Austrian Archduchess Marie Theresa (widow of the Archduke Ludwig, and mother to the Archduke Otto, heir to the Imperial throne). The Countess Bardi was very cordial—very beautiful, too, in both body and spirit—and so we took counsel of the wise and the knowing, and learned that it would be proper etiquette for us to drive to the Palace between 12 and 2 today and write our names in her visitors' book in the portier's office.

So we drove there; got by the sentinels without accident, and told the finely uniformed portier what our errand was. He said:

"You are Americans?"

"Yes."

"You are expected. Her Royal Highness is out, but she will be in in a minute."

And he was taking us toward a liveried manservant who stood at the foot of the stairs with an expectant look on his face. But Livy hung back and said:

"No, it is a mistake. We are not expected—we have only come to write in the book."

The portier said again:

"You are Americans, is it not so?"

"Yes, but we are not expected."

"There can be no mistake, *gnädige Frau;* Her Royal Highness left particular orders that her absence must be explained and that you must be shown upstairs. It is but a few minutes—she will come almost at once."

The other servant also insisted—and beguiled us upstairs; but when we found that he was taking us to a drawing-room, Livy drew the line—she would go no further—"Let us have the visitors' book and get away," and down she went again. There was no book—would we write on a piece of paper? Yes, that would do. So the portier was commanded to furnish a paper and a pen. But he was going to obey his higher orders or die at his post. He would hear of none of these arrangements: we *must* go upstairs, and wait. The sentinels were close by, with their guns. I am a prudent man. I said we would obey.

So we went up again, laid off our wraps, and were conducted through one drawing-room (saw a gown skurrying out of the door) and left alone in another. Livy was in a great fright, and made the servant promise to inquire, and if it was a mistake come back and tell us and give us a chance to fly before being ordered out.

But I was not troubled; I was charmed with the situation, charmed with the fine literary flavor of it, and with the story-book completeness of it. I believed there was a mistake—I was sure of it—but I wouldn't have missed it for anything. I was full of eager curiosity to see how it would turn out; and I could hardly enjoy a beautiful oil-painted lake scene which fascinated me, my mind was so luxuriously busy imagining what was going to happen. And I had one deep, deep, regret—that Howells was not there—there to fill the occasion with colossal blunders, and make it too funny for this world! Howells or Rev. Twichell—or both. However, with three born blunder-makers together, perhaps that would have been too much.

I imagined the Princess coming home and finding that a couple of innocent wild Americans, who were meaning no harm, had been mistaken for somebody who was really expected, and had gotten themselves into a situation common to the mendacious stage, but wholly impossible in real life. I knew that the ordinary princess of books and the stage would have no difficulty in dealing with this matter—it would be quite civil: order up the sentinel and clear these foolish intruders out. But this was not that kind of a princess—she was made of finer fiber than that. Her first thought would be, how to get us out of there without humiliating us. *She* would be troubled now; and the sorrowful comedy would be exhaustively complete and perfect all around. How would she proceed? I set myself the pleasant entertainment of ciphering that out. I said to myself, "In the first place, she . . ."

And then she came in! And I got no further with my plot. But I *could* have ciphered it out—I know it. With her came her sister the Archduchess—eloquent, deep eyes, and the face a book where the records of a right heart are clearly written. She had suffered a bereavement and if I had had more German at my command, *there* was a subject which was close to my heart! Her daughters were with her, and also the children of her sister—that princess who assists her husband in his noble work of affording relief to people whose eyes have suffered from disease. It was a splendid pleasure to be this close to that prince and his princess, whom I have so long held in such deep honor and reverence. To relieve pain—that is an exalted office; and when a prince does it, and doesn't *need* to do it, it makes the princely dignity ideal.

It was a charming twenty minutes we spent there. There are princes which I cast in the *Echte* (genuine) princely mold, and they make me regret—again—that I am not a prince myself. It is not a new regret but a very old one. I have never been properly and humbly satisfied with my condition. I am a democrat only on principle, not by instinct—nobody is *that*. Doubtless some people *say* they are, but this world is grievously given to lying.

When we got back home we found out that we *were* the Americans who were expected, after all—but at two o'clock, not 12:30. But no matter, nothing could have improved the episode. I was sure we were the wrong ones, but there was nothing to make me sorry it had happened.

> At the hotel they found a written invitation for them to come to the Palace. Mark Twain appears to have entirely forgotten how rabidly democratic he had been when writing of King Arthur's Court, some ten years earlier.

March 18, '98. On the 15th I heard by accident, through a chance remark of Miss Levitus, that the American patents on Szczepanik's designing-machine were not sold. I sent a note at once to Miss Levitus and asked her to arrange an interview for next night, here in the Hotel Metropole, in our room. I spent the 16th in gathering American statistics at our Consulate-General (the youngest were 18 years old) and British ones, through Mr. Wm. Lavino, correspondent of the London Times: he got others for me by telephoning the British Consul.

I ciphered on the date and wrote eleven pages of questions; and when the inventor and his capitalist arrived at nine with Miss Levitus and Dr. Winternitz, I was ready for business and rich with my new learning. My extraordinary familiarity with the subject paralyzed the banker for a while, for he was merely expecting to find a humorist, not a commercial cyclopedia—but he recovered presently.

We talked till midnight and then parted: I to think over the data and the price, $1,500,000, and we to meet again at 4 P.M. today. By breakfast time I had thought it over sufficiently; so that I sent word and Mr. Kleinberg came and we entered into an agreement.

> He could never resist a patent right. This one —a designing-machine to be used in the manufacture of carpets, etc., was particularly alluring. Again the air was full of gold—even the typesetter had never held out such prospects as this. The whole industry of carpet-making was to be revolutionized. When he had his option properly signed, sealed and delivered, he accounted himself a billionaire. In his notebook he writes that when a certain Mr. Wood representing American carpet interests called and inquired how much he would take for his option, he could not think of a price big enough.

I declined and got away from the subject. I was afraid he would offer me half a million dollars for it. I should have been obliged to take it. But I was born with a speculative instinct and I did not want that temptation put in my way.

Wood said he knew but one man in Vienna—had met him some years ago in Constantinople—Major X—an American gentleman who has served in the Austrian Cavalry 32 years. He had taken the Major along as interpreter, when he had his talk with Mr. Kleinberg this morning. And now I find that Major X is to be one of the guests who I am to meet at Dr. Otis's tonight. It *is* a small world.

> A small world, and a peculiar one. Perhaps there was nothing suspicious in the facts of Mr. Wood's slight acquaintance in Vienna and Major X's presence at the dinner—perhaps Mr. Wood really did contemplate taking over the option, but there is something in it all that suggests an "arrangement"—the kind of arrangement that suggests Paige.

I wrote all about the Option to Mr. H. H. Rogers (reserving 1/10 of the eventual stock for myself) Sunday morning and mailed the letter, to catch the Wednesday steamer. I asked Mr. Rogers to come over and if he was not sufficiently impressed he could cable me the word "London." I would then try to sell the Option there. I should expect to succeed.

> Apparently Mr. Rogers was not impressed—even after careful investigation. He did not put any money into the carpet-designing patent or permit Mark Twain to do so. The pages of the notebook glow with matter concerning the invention, inventors, and the like, for a time, and then these things are heard of no more. If there was a fortune to be made from the designer it escaped him, but more likely he escaped *losing* one.

"The Princess Hohenlohe wishes you to write on her fan."

"With pleasure—where is she?"

"At your elbow."

I turned and took the fan and said:

"Your Highness's place is in a fairy tale; and by and by I mean to write that tale."

Whereat, she laughed, a happy girlish laugh, and we moved through the crowd to a writing table and to get a stronger light, so that I could see her better. Beautiful little creature, with the dearest friendly ways and sincerity, and simplicity, and sweetnesses—the ideal princess of the fairy tales. She is 16 or 17, I judge.

Kaltenleutgeben, May 27, '98.

We have some insane customs, of course. All countries have insane customs. The stranger notices that they are insane—the native doesn't; he is used to them, hardened to them, they are matters of course to him. In Vienna when you take a flat you pay the rent twice a year in advance. In the country when you take a villa you pay the whole year in advance. "It may burn down the first night," you say, "what then?" The proprietor answers—"I have other houses; you can have one of those."

"It would not suit; we examined every house in the place—there is not another house that would *begin* to suit."

"I should do the best I could for you."

"The best you could do would be a long way from satisfactory."

"One can but do one's best."

"You don't suggest refunding the money."

"It is not the custom."

"When a man comes to the cure, he knows his term is six weeks, and he must be under the doctor's advice all the time. Does the doctor collect the whole fee in advance?"

"Oh, no."

"Why not?"

"The man—"

"Go on. You were going to say the man might die the first day."

"Yes."

"Just as the house might burn down."

The Being who to me is the real God is the One who

created this majestic universe and rules it. He is the only Originator, the only originator of thoughts; thoughts suggested from within not from without; the originator of colors and of all their possible combinations; of forces and the laws that govern them; of forms and shapes of *all* forms. Man has never invented a new one; He is the only Originator—He made the materials of all things; He made the laws by which and by which only, man may combine them into machines and other things which outside influence may suggest to him. He made character—man can portray it but not "create" it, for He is the only Creator.

He is the perfect artisan, the perfect artist. Everything which he has made is fine, everything which he has made is beautiful; nothing coarse, nothing ugly has ever come from His hand. Even His materials are all delicate, none of them is coarse. The materials of the leaf, the flower, the fruit; of the insect, the elephant, the man; of the earth, the crags and the ocean; of the snow, the hoarfrost and the ice—may be reduced to infinitesimal particles and they are still delicate, still faultless; whether He makes a gnat, a bird, a horse, a plain, a forest, a mountain range, a planet, a constellation, or a diatom whose form the keenest eye in the world cannot perceive, it is all one—He makes it utterly and minutely perfect in form, and construction. The diatom which is invisible to the eye on the point of a needle is graceful and beautiful in form and in the minute exquisite elaboration of its parts it is a wonder. The contemplation of it moves one to something of the same awe and reverence which the march of the comets through their billion mile orbits compels.

This is indeed a God! He is not jealous, trivial, ignorant, revengeful—it is impossible. He has personal dignity—dignity answerable to his grandeur, his greatness, his might, his sublimity; He cares nothing for men's flatteries, compliments, praises, prayers; it is impossible that he should value them, impossible that he should listen to them, these mouthings of microbes. He is not ignorant, He does not mistake His myriad great suns, swimming in the measureless ocean of space for tallow candles hung in the roof to light this forgotten potato which we call the Earth, and name His footstool. He cannot see it except under His microscope. The shadow does not go back on His dial—it is against His law; His sun does not stand still on Gibeon to accommodate a worm out on a raid against other worms—it is against His law. His real character is written in plain words in His real Bible, which is Nature and her history; we read it every day, and we could understand it and trust in it if we would burn the spurious one and dig the remains of our insignificant reasoning faculties out of the grave where that and other man-made Bibles have buried them for 2000 years and more.

The Bible of Nature tells us no word about any future life, but only about this present one. It does not promise a future life; it does not even vaguely indicate one. It is not intended as a message to us, any more than the scientist intends a message to surviving microbes when he boils the life out of a billion of them in a thimble. The microbes discover a message in it; this is certain—if they have a pulpit.

The Book of Nature tells us distinctly that God cares not a rap for us—nor for any living creature. It tells us that His laws inflict pain and suffering and sorrow, but it does not say that this is done in order that He may get pleasure out of this misery. We do not know what the object is, for the Book is not able to tell us. It may be mere indifference. Without a doubt He had an object, but we have no way of discovering what it was. The scientist has an object, but it is not the joy of inflicting pain upon the microbe.

The Law of the Distribution of Comfort and Pain shows an entire absence of sentimental justice. The proportion of punishments to the size of the infractions has been ignored; this again shows the absence of anything representing sentimental justice. I knew an unspeakable villain who was born rich, remained rich, was never ill a day, never had a bone broken, led a joyous life till 80, then died a painless death by apoplexy. I knew a man who when in his second year in college jumped into an ice-cold stream when he was overheated and rescued a priest of God from drowning; suffered partial paralysis, lay in his bed 38 years, unable to speak, unable to feed himself, unable to write; not even the small charity of quenching his mind was doled out to him—he lay and thought and brooded and mourned and begged for death 38 years. There are no laws founded upon sentimental justice; the laws are all hard and fast. If it so happen that you are just in the right condition to bring on 38 years of paralysis by a sudden cold bath, that is what the bath will produce—no allowance will be made even if you take the bath to save the Virgin Mary.

June 11, '98. Clara's birthday three days ago. Not a reference to it has been made by any member of the family in my hearing; no presents, no congratulations, no celebrations. Up to a year and ten months ago all our birthdays from the beginning of the family life were annually celebrated with loving preparations followed by a joyous and jovial outpouring of thanksgivings. The birthdays were milestones on the march of happiness. Then Susy died. All anniversaries of whatever sort perished with her. As we pass them now they are only gravestones. We cannot keep from seeing them as we go by but we can keep silent about them and look the other way and put them out of memory as they sink out of sight behind us.

The Lost Sweetheart

I was 22 when I met her and she 16. It was in a dream. Go on with the story. Meetings extended over years. Both are as young as ever, always. First time she jumps across a brook ahead, and when I am about to follow a steamboat rushes along and when it gets by she has vanished and the brook is a mile wide. Put in such things.

Aug. 4, '98. Finished "My Platonic Sweetheart" a day or so ago.

> This was the story outlined as the Lost Sweetheart—a lovely dream fancy, published in Harper's Magazine two years after his death, and now included in his collected works.

Aug. 7, '98. I think a few monarchs have died here and there during the past year, I do not remember. It made a great silence. Bismarck has been dead five or six days now, but the reverberatings from that mighty fall still go quaking and thundering around the planet.

If a king should jump overboard from a ship and save a life, it would last in history ten thousand years. A sailor who should jump over and save a ham would risk his life, be just as heroic and would be moved by the same impulse.

For man to risk his life (and lose it) for the sake of a friend, a child, a battalion, a king, a country, is no large matter, it has been done a billion times, it is done every day by firemen and by soldiers at $8 a month (1898). For a God to take three days on a Cross out of a life of eternal happiness and mastership of the universe is a service which the least among us would be glad to do upon the like terms. The world's population is 1,500,000,000; if the offer was made there would be 1,500,000,000 takers. Charlotte Corday—she risked and got, hell—as she believed.

No man that ever lived has ever done a thing to please God—primarily. It was done to please himself, then God next.

A man's brain (intellect) is stored powder; it cannot touch itself off; the fire must come from the outside.

Aug. 10, '98. Last night dreamed of a whaling cruise in a drop of water. Not by microscope, but actually. This would mean a reduction of the participants to a minuteness which would make them nearly invisible to God, and He wouldn't be interested in them any longer.

Lying thinking about this, concluded to write a dispute between a microscope and a telescope—one can pull a moral out of that.

The lowest form of the embarrassed laugh is when you do it when soliloquizing; when you use it involuntarily—to cover a naked and poor remark made to a person who is present in your imagination only. (I wish the word "*only*" was in hell.)

Sept. 10. News came at 6 P.M. that the Empress was assassinated at Geneva, just after noon.

Sept. 17. Friday—funeral of the Empress—in the church opposite the Hotel Kranz windows. [That is, those of Mark Twain's apartment—season 1898-99.]

THE BELLS.

At twelve noon the little square was suddenly emptied.

At 1:05 building the fence—with soldiers—a wall of them, elbow to elbow, double rank, against every sidewalk, and a double rank across the square in front of the Kranz. Done in three minutes.

Sanding the street in front of the plain little white village church of the Capuchins—white plastered, its only ornament a statue of a monk in a niche.

Officers of all breeds drifting about on business and some in black cloaks and caps with a single feather (long) sticking up, otherwise gorgeous. In other cases with much gold and a paint-brush plume, some like a tall delicate puff of steam. Long black cloaks, silver cross on them. Wagons arriving with flower wreaths. Many picturesque Hungarian costumes.

Three Archdukes below on balcony. No noise of hoofs. All traffic shut off at two.

Vast windows of a corner store, with people in masses behind them, balconies overflowing. People in windows dim like folk under water.

All the military movements beautifully done—

Knights of Malta—beautiful red uniform—a broad white cross covering breast and a gush of white plumes. Here one sees the Golden Fleece, 1431. No end of coachmen and footmen in black cocked hats and mourning.

At 2:30 a long black wagon with six mourning servants—something taken out and carried in—wish I knew what it was.

On this side of the middle of the square I see none but a great crowd of uniforms—no civilians, only officers. This space is fenced off by oblong double fence of soldiers.

2:40. Small procession of bare-headed monks, the head one with a white shirt and a cross.

Not many smoking today.

Display of mourning not great. Ladies generally in black.

2:45. Carriages passing in a continuous stream.

A Cardinal in purple with two attendants arrives and enters.

Dress these people differently (Church all right) and it is a funeral in Hannibal, fifty years ago. For evidently all these gorgeous folk know each other from babyhood—greet, kindly and cordially.

3:05. It is a fine picture now—a solid mass of blue and green and gold with that splotch of stunning red and white and gold in front of church.

1600 years ago the Emperor Marcus Aurelius died here—it was a Roman Camp then, and the country had been under the Roman Dominion something over 400, possibly 600, years.

3:58. An interval. The crowd waiting.

Pause—waiting.

(I suppose that no one past 45 attaches high value to his life, but would not like to have it taken in a horrible way.)

Essentially, nobilities are foolishnesses, but if I were a citizen where they prevail I would do my best to get a title, for the consideration it furnishes—that is what we want. In Republics we strive for it with the surest means we have—money.

4:12. *The* procession is coming—cavalry, four abreast, to spread the crowd apart—25 men.

Great body of Lancers—blue, and gilt helmets. Hardly a sound of hoofs.

Three 6-horse mourning coaches. Outriders and coachmen in cocked hats and white wigs. Troops in red, gold and white—splendid.

The hearse—eight black horses, plumed—all uncover. The military salute. Drums. Hungarian bodyguard with leopard skins.

Candles.

The little coffin borne in.

That scalawag caused it.

The crowd has surged together. Solid. Splendid mass of color.

Maria Theresa and Duke of Reinchstadt lie in that little church-vault, and others of the family.

4:45. Coming out of the church.

Who is the principal? The guilty one? This man? No—Militarism, which burdens and impoverishes and maddens. Royalty is itself the Empress' murderer before the fact.

He "always intended to kill a queen."

They have shown him his photograph: "Henceforth I shall be celebrated."

Imprison for life. It is severer than death.

Celebrity was what he wanted, at any cost.

Everywhere are people glad to be able to say they knew him—vain of it. If you and I had known him we should tell about it—and at bottom this would be vanity.

The gypsy who told her at 13 she would ascend a throne, suffer hard blows and die a violent death.

Emperor William lays it on the Lord, but it was Militarism. Williams says "so ordained from Above." It is no compliment to God. The remark acquits the prisoner. No different meaning can be given it. It was always a fool remark—for, if God does a thing His agent is guiltless and by no logic can he be made responsible.

But we are all insane, anyway.

Note the mountain-climbers.

The suicide seems to me the only sane person.

If it is a crime, "ordaining it from On High" *leaves* it a crime. It is God's crime. The agent is secondary. When people lay it on God they should forebear to call it a crime. But William calls it "a deed unparalleled for ruthlessness." Queer!

From the material collected that day he made an article on the assassination of the Empress, now included in his collected works.

Sept. 21. Mental Telegraphy.

Mrs. Clemens was pouring the coffee this morning: I unfolded the Neue Freiepresse, began to read a paragraph and said—

"They have found a new way to tell genuine gems from false ——"

"By the Roëntgen Ray," she exclaimed.

That is what I was going to say. She had not seen the paper and there had been no talk about the ray, or gems, by herself or by me. It was a plain case of telegraphy.

Story of little Satan Jr. who came to Hannibal, went to school, was popular and greatly liked by those who knew his secret. The others were jealous and the girls didn't like him because he smelled of brimstone. He was always doing miracles—his pals knew they were miracles, the others thought they were mysteries.

> This is a more definite hint of the story of *The Mysterious Stranger* which he presently began and partly finished, in three different forms. Just when he finished it is not certain. The writer of these lines recalls a day in 1909 when Mark Twain, pointing to a drawer containing some manuscripts, said: "There are a few things there which might be published, if I could finish them; but I shall never do it, now. There is one, *The Mysterious Stranger,* that I could finish very easily, almost any time. Perhaps I shall do that one, and then some day you can get it in shape for publication." He died the following April. So far as I then knew he had not added anything to the story, which it seemed he had undertaken in several forms. But two or three years later, among some loose papers, I found that amazing final chapter, of the best version, probably written (and forgotten, for his memory had become very uncertain) about the time

of our conversation. The story was published serially in Harper's Magazine, and later in book form. It has been called his literary "high-water mark."

March 14, '99. Received letter from Mr. Rogers. Last sale (of stocks) brought $3586. Total in his hands $51995. Brooklyn Gas is up to $155—cost us $75.

March 23, '99. Budapest. Speech at Jubilee of Emancipation of the Hungarian Press. Banquet.

CHAPTER XXXII

England Again

The Clemens family spent some months in Sweden (summer of 1899), then located in London (30 Wellington Court—later at Dollis Hill) for the remainder of their European sojourn.

TRUE love is the only heart disease that is best left to "run on."—The only affection of the heart for which there is no help, and none desired.

Happiness is a Swedish sunset—it is there for all, but most of us look the other way and lose it.

Portions of a Speech delivered at the Savage Club, London

Fellow Savages: It is 27 years since I was here before. Some of you have grown gray since then, others baldheaded. I was six feet four then—now five feet 8½ and daily diminishing in altitude. Also in principles—the shrinkage still goes on. I have not professionally dealt in truth. Many when they come to die have spent all the truth that was in them, and enter the next world as paupers. I have saved up enough to make an astonishment there.

I recognize changes. Irving was here then—is here now—may he long abide. Hyde Park was only half as large as it is now. The shilling was only half as big as it is, but you could buy twice as much with it. Since then you have borrowed our telephone, phonograph, and some other necessaries of life and we have borrowed your perfecting press. Stanley is here, and Douglas Straight; but Charles Reade is gone and Tom Hood and Harry Lee, and Canon Kingsley. Stanley was only the creator of Africa then, the comrade of kings, the admiration of the world—now he is G.C.B. In those days you could have carried Kipling around in his lunch-basket—now he fills the world.

I was young and foolish then—now I am old and foolisher. My hair was as the lurid crimson of the sun—now it has paled to the cold gray of the dawn.

These are merely notes that he made for a speech he was to deliver and did deliver, a day or two later!

Greeting to 1900

The 20th Century is a stranger to me—I wish it well but my heart is all for my own century. I took 65 years of it, just on a risk, but if I had known as much about it as I know now I would have taken the whole of it.

There are no wild animals till man makes them so.

To the pure all things are impure.

Relief of Mafeking. The news came at 9:17 P.M. Before ten all London was in the streets gone mad with joy. By then the news was all over the American continent.

Speech at Lotos

Thank my 95 creditors only one of whom was a Shylock.

Irving Underhill wants to pay me $500—owing seven years. Cannot allow it. He has had a hard time.

Offered $10,000 a year to edit Judge—the labor required estimated at "one hour of my time per week." Can't accept.

Mailed letters to William M. Clemens, P.O. Box 1716, N.Y. and the Bowen Merrill Co. Indianapolis, warning them not to issue those books.

> "Those books" were copies of a biography of Mark Twain, prepared by W. M. Clemens against Mark Twain's wishes. This Clemens, known as a "nephew" or "cousin" of Mark Twain's, was neither: or, if the latter, the degree of cousinship was very remote.

When you climb the hill of happiness may you never meet a friend.

Drove out to Dollis Hill (4:35 to 5:10) in the rainstorm and took possession. It is certainly the dirtiest dwelling-house in Europe—perhaps in the universe.

> This was a furnished house just outside of London, taken for the summer of 1900. It was at one time a favorite retreat for Gladstone, and the place, today public property, is now called "Gladstone Park."
>
> He loved Dollis Hill, once he was established, and left it with regret.

Better sixty days of Dollis than a cycle of Cathay.

CHAPTER XXXIII

Back in America

OCT. 14, 1900, Sunday noon. About 500 miles to make. A spacious ship and most comfortable. Rides the seas level, hardly any motion, no seasickness aboard. No table racks.

> The Mark Twain party had left Dollis Hill early in October, sailing on the 6th, for America by the steamer *Minnehaha*, arriving October 15, after a foreign residence of more than nine years.

M.H. has gradually six bastards put upon him by the courts, some on no good evidence but his lecherous character. Then dies and turns out to be a woman.

April 17. In N. Y. in 1895 when I was 60, Cheiro the palmist told me that I should become very wealthy in my 68th year. I was a bankrupt and heavily in debt at the time and I properly thanked him. He said it again in London, two years afterward and I properly thanked him again. Shall I be able to complete my thanks next year? If not can I sue him for breach of promise?

Name the greatest of all the inventors: Accident.

Story of the coward who did one stupendously brave deed—and then had to go on all his life in like manner to live up to his reputation. His monument "To the bravest of the brave" moves his old friends to reveal his secret to me, a stranger.

> He could not resist from investing in doubtful enterprises. The next entry supports this.

Jan. 9, 1902. 200 shares stock in the Booklovers Library —half to Jean and half to Clara. —Will arrive presently.

Wednesday June 4. Columbia, Mo. University degree LL.D.

> He made the trip to Hannibal and to Columbia, for the degree, but this is his only note of it. For a fuller account see "Mark Twain—a Biography," Chapter CCXXI.

Thursday Aug. 2. Dined at the deEste Villa, York Harbor, Maine, guest of John Cadwalader of Philadelphia. An incident related.

Chief Justice John Marshall died in Phila. in 1835, aged 80. Meeting of Bar asked for one dollar from each lawyer in America, for a monument. Dollars came in fast at first, then interest perished, with $900 collected. The trustee invested it in safe securities; reinvesting when they fell in; always investing the little dabs of interest. He died in 1880, and Mr. Cadwalader was executor of the old lawyer's will. Among a carefully kept mass of ancient papers he found everything connected with the matter (now long ago forgotten). He was able to put his hand at once upon every dollar. The $900 had grown to $45000.

No one knew of this secret. At the next important meeting of the Bar Mr. C. rose to reveal it, but Mr. Daugherty rose at the same time. In deference to his great fame and character Mr. C. yielded the floor. D. said—"Mr. Chairman, there is no monument to the greatest legal light, etc., while there are monuments to inconsequential men. Before another word is uttered here we must remove this stain.

The Bar of America must at once raise money, etc." (Applause)

Then Mr. C. got up and told his beautiful secret.

Aug. 11. The Queen of Roumania's friend was here.

Tuesday Aug. 12, 1902. At 7 A.M. Livy taken violently ill. Telephoned, and Dr. Lambert was here in half an hour. She could not breath—was likely to stifle. Also she had severe palpitation. She believed she was dying. I also believed it.

August 25. Livy's illness hangs on and on from day to day and there is never any great improvement—never anything to rouse us and make us jubilant.

Wednesday, Sept. 3. Always Mr. Rogers keeps his yacht (Kanawha) in commission and ready to fly here and take us to Riverdale on telegraphic notice.

Tuesday Sept. 9. Livy getting along pretty well, though it is a case of up and down, and down and up, no certainty about it.

Cadwalader. Precepts and principles for a New Religion: Having for its base God and Man as they are, and not as the elaborately masked and disguised artificialities they are represented to be in most philosophies and in all religions.

Corrected original ms. of "Heaven and Hell" and mailed it. Jean is typing "The Belated Russian Passport."

Sept. 18, 1902. Telegram from Duneka:[1] "Thank you very much for Heaven or Hell. It is great. Have you sent

[1] Frederick A. Duneka, general manager of Harper & Brothers, New York City.

Russian Passport yet? If not won't you please?" (Am mailing it to him now).

Sept. 20. Letter yesterday from Mr. Appleton. We can have Riverdale House till April, at $250 a month, and from Munsey at same rate to June 1—and maybe a month longer, Munsey thinks.

Monday Sept. 22. Our dear prisoner is where she is through overwork—day and night devoted to the children and me.

Wednesday 24. Dr. Allen came yesterday and raised our spirits. A marked change followed. Dr. Putnam this morning said no sort of reason she should not become as well as before. He ordered nurse and she came. Recovery begun. Very briskly.

> During nearly two years their hopes would rise and fall, almost daily.

We are a drifting ship without a captain. We survive by accident.

Thursday, 25th. Lunch. Mrs. Mercer's, to meet Mrs. Bell and a Mrs. Pratt. I could not make the arrangement positive (later I went).

Helmer (osteopath) came from Vermont. Gave Livy a severe treatment—left her sore and lame, and she slept but little, the night. She is weak and frail but she has been that for 45 days.

Again banished from the house, last night. By the new nurse. She allows no one in the sickroom, day and night, but herself. If we had had her in the beginning Livy would be well now.

(Added note, three weeks later: Too sudden a verdict. The above nurse turned out to be mechanically competent (rule of thumb), but vain, silly, self-important, untrustworthy, a most thorough fool, and a liar by instinct and training. I discharged her Oct. 23.)

Yesterday went to Boston, with Howells, and completed railroad arrangements, as follows:—

Invalid car from York Harbor to Riverdale without change. Time 8:45 A.M. (York) 5:40 P.M. Grand Central; about 6, Riverdale.

Oct. 16. Yesterday we left York in a special invalid car at 8:45 and came through to Riverdale without delay or change in 9½ hours. Special locomotive at both ends.

Nov. 25. Julie's wedding.

> This was the marriage of Julia Langdon, Mrs. Clemens' niece, to Edward E. Loomis, today (1931) president of the Lehigh Valley Railroad.

Nov. 27. Livy's birthday.

Dec. 23, 1902. Jean was hit with a chill. Clara was completing her watch in her mother's room and there was no one able to force Jean to go to bed. As a result she is pretty ill today. Fever and high temperature.

Dec. 28. It was pneumonia. For five days Jean's temperature ranged between 103½ and 104 2/5, when it got down to 101. She looks like an escaped survivor in a forest fire.

Sunday evening. For six days now my story in the Christmas Harper ("Was it Heaven or Hell") has been enacted in this house: every day Clara and the nurses have lied about Jean to her mother—describing the fine time she is having out of doors in the winter sports.

> It is not easy to picture that afflicted household, or the state of Mark Twain's mind during this period. Forbidden by doctor and nurse to see Mrs. Clemens, he was like a soul in purga-

tory. He often sat outside her door or pushed little notes under it.

Dec. 30. 2:40 P.M. Saw Livy five minutes by the watch.—The first time in more than three months. A splendid five minutes.

Jean passed what the nurse called a splendid night and is doing well. The doctor stayed all night.

One of the proofs of the immortality of the soul is that myriads have believed it. They also believed the world was flat.

The gods offer no rewards for intellect. There was never one yet that showed any interest in it. Which is singular, for they themselves *have* possessed it, some of them in a considerable degree; not transcending the human limit in any instance, but quite often reaching it.

What is the difference between a taxidermist and a tax collector? The taxidermist takes only your skin.

To create man was a fine and original idea; but to add the sheep was tautology.

None of us can be as great as God, but any of us can be as good.

All gods are better than their conduct.

Only he who has seen better days and lives to see better days again knows their full value.

Circumstances make man, not man circumstances.

You must not pay a person a compliment and then straightway follow it with a criticism.

Do not offer a compliment and ask a favor at the same time. A compliment that is charged for is not valuable.

The man who is a pessimist before 48 knows too much; if he is an optimist after it, he knows too little.

On the whole it is better to deserve honors and not have them than to have them and not deserve them.

The human race consists of the dangerously insane and such as are not.

The time to begin writing an article is when you have finished it to your satisfaction. By that time you begin to clearly and logically perceive what it is that you really want to say.

Cheiro's prophecy fulfilled
End of 1902

My cash income from my books for 1902 was $60,000 (both publishers). Cash from all sources something over $100,000.

Jan. 1, 1903. Saw Livy again. Am to see her five minutes every day if she continues to improve.

Feb. 2, 1903. 33d wedding anniversary. I was allowed to see Livy five minutes this morning in honor of the day. She makes but little progress toward recovery; still there is certainly *some*—we are sure.

The time in St. Louis, in '53, age 17½ that I took the shy pretty girl from up country to Ben de Bar's theater, and had on new 6's when my number was 7, and slipped them off and couldn't get them on again, and walked home with them under my arm—white sox, and it was raining.

We may not doubt that society in heaven consists mainly of undesirable persons.

Thursday March 19. Susy's birthday. She would be 31, now.

The Prophecy

In 1895 Cheiro, the palmist, examined my hand and said that in my 68th year (1903), I would become suddenly rich. I was bankrupt and $94,000 in debt at the time, through the failure of Chas. L. Webster & Co. Two years later—in London—Cheiro repeated this long-distance prediction and added that the riches would come from a quite unexpected source. I am superstitious. I kept the prediction in mind and often thought of it. When at last it came true, Oct. 22, 1903, there was but a month and nine days to spare.

The contract signed that day concentrates all my books in Harpers' hands and now at last they are valuable: in fact they are a fortune. They *guarantee* me $25,000 a year for five years, but they will yield twice as much as that for many a year, if intelligently handled.

Adam, man's benefactor—he gave him all he has ever received that was worth having—Death.

May 23 '03. Martyrdom covers a multitude of sins.

Man was made at the end of the week's work, when God was tired.

Only one thing is impossible for God: to find any sense in any copyright law on the planet.

Whenever a copyright law is to be made or altered, then the idiots assemble.

Wednesday July 1 '03. The yacht sailed with us at 9 A.M. [from Riverdale] reached the D.L. & W. pier 9:45. —Mr. and Mrs. Rogers were on board. Refreshing sail, but railroad journey suffocating and awful. We got to the farm (Elmira) about 6 P.M. Cool and pleasant here.

July 2. Livy weak and exhausted from the journey. Melancholy and homesick.

Saturday Oct 3. Monday we leave for N.Y. Oct. 24 we sail for Italy. Today I placed flowers on Susy's grave for the last time, probably; and read the words—"Good Night, Dear Heart, Good Night."

CHAPTER XXXIV

Italy Again

Oct. 24, 1903. Sailed in the Princess Irene for Genoa at 11. Flowers and fruits from Mrs. Rogers and Mrs. Coe. We have with us Katy Leary in our domestic service 22 years and Miss Margaret Sherry (trained nurse).

> Mrs. Clemens had happy memories of Florence, and believed if she could be there again her health would improve. Eleven years before they had spent a winter at the beautiful Villa Viviani, and her husband had written there a large portion of his "Joan of Arc," her favorite of his works.

Sunday Oct. 25. Heavy storm all night. Only two stewardesses. Ours served sixty meals in rooms, this morning.

Tuesday Oct. 27. Livy is enduring the voyage marvelously well. As well as Clara and Jean, I think, and far better than the trained nurse.

3 P.M. She has been out on deck an hour.

Oct. 28. Youth in smoking-chapel talking nursery German in loud voice, to be heard and envied of men.—The old familiar simple words of the textbook vocabulary, uttered with painful distinctness. Yet there are those who say there is no hell.

Thursday Oct. 29. Two men—a giant and a Shetland pony—also a giraffe, six feet four, tramped the deck after midnight, talking loudly. On the port side four sat under Mrs. Miller's open port and told unclean anecdotes, in the national yell, swore, laughed like demons, and sang. The Captain is going to prevent these freedoms after 11:30 hereafter.

Oct. 30. There should be no first come, take choice, in location of steamer chairs. The chair space outside of a stateroom should be the property of the occupant. People under our port chatter till 11—if these were our chairs we could have tranquillity, for we retire at 9:30.

In 1894 Harpers Monthly paid me only $75 a page for Joan of Arc.

Passed the Azores at 8.

Monday. Due at Gibraltar ten days from N.Y., three days to Naples, then one day to Genoa.

At supper the band played Cavalleria Rusticana (the Intermezzo) which is forever associated in my mind with Susy. I love it better than any other, but it breaks my heart.

Arrived at Gibraltar 7 A.M. Left at 2 P.M. A pest of flies. Thought they did not have them in Europe.

Saw at Gibraltar Michael Benunes, our guide of 36 years ago—still the most distinguished-looking man in that town. He took Jackson, Dan, Jack, Miss Newell, and me, into Spain—all dead now but me, I believe.

NEVER take a promenade-deck room again, at any price: a madhouse is preferable. Get the Captain's apartment or go down cellar, and NEVER travel in an emigrant ship.

Dec. 7 '03. Villa Quarto, Florence. Miss Margaret Sherry, Livy's trained nurse for the past twelve months and more, left for America today. We can never forget her and shall always be grateful to her.

Dec. 22 '03. "What is so rare as a day in June?" That is this day, exactly. Brilliant sun, balmy air, heavy with the odor of roses.

In the early days I was a correspondent and it was a lucrative respectable industry; but now by merely dropping an *r* out of it, it has so lost ground in the public demand that one can hardly make a living at it.

There is no sadder sight than a young pessimist, except an old optimist.

When one reads Bibles, one is less surprised at what the Deity knows than at what he doesn't know.

It is not in the least likely that any life has ever been lived which was not a failure in the secret judgment of the person who lived it.

It is not likely that there has ever been a civilized person 65 years old who would consent to live his life over again.

If man had created man he would be ashamed of his performance.

Jan. 1, 1904. Lay abed nearly all day but wrote 3000 words, earning $900.

> He took a boyish interest in the calculation of how much copy he was turning out and what he would receive for it. Quantity seemed more important to him than quality—in fact he was not always clear as to the difference.

Jan. 14. Died at Keokuk, Mrs. Orion Clemens.

Cablegram "Molly died today." She survived Orion six years, and was about 78 years old.

Feb. 16. Curious dream last night that our former cook became frightened and said "The Countess has bitten the murderous donkey, and it is dead."

Feb. 22. At midnight Livy's pulse went to 192 and there was a collapse. Great alarm. Subcutaneous injection of brandy saved her.

April 9. Sunday. About ten tonight awful attack—for more than an hour. Livy struggled for breath. Clara was in there. Jean and I listened at the door.

April 27. The Gelli portrait for the St. Louis Fair finished. It hasn't a defect.

Livy likes the portrait. It spent the day in her room. It is mine for sitting for it, therefore it is hers. She requires that it be brought back here from St. Louis. It will be as she desires.

May 29. Villa-hunting these many, many days. We can't stay in this neighborhood.

English and Americans are foreigners, but in a lesser degree than is the case with other peoples. Men and women—even man and wife are foreigners. Each has reserves that the other cannot enter into, nor understand. These have the effect of frontiers.

Father Stiatlesi has suppressed his fancy cocks and hens because they disturb Mrs. Clemens. He is the best man I know.

June 4. I have secured an option on two villas, one at

115,000 francs, the other at 160,000 francs, cash. But both of these submitted to Livy, for her decision.

And then the end.

June 5. At a quarter past nine this evening, she that was the life of my life, passed to the relief of heavenly peace of death, after 22 months of unjust and unearned suffering. I first saw her near 37 years ago, and now I have looked upon her face for the last time. Oh, so unexpected!

June 6. At 12:20 P.M. I looked for the last time upon that dear face—and I was full of remorse for things done and said in the 34 years of married life that hurt Livy's heart.

June 7. We had kept Mrs. Orion Clemens's death from Livy. She never learned of it. Later we kept Sir Henry M. Stanley's death from her. She died without ever finding out that a year and a half ago Jean and afterward Clara passed through serious illnesses under the same roof with her.

Fifty-four lamenting cablegrams have arrived—from America, England, France, Austria, Germany, Australia. Soon the letters will follow. Livy was beloved everywhere.

June 10. Livy's last gift to the children was a pair of riding-horses—six or eight weeks ago. Ugo (the butler) will sail with them for America, from Leghorn, June 22.

June 18. I got up in a chair in my room on the second floor and lost my balance and almost fell out (the window). I don't know what saved me. The fall would have killed me; in my bereaved circumstances the world would have been sure it was suicide.

June 21. Left the villa. All arrived with the baggage at the Hôtel de la Ville. First day of the sad journey home.

June 26. When we were ready to leave the hotel at noon Jean was not well enough. We canceled all arrangements. Wait over till tomorrow at 1:20 P.M.

Our ship is the Prince Oscar. Our dear casket went on board at Genoa, yesterday.

June 27. Came down to Naples. Hôtel du Vesuve, good. The green tin box (1870) then the two black tin boxes (1896) all three now succeeded by the plain tin box (June 1904). After a little who will care for these so hallowed treasures?

How all values have shrunken.

June 29. Sailed last night, at ten. The bugle called to breakfast. I recognized the notes, and was distressed. When I heard them last Livy heard them with me; now they fall upon her ears unheeded.

This ship is the Prince Oscar, Hamburg American.

June 30. Clara keeps her bed and cannot bear to see any strangers.

The weather is beautiful, the sea is smooth and curiously blue.

In my life there have been 68 Junes—but how vague and colorless 67 of them are contrasted with the deep blackness of this one.

July 1. I cannot reproduce Livy's face in my mind's eye—I was never in my life able to reproduce a face. It is a curious infirmity—and now at last I realize that it is a calamity.

July 2. In these 34 years we have made many voyages together, Livy dear, and now we are making our last. You down below and lonely, I above with the crowd and lonely.

July 3. Ship time 8 A.M. In 13¼ hours it will be four weeks since Livy died. 31 years ago we made our first voyage together and this is our last in company. Susy was a year old then. She died at 24 and has been in her grave 8 years.

July 4. We did not come out of our room during the day and evening. We were full of memories of other Fourths.

July 8. A wonderful day. Brilliant sun, brilliant blue water, strong and delightful breeze. In middle of Gulf Stream. Temperature of water 73½ degrees Fahrenheit. We had such days in the Indian Ocean, and Livy so enjoyed the exaltation of spirits they produced.

July 10. Tonight it will be six weeks. But to me it remains yesterday as it has from the first. But this funeral march—how sad and long it is.

Two days more will be the second stage of it.

July 12. Due to finish this melancholy voyage at 7 or 8 this evening.

Smallpox discovered this morning; five cases in steerage; every soul on board being vaccinated.

People who travel in an immigrant ship belong in insane asylums.

July 13. Orders from President Roosevelt and the Secretary of the Treasury passed us swiftly ashore and we went to the hotel with Charlie Langdon and Mr. and Mrs. Loomis. Mrs. Loomis is my niece by marriage. Loomis is Vice-President of the D L & W RR and we all go to

Elmira in his private car tomorrow—taking Rev. J. H. Twichell of Hartford, who married us.

July 14. Funeral private in the house of Livy's young maidenhood. Where she stood as a bride 34 years ago, there her coffin rested; and over it the same voice that had made her a wife, then, committed her departed spirit to God, now.[1]

[1] For a more detailed account of Mrs. Clemens' last days from York Harbor to Florence and of the voyage home, see Chapters XVII, XVIII, XIX of *My Father, Mark Twain*, by Clara Clemens, and Chapters CCXXIII, CCXXVI, CCXXIX to CCXXXI, of *Mark Twain, A Biography*.

CHAPTER XXXV

Closing Years

July 16. Clara and Teresa (Italian maid) went to the summer home, Lee, Mass., in the Berkshire Hills.

July 18. At 9:15 I and Ugo, butler (he arrived from Italy with the horses on Friday) left for Lee and arrived at 1:07. Jean and Katy left at 3:30 and arrived about 7.

July 22. Clara, sick, heart-broken, unrestful, returned to N. Y. with Katy to rest awhile with Miss Dr. Parry.

Katy Leary was with Susy when she died in '96, and with Livy when she died. She has been in our service 23 years.

July 24. Cold. We built a fire in my room. Then clawed the logs out and threw water, remembering there is a brood of swallows in the chimney. The tragedy was averted.

Lee, Mass. Berkshire Hills, July 31, 1904.

Last night the young people out on a moonlight ride. Trolley frightened Jean's horse. Collision. Horse killed. Rodman Gilder picked Jean up—unconscious; she was taken to the doctor per the car. Face, nose, side, back, contused; tendon of left ankle broken.

August 10. New York. Clara here sick—never well since June 5. Jean is at the summer home in Berkshire Hills, crippled.

August 11. Two years ago Livy was stricken at York Harbor 7 in the morning. From that time until the fatal 5th of June 1904, she never saw a well day.

Sept. 1. Died at Greenwich, Ct. my sister, Pamela Moffatt, aged about 73. She had been 60 years an invalid. Death-dates this year: Jan. 14, June 5, Sept. 1.

Oct. 13. Executed my last will.

Now, I have got a word for it when "purring" is a shade too strong to properly describe that almost undetectable soft rumbling sound, which you feel rather than hear, when you press a kitten to your ear. I pressed the kitten to Clara's ear and said, "There—now you can hear him *smoldering*."

The only very marked difference between the average civilized man and the average savage is that the one is gilded and the other painted.

The critic's symbol should be the tumble-bug: he deposits his egg in somebody else's dung, otherwise he could not hatch it.

The course of free love never runs smooth. I suppose we have all tried it.

An uneasy conscience is a hair in the mouth.

God, so atrocious in the Old Testament, so attractive in the New—the Jekyl and Hyde of sacred romance.

Let us so live that when we come to die even the undertaker will be sorry.

The skin of every human being contains a slave.

I am a pretty versatile fool when it comes to contracts, and business and such things. I have signed a lot of contracts in my time, and at sometime I probably knew what the contracts meant, but six months later everything had grown dim and I could be *certain* of only two things, to wit:

One, I didn't sign any contract.

Two, the contract means the opposite of what it says.

Maxims in the Rough

A miracle is by far the most wonderful and impressive and awe-inspiring thing we can conceive of, except the credulity that can take it at par.

There is nothing more impressive than a miracle, except the credulity that can take it at par.

There is nothing more awe-inspiring than a miracle except the credulity that can take it at par.

None but the dead have free speech.

None but the dead are permitted to speak the truth.

In America—as elsewhere—free speech is confined to the dead.

The Majority is always in the wrong.

Whenever you find that you are on the side of the majority, it is time to reform—(or pause and reflect).

Geological time is not money. A pity too; for it would have abolished poverty from the earth.

Let us adopt geological time, then time being money, —there will be no more poverty.

We are all missionaries (propagandists of *our* views). Each of us disapproves of the other missionaries; in fact detests them, as a rule. I am one of the herd myself. It is noticeable that the professional always uses the one license: "Go ye into all the world," and ignores the Golden Rule which would restrain him from entering China and one or two other countries where he is not wanted and is not welcome.

Man has not a single right which is the product of anything but might.

Not a single right is indestructible: a new might can at any time abolish it, hence, man possesses not a single *permanent* right.

God is Might (and He is shifty, malicious, and uncertain).

"In God We Trust." It is the choicest compliment that has ever been paid us, and the most gratifying to our feelings. It is simple, direct, gracefully phrased; it always sounds well—In God We Trust. I don't believe it would sound any better if it were true. And in a measure it is true—half the nation trusts in Him. That half has decided it.

"Pop's down in the sty. You will know him from the hogs because he's got his hat on."

In the beginning of a change the patriot is a scarce man, and brave, and hated and scorned. When his cause succeeds, the timid join him, for then it costs nothing to be a patriot. The soul and substance of what customarily ranks as patriotism is moral cowardice—and always has been.

In any civic crisis of a great and dangerous sort the common herd is not privately anxious about the rights and wrongs of the matter, it is only anxious to be on the winning side. In the North, before the War, the man who opposed slavery was despised and ostracized, and insulted. By the "Patriots." Then, by and by, the "Patriots" went over to his side, and thenceforth his attitude became patriotism.

There are two kinds of patriotism—monarchical patriotism and republican patriotism. In the one case the government and the king may rightfully furnish you their notions of patriotism; in the other, neither the government nor the entire nation is privileged to dictate to any individual what the form of his patriotism shall be. The Gospel of the Monarchical Patriotism is: "The King can do no wrong." We have adopted it with all its servility, with an unimportant change in the wording: "Our country, right *or* wrong!"

We have thrown away the most valuable asset we have —the individual right to oppose both flag and country when he (just *he* by himself) believes them to be in the wrong. We have thrown it away; and with it all that was really respectable about that grotesque and laughable word, Patriotism.

Sixty years ago optimist and fool were not synonymous terms. This is a greater change than that wrought by science and invention. It is the mightiest change that was ever wrought in the world in any sixty years since creation. Jan. 1905.

Sept. 24 '05. At 8 A.M. a beautiful dream and vividly real. Livy. Conversation of two or three minutes. I said several times "Then it was only a dream, only a dream." She did not seem to understand what I meant.

1906. Paine: "Why is the king's mind [M.T. was frequently referred to as the king] like a railroad time-table? Because it is subject to change without notice."

It will be seen from the foregoing that the present writer was by this time on the scene. Early in January I had become Mark Twain's biographer and he had begun daily dictation—notes for my use, later to become his *Autobiography*. He seldom made entries now in his notebooks, using a pad of paper for such memoranda as he wished to jot down between dictations. When it was possible I saved these things, but I have not been able always to keep them nor the few remaining notebook entries in chronological order. He made notes in any book or on any pad that came handy.

SOME WASHINGTON NOTES

Early in December (1906) I accompanied Mark Twain on a copyright lobbying expedition to Washington, an account of which is elsewhere set down and need not be repeated here. Looking through the notes of that journey, however, I find one or two that may be added, now.

We arrived in the evening and went to the New Willard, a hotel boasting certain "latest improvements." For one thing, you were sure of getting boiling water from the "Hot" faucet almost instantly—it wasn't necessary to feel of it. Early next morning he was in the bathroom. I heard the water turned into the tub, followed by a wild blast of profanity: "God-damn the God-damned son-of-a-bitch that invented that faucet! I hope he'll roast in hell for a million years!" It appeared that he had sampled the temperature of the flow, as was his custom at home—ordinarily singing a little at such a moment.

It was not much of a start for the day. When coffee came up his tray was placed on a little table by his bed, which he had got back into as soon as possible. The hot milk was in a good-sized pitcher—of narrow-neck, wide-bottom design, something the shape of a pear or a gourd. Seizing it with a jerk he slopped an unnecessary amount of the contents into his coffee, and a good deal into the tray. He banged down the pitcher and glared at it helplessly. "That hell-fired thing," he said, "one might as well try to pour milk out of a womb!" And a moment later, "I get so damned short of profanity at a time like this."

Notes for "Letters from the Earth," an unfinished manuscript. Letters supposed to have been written by an angel visiting the earth, to another angel, in Heaven. Subject, Man:

"His (man's) heaven is a curious place. It has not a single feature in it that he values on earth. It consists wholly of diversion which on earth he cares for not at all. For example:

"Most men do not sing—cannot sing—will not stay where others are singing; many men do not pray, or like to; fewer still go to church. To most men Sunday is a bore—all sane men detest noise—also, monotony.

"Very well, in Man's heaven it is *always* Sunday. Always Sunday, and everybody either prays or sings. Continually. Especially sings. The man who could not sing a note on earth sings there. Hymns! *One* hymn! 'Hosannah, hosannah unto the highest!' And everybody banging a harp—a hurricane of sound—a praise service—a service of flattery, adulation. You will wonder who would endure this insane compliment—not only endure it but like it, require it. Hold your breath—it is God; Man's God, his own pet invention.

"Man's heaven is a place of reward—of previous delights—made it himself, mind you—all out of his own head. Very well; of the delights of *this* world man cares *most* for sexual intercourse. He will go any length for it—risk fortune, character, reputation, life itself. And what do you think he has done? In a thousand years you would never guess—*he has left it out of his heaven! Prayer takes its place.*"

He wrote several chapters of the book—it was to have been that—but he was tired, and no longer well. He had exhausted the topic, first and last—it could not amuse or interest him long.

What seems to be his final notebook entry was made about this time, or a little earlier.

"All schools, all colleges, have two great functions: to confer, and to conceal valuable knowledge. The Theological knowledge which they conceal cannot justly be regarded as less valuable than that which they reveal. That is, if, when man is buying a basket of strawberries, it can profit him to know that the bottom half of it is rotten. Nov. 5, 1908."

He still made notes, now and again, on the little pads that were always near his bed, where he spent most of his time. Among the later memoranda was this one, written doubtless at some moment when he considered his acceptance of the swiftly approaching (and, to him, welcome) change:

"He had arrived at the dignity of Death—the only earthly dignity that is not artificial—the only safe one. The others are traps that can beguile to humiliation.

"Death, the only immortal who treats us all alike, whose pity and whose peace and whose refuge are for all—the soiled and the pure, the rich and the poor, the loved and the unloved."

And once he wrote:

"Obscurity and a competence—that is the life that is best worth living."

AFTERWORD

And so the record closes. It is Mark Twain—at his best and at his worst. I cannot discover anything more to add, and I am not prompted to take anything away. Those who have wanted Mark Twain as he was—to himself, and to those nearest him—have him now—in his daughter's memories, *My Father, Mark Twain*, and in these desultory memoranda, the fitful record of fifty years. Whatever he may appear to the rest of the world, to those in his daily life he was the kindest and wisest of men. We thought him also the handsomest. He was an extremist, of course, but when has there ever been a genius who was not? The words are nearly synonymous.

He had every human attribute. Once he wrote:

"I have found there is no ingredient of the race which I do not possess in either a small or a large way. When it is small, as compared with the same ingredient in somebody else, there is still enough of it for purposes of examination."

Some there were who never understood him—who saw only his weaknesses—who thought because of his great gifts he should be above weaknesses, which to them were only flaws. They had little conception of a nature like his. The chicken does not understand the eagle, save now and then, a little, when the eagle catches the chicken and takes him on a trip through space. Then the chicken may get a dim idea of what the eagle's life is like, though on the whole the fowl is unlikely to enjoy the excursion.

His soul was built of truth. If his tricky memory and unfailing imagination led him into many misstatements, he was always eager to correct, when he became conscious of them. Howells once said to me:

"He was the most truthful man, when it was a question of fact, I have ever known, particularly when it was a relation of some discreditable occurrence in which he had been concerned. I remember once at dinner, when the conversation turned to the subject of jails and the experience of occupying a cell, he said:

" 'I passed a night in jail once.'

"Clara, who was present, was shocked.

" 'Why, Father,' she said, 'how in the world did you come to be in jail?'

"He did not make any excuse; he did not say that it had been a mistake and that he had made it warm for the authorities afterwards. Most of us would have qualified, palliated, let ourselves down easy. Nothing of the sort; he looked mildly at Clara, and replied:

" 'Drunk, I guess.' "

He believed others to be as truthful as himself, until he found his confidence misplaced. Then, for the time suspicious, he was apt to distrust those who were loyal, to discredit that which was truth. It was largely because of his disappointment in persons taken too easily on trust that he was moved at times to rail at mankind in general, the falsity of the human race at large. Yet, to the last, his confidence was easily won, and not always by those entitled to that great honor.

Always from youth to age he strove against oppression, superstition, sham, hypocrisy, evil in every form. He fought in the open, with that most powerful of all weapons, truth—unanswerable logic supplemented by ridicule. He believed that no abuse could withstand ridicule, and he went far toward proving it.

He saw life at a quizzical slant, but he was not, first of all, a humorist. His phrase was likely to carry a laugh with it, but more often than not it carried some deep revealment of human truth, or human injustice. A hundred maxims in the foregoing pages testify to this. The expression that is merely humorous does not long survive. There must be substance beneath it. Cervantes would not be remembered today if Don Quixote and Sancha Panza underneath all the absurdities of their literary dress had not been vital in their philosophy. If humor survive, it is because it decorates something that is alive and will continue to live through the generations—in a word, truth. The decoration alone will not endure.

Any attempt to discover a hidden, subtle psychology in the writings of Mark Twain I think must be an effort far afield. I think so because of my knowledge of him and because of his knowledge of himself. Once when he came upon something of the sort he said:

"I wish I could understand what in the nation that man is driving at. He has a superstition that he means something, but it misses me altogether."

If there ever was a man who said what he meant, in the fewest number of words, it was Mark Twain.

Many have sought to compare him with other laughing philosophers, ancient and modern. He does not lend himself to that, either. Now and then, from the remoter distances there comes to this flitting island a mysterious visitant, a superhuman soul. Such a stranger is not to be classified, not to be compared. He may leave a class behind him, but he does not enter one on arrival; and such arrivals are too infrequent to admit of duplication.

One must wonder, at times, where Mark Twain will rank in the long eons of the ages. When so many have gone by that the student will have to think a little before he can decide whether Mark Twain was a contemporary of Aristophanes or of William Shakespeare. Little of the mighty ruck of literature of this day—of any day—can survive. One may believe that something of Mark Twain's will be among that little.

For he was a giant in his day; he struck deeply into the earth and digged up gold. We do not destroy gold, and it does not disintegrate. It is preserved and remains the same, untarnished by the forever. It is not all gold that he has left us—oh, by no means—but little by little the alloy will disappear, and in the long ten thousand years there will be those who will recognize and preserve the metal of the gods.

THE END

INDEX

INDEX

INDEX

INDEX

INDEX

INDEX

INDEX

INDEX

INDEX

INDEX